DEVIANT BEHAVIOUR

Paul Rock

Lecturer in Sociology in the London School of Economics and
Political Science

HUTCHINSON UNIVERSITY LIBRARY
LONDON

HUTCHINSON & CO (*Publishers*) LTD
3 Fitzroy Square, London W1

London Melbourne Sydney Auckland
Wellington Johannesburg Cape Town
and agencies throughout the world

First published 1973

*This book has been set in Times type, printed in Great Britain
on smooth wove paper by The Camelot Press Ltd, London and Southampton,
and bound by Wm. Brendon, of Tiptree, Essex*

ISBN 0 09 115440 5 (cased)
0 09 115441 3 (paper)

For

Barbara and Matthew

CONTENTS

ACKNOWLEDGEMENTS

This book is a crystallisation of ideas which emerged from two settings. First, I am enormously indebted to members of the National Deviancy Conference; and although they will probably disown many of the perspectives which I have adopted, our meetings led me to structure what I had initially experienced as no more than a set of intuitions. The other setting was the graduate seminar held by David Downes, Frances Heidensohn and myself at the London School of Economics between 1969 and 1970. The book was originally conceived as a joint work to be written by Frances Heidensohn and me: it is a great pity that she was unable to collaborate. Kit Carson and Bill Chambliss were most helpful in commenting on sections of the book, as was Percy Cohen, who suggested it in the first place.

I am grateful to the following for permission to use copyright material: Basic Book, Inc., Publishers, New York, from *Deviance and Respectability: The Social Construction of Moral Meanings*, Ed. Jack D. Douglas, 1970; the Free Press, New York, from *The Other Side*, Ed. H. Becker, 1964, and from *The Legislation of Morality* by T. Duster, 1970; Martinus Nijhoff, The Hague, from *Alfred Schutz: Collected Papers*, Ed. M. Natanson, 1967; John Wiley & Sons, Inc., from *The Police: Six Sociological Essays*, Ed. David J. Bordua, 1967.

Crouch End   P. R.

INTRODUCTION

The study of crime has conventionally dwelt on the pathology of the individual offender or on the groups in which he organises his behaviour. Heavily dominated by a statistical approach, it was never the peculiar province of any one discipline. Psychology, psychoanalysis, anthropology, law, applied statistics and sociology all laid claim to criminology. Many criminologists were tacitly committed to multidisciplinary syntheses[1] whose goals were dictated by practical correctional objectives rather than the refinement of theoretical understanding.[2] The rules, whose infringement constituted deviancy, were simply taken for granted. They were not only absolute but also unproblematic. Similarly, social control and nondeviant behaviour were treated as only the backcloth against which pathology was displayed. They were discrete, isolated and unworthy of analysis.

In the main, criminology has been estranged from prevailing sociological concerns and stances. It has bracketed or ignored vast areas of social process which any practising sociologist would consider integrally linked to criminal behaviour. Disregard has largely been exchanged. Social rules, deviancy and formal agencies of control have never been of much interest to sociologists. Most sociologists would be ashamed to know nothing about academic writings on religion, politics or development. It is not a matter of professional shame to be devoid of competence in the field of deviancy theory.[3]

Of course, there *have* been abundant exceptions to the general alienation of criminology: instances are Durkheim's preoccupation with moral order and deviancy; occasional ethnographic studies such as Whyte's *Streetcorner Society*; the structural-functionalist work of Parsons, Merton, Cohen, Cloward and Ohlin; the Chicago

[1] Superior figures refer to end-of-chapter notes.

ecologists; and sophisticated institutional studies of prison structure. Above all, there has been the continuous but slender tradition of thought which originated (arbitrarily) in Simmel, and continued through Park and the Chicago School, Tannenbaum, Sutherland, Cressey and, most important, Lemert. The tradition ultimately developed into what has been called the interactionist sociology of deviancy. Interactionism was not itself markedly sophisticated, but it did galvanise criminology. Its chief significance was the transformation of *criminology* into the *sociology* of deviancy. The change denoted a shift in the nature of the substantive area studied. Crime simply became one of a number of rule-breaking phenomena whose particular characteristic was the infraction of criminal law. The invocation of criminal law as a means of social control became an event worthy of explanation in its own right. Social control became the chief focus and its connections with power became salient.

The change connoted a redefinition of crime and deviancy as social occurrences which can be studied with conventional sociological concepts and techniques. Deviancy is a widespread activity and, *a priori*, it should not be regarded as intellectually sacred or mysterious. Connections between events in nondeviant settings are not magically severed when the events are produced in deviant settings. The interactionists destroyed the absurd barrier which has hindered the application of normal sociology to this one reserved area of crime. Sociologists ceased merely to *take* problems from the field of deviancy, they began to *make* them according to their own analytic criteria. They did so by transposing ideas derived from the sociologies of work, institutions and medicine. The transposition was revolutionary because deviancy became no longer pathological or extraordinary.

My book represents an attempt to synthesise and order some of the ideas which are now taken to constitute the sociology of deviancy. It is a short introduction to the field and necessarily neglects vital issues. It cannot pretend to be comprehensive but, if its intention is realised, it should permit those who are unversed in the writing on deviancy to organise their understanding and detect underlying themes.

My argument is principally based on the belief that the sociology of deviancy is enhanced when it focuses on the meanings which are linked to the regulation of behaviour. This stance will enable me to pay attention to important properties of the field which become neglected when meaning is relegated to a secondary position. A sociology which lacks such a focus confronts several intellectual difficulties.

The first difficulty is that inferences about the way in which an abstractly conceived social structure affects action[4] must either be unstated (and thereby left problematic)[5] or else must rest upon a tacit use of a commonsense empathy. Schutz remarks of the first alternative:

> The achievements of modern economic theories would make it preposterous to deny that an abstract conceptual scheme can be used very successfully for the solution of many problems. And similar examples could be given from the field of almost all the other social sciences. Closer investigation, however, reveals that this abstract conceptual scheme is nothing else than a kind of intellectual shorthand and that the underlying subjective elements of human actions involved are either taken for granted or deemed to be irrelevant with respect to the scientific purpose at hand—and are, therefore, disregarded.[6]

Coser quite frequently exemplifies a resort to the second alternative. He makes use of a sociological equivalent of economic or legal man, an entity devised to aid analysis. Coser's sociological man reacts to problematic situations in a way that is both rational and transparent to any sensible observer. In a discussion of the social functions of violence, for instance, he states:

> since Negroes are assigned lowest position in all three major dimensions of the American status system—and since their mobility chances are nil in the first and minimal in the second and third, it stands to reason that achievement in the area of interpersonal violence might be seen as a channel leading to self-regard and self-enhancement. . . .[7]

The phrase 'it stands to reason' is most significant. It means, in effect, that any rational and understanding member of society might react in the same way as the deprived Black. The covert assumption that the Black and the understanding member share the same perspectives makes Coser's analysis possible. Yet the grounds upon which it is based are left entirely unspecified and they could be sociologically implausible. Indeed, the particular interpretations of violence and deprivation made by the American Black are precisely what is problematic.

Inferences about the impact of social phenomena on individuals must, however, be made because the phenomena would not exist at all if they were not sustained by innumerable people intentionally or unintentionally constructing social order. It is usually helpful, and often imperative, to refer back to the meanings employed by these people. Unless such reference takes place, social affairs may become reified. They may be thought to have a source of vitality which does not emanate from individuals in concrete social settings.

In one sense, all major social phenomena are merely constellations of individual actions viewed at a low level of magnification. Social

structure exists only because people routinely experience the world
in particular ways, respond and, through their concerted activity,
produce effects which can be interpreted as patterns. When the
intimate connections between these experiences and their patterned
consequences are ignored, bizarre analysis can result. In particular,
certain kinds of model can dominate thinking and turn it away from
an acknowledgment of the reflexivity which distinguishes man. As
Blumer argues,

the question remains whether human society or social action can be
successfuly analyzed by schemes which refuse to recognize human beings
as they are, namely, as persons constructing individual and collective
action through an interpretation of the situations which confront them.[8]

Even if it is assumed that large-scale social structures have a
logic and organisation which are, *sui generis*, attempts to predict
their development may falter unless they employ material derived
from the micro-sociological plane. Paradigms for explaining macro-
structural events depend, like all paradigms, upon metaphor for their
animation. Whether the explicit or implicit metaphor be mathematical, anthropomorphic, mechanical, cybernetic, organic or
ecological in nature, it is necessarily misleading. Such models of
large-scale processes can never be completely adequate because they
are, at best, limited descriptions whose utility is circumscribed by the
fact that social affairs are *not* mathematical systems, men or cybernetic systems. Because the logic of the metaphor is not identical to
the logic of the thing to be explained, its working must be taken as
only a tentative guide to understanding social process. Society cannot
be explained by mathematical metaphor alone.

It can be argued, for instance, that man's capacity to reason and
interpet makes him an object which cannot be easily tackled by
concepts of 'immanence'. Thus Davis, in his study of families faced
with the crisis of disease, organised his analysis around the competing concept of 'emergence':

. . . the reactions of the families can best be described in terms of an
ongoing developmental process—an improvisatory 'building up', as it
were, in which each new event posed new problems that in turn generated a
trial-and-error search for new interpretations and definitions of the
situation. This search resulted not only in perceptual modifications of the
existing situation, but an unwilling re-evaluation of the relevant past and
impending situations as well. Thus, the actual undergoing of the process
set its own conditions for further action, the conditions themselves being
an existential amalgam of previously emergent responses and events. This
process . . . defies simple causal reduction to some original state of immanence or fixed set of determining events. Although it is possible to

detect, *post hoc*, certain regularities in the process, this is not to say that its end-states are wholly contained in its beginnings.[9]

If ideas of emergence *are* appropriate to sociological analysis, it follows that all macro-structural metaphors must be treated with enormous circumspection. Not only do these metaphors generally rest on immanence, they also restrict access to important sectors of enquiry. That is, their operations are foreign to human affairs and lead to mistaken deduction. They also warp the field which is visible to the sociologist. As Burke says, 'A way of seeing is always a way of not seeing'.[10] The cost of elevating a suggestive approach to a pre-eminent position are the ideas which are necessarily neglected. The metaphors make the cybernetic, mathematical or mechanical aspects of social structure most salient; produce ideal-types of men and institutions which are cybernetically, mathematically or mechanically plausible; and ignore what does not comfortably fit into the general interpretative scheme. If such metaphors are employed, it must be on the assumption that they are adequate for the purposes at hand. When matters require more exhaustive examination, further generalisation or prediction, however, the constraints imposed by the metaphor's partial vision may become acute. Anything but a very simplified description is likely to suffer because the metaphor cannot account for a multitude of phenomena and because it is a model whose workings are qualitatively different from those of the thing described.

The selection of one paradigm always entails the rejection of others, and it may be that the decision to choose one which cannot accommodate man's distinctive reflexivity will lead to too great an impoverishment. No macro-structural metaphor can make this accommodation and it must therefore be supported by a complementary understanding of meanings organised in interpersonal situations. Matza, who also resorts to concepts of emergence, uses the term 'naturalism' to refer to a style of enquiry which remains 'true' to the nature of the matter studied. He states:

Man participates in *meaningful* activity. He creates his reality and that of the world around him, actively and strenuously. Man *naturally*—not supernaturally—transcends the existential realms in which the conceptions of cause, force, and reactivity are easily applicable. Accordingly, a view that conceives man as object, methods that probe human behavior without concerning themselves with the meaning of behavior, cannot be regarded as naturalist. Such views and methods are the very *opposite* of naturalism because they have molested in advance the phenomenon to be studied.[11]

The complications involved in employing unqualified metaphors are exacerbated by reification. When intellectual questions are tackled by elaborate metaphor, the vital 'as if' clause often becomes deleted and the scheme is confused with the thing it explains. Instead of viewing social life *as if* it were a cybernetic or mechanical system, it is treated as just such a system. The artifice in model construction can be forgotten. When answers derived from exploring a metaphor are taken to be necessarily true of the 'real world', the hazards are obvious. The larger weight will always fall to the ground before the smaller.

The sociology of deviancy has frequently suffered from such misplaced concreteness. Deviant events have been discussed as if they were medical pathologies, for example. Rule-breaking has been described by the language of epidemic, disorder and diagnosis. When the metaphor becomes reified, deviancy *becomes* pathology. For instance, drug usage has been treated as an epidemic which spreads from one person to another by simple contagion. A whole array of potentially enlightening concepts is thereby displaced. The logic of the disease epidemic becomes regarded as absolutely appropriate to the analysis of drug consumption. There is nothing in this paradigm which would lead one to question whether the spread of drug-taking *is*, in fact, an epidemic. The conclusions that can be drawn from this kind of scheme, although internally logical, tend merely to confuse. An alternative stance has been fostered by Young, who argues 'people accept socialization into drug culture because they find the cultures attractive in terms of solving problems which they face; they do not "catch" drug addiction, they *embrace* it'.[12]

Non-naturalistic metaphors of the medical sort must be treated with caution and independently checked unless it can be demonstrated that in all relevant details social influence is communicated by means which are directly analogous to the germ or virus; that people have no real control over its diffusion; that their own understanding of the situation is not a determinant of their receptivity; and so on. It is clear that a set of propositions which are independent of the metaphor must be used to examine the degree of correspondence between the logic of the metaphor and the logic of the problematic situation.[13] Of course, these propositions must be metaphorically phrased themselves, but they will serve as an important corrective if they are grounded in the world of meanings which is open to Matza's naturalism.

A resort to simple induction is not much of a refuge from the problem posed by neglecting meanings. Connections between events can, in the last resort, be demonstrated only at the level of meaning. For example, unless Catholicism and large families are shown to be linked by religious beliefs about the propriety of contraception, the seeming connectedness of the two 'facts' may be simply fortuitous.

Similarly, whilst events which seemed to be connected in the past may again appear together, there are no good grounds for arguing *why* this should be so unless the meanings of the events to the actors are apprehended by the sociologist. *Causal* necessity can be claimed in sociology only by invoking the subjective transformations which accompany and generate social change. Thus a group which is confronted by external threat may strengthen its boundaries and display increased solidarity, but these events cannot be fused into a causal system until the group's system for identifying threat and its reading of the meaning of the threat are grasped. Without this kind of apprehension, social phenomena must always be regarded as discrete and unrelated.

This approach will inform my general treatment of deviancy. I shall build my analysis around the manner in which understandings of deviancy give rise to orderly patterns of rule-making, rule enforcement and rule-breaking.

1. For an example of a plea for a multidisciplinary criminology, see M. Wolfgang and F. Ferracuti, *The Subculture of Violence*, Tavistock, London, 1967.

2. cf. C. Wright Mills, 'The Professional Ideology of Social Pathologists', *American Journal of Sociology*, September 1943, vol. 49, no. 2.

3. cf. S. Cohen, 'Criminology and the Sociology of Deviance in Britain', in P. Rock and M. McIntosh (Ed.), *Deviance and Social Control*, Tavistock, London, forthcoming.

4. Of course there is only an analytic difference between social structure and action.

5 cf. J. Douglas, *The Social Meanings of Suicide*, Princeton University Press, New Jersey, 1967.

6. A. Schutz, 'Commonsense and Scientific Interpretations of Human Action', in M. Natanson (Ed.), *Alfred Schutz: Collected Papers*, Martinus Nijhoff, The Hague, 1967, vol. 1, p. 35.

7. L. Coser, *Continuities in the Study of Social Conflict*, Free Press, New York, 1967, p. 80.

8. H. Blumer, 'Society as Symbolic Interaction', in A. Rose (Ed.), *Human Behaviour and Social Processes*, Routledge & Kegan Paul, London, 1962, p. 192.

9. F. Davis, *Passage Through Crisis*, Bobbs-Merrill, Indianapolis, 1963, p. 10.

10. K. Burke, *Permanence and Change*, New Republic Inc., New York, 1935, p. 70.

11. D. Matza, *Becoming Deviant*, Prentice-Hall, New Jersey, 1969, p. 8.

12. J. Young, *The Drugtakers*, MacGibbon & Kee, London, 1971, p. 42.

13. The solution offered by ethnomethodology is to adopt a conscious sociology of sociology as a check: 'realise the nature of the game *you* are playing, the rules and meanings *you* are invoking in the undertaking of the game you are observing'. Secondly, 'realise that the games you observe may have very different rules, and that what constitutes a rational move in one game may be totally irrelevant to what constitutes a rational move in another'. And finally, 'in order to understand these games, forget your pre-suppositions and learn the rules that constitute meaningful and rational action in the game, learn the game in fact'. M. Phillipson

and M. Roche, 'Phenomenological Sociology and the Study of Deviance', in P. Rock and M. McIntosh (Ed.), *Deviance and Social Control*, Tavistock, London, forthcoming. Of course, not only is there a problem of an infinite regress of sociologies of sociologies, there is also the difficulty posed by the implicit assertion that the meanings understood by the game's players (or 'first-order constructs') can be understood without obfuscating metaphor by the sociologist. No sociologist can confront the reality of a problematic situation in a stance of pure naïvety. He must organise his perspective on the situation in terms of some model which is not identical to the model employed by the players.

I

DEFINITIONS OF DEVIANTS AND DEVIANCY

A sociological conception of deviancy must dwell on its peculiarly social qualities. As a significant social entity, the 'deviant' is the occupant of a special role which is recognised and ordered in a process of interaction. If a person is not assigned to this role and not treated as deviant, he cannot be regarded sociologically as a deviant. No matter how much he may be assumed by some to be a disturbed, disruptive or atypical individual, his *social* meaning is not that of deviancy but something else. Those who would explain his behaviour do not account for social deviancy or a deviant role, but disturbance, disruptiveness or atypicality as they conceive it. Deviancy is a social construct* fashioned by the members of the society in which it exists. They endow it with importance and distinctiveness and they assign it to a special place in the organisation of their collective lives. As Quinney remarks:

... a thing exists only when it is given a name; any phenomenon is real to us only when we can imagine it. Without imagination there would be nothing to experience. So it is with crime. In our relationships with others we construct a *social reality of crime*. This reality is both conceptual and phenomenal, a world of meanings and events constructed in reference to crime.[1]

Deviant roles are given names (whether Student Militant, Hooligan, Criminal, Homosexual or simply Deviant) which single them out for purposes of elucidation, action and, often, the justification of action. In one study, for instance, Turner and Surace argued that the presence and behaviour of young Mexican 'zootsuiters' in California

---

* Social constructs are the interpretations which men collaboratively give to the objects and events around them. They are rather more than interpretations, however, because they are also the social phenomena which men create through their activities and as a result of these interpretations.

evoked hostility. The hostility was marked by ambivalence because, whilst 'zootsuiter' conjured up images of delinquency and violence, 'Mexican' evoked images of the romantic and exciting. Collective action against the deviants became possible only when they were referred to as 'zootsuiters' and their Mexican facet was ignored. Condemnatory symbols which are unambiguous can thus mobilise a punitive response.[2]

[The deviant role is given a recognised place in the social structure and those who assume it are led to expect that becoming deviant will be a fateful process.] One of the basic problems in sociology is to explain the origins, maintenance and effects of these acts of social placement. [Deviancy is a part of the social reality which organises people's lives, and this social reality must be the primary material of analysis.] As Schutz states:

[The social scientist's] observational field, the social world, is not essentially structureless. It has a particular meaning and relevance structure for the human beings living, thinking, and acting therein. They have preselected and preinterpreted this world by a series of common-sense constructs of the reality of daily life, and it is these thought objects which determine their behavior, define the goal of their action, the means available for attaining them. . . . The thought objects constructed by the social scientists refer to and are founded upon the thought objects constructed by the common-sense thought of man living his everyday life among his fellow-men. Thus, the constructs used by the social scientist are, so to speak, constructs of the second degree, namely constructs of the constructs made by the actors on the social scene. . . .[3]

[If deviancy is a social reality, then, it is deviancy as it is construed, responded to and generated by members of society. It is not deviancy which the social scientist would independently choose to study. Deviant roles and behaviour are prestructured for his inspection whatever he may think about the rationality or morality of their making. Marihuana smokers, witches, usurers, nationalists, internationalists and the Jews have all been variously defined as deviants in different societies.* The definitions have been of great consequence to them.]

* A list of other deviancies has been compiled by Sutherland and Cressey: 'It was a crime in Iceland in the Viking age for a person to write verses about another, even if the sentiment was complimentary, if the verses exceeded four strophes in length. A Prussian law of 1784 prohibited mothers and nurses from taking children under two years of age into their beds. The English villein in the fourteenth century was not allowed to send his son to school, and no one lower than a freeholder was permitted by law to keep a dog. The following have at different times been crimes: printing a book, professing the medical doctrine of circulation of the blood, driving with reins, selling coins to foreigners, having gold in the house, buying goods on the way to market or in the market for the purpose of selling them at a higher price, writing a cheque for less than one dollar.'

Of course, a sociologist who organised his study at the level of commonsense thought alone would be able to contribute little, if anything, to understanding about social processes. His task is to transcend the commonsense world and discern patterns and relationships which may not appear to those involved in the problematic situation. Moreover, the problem of eliciting meanings from those involved is an enormously complicated one. Not only may meanings be disguised, unclear or confused. Worse still, the very assumption that there is a set of clear meanings guiding a particular course of action may be thoroughly misleading.

It may be the case that the conceptions which people hold about deviancy are in some sense erroneous and that their placement of specific individuals in deviant roles is also misguided. Through their act of appraisal, however, they will have important social effects on those whom they condemn. Lemert contends that deviation can be divided into a primary form, the initial act of rule-breaking, and a secondary form, the set of adjustments which the rule-breaker may have to make to cope with the reactions which his rule-breaking engenders:

. . . if the deviant acts are repetitive and have a high visibility, and if there is a severe societal reaction, which, through a process of identification, is incorporated as part of the 'me' of the individual, the probability is greatly increased that the integration of existing roles will be disrupted and that reorganization based upon a new role or set of roles will occur . . . when a person begins to employ his deviant behavior or a role based upon it as means of defense, attack, or adjustment to the overt and covert problems created by the consequent societal reaction to him, his deviation is secondary.[4]

The assignment to a deviant role may be based on imperfect wisdom but the consequences of such an assignment are still of the greatest importance to the new role-player. To others he will *be* a deviant, whether or not an outsider could argue that he did not commit the acts imputed to him. '. . . It should be clear that *secondary deviation can be produced when an individual is not himself motivated to adopt it, and when no "objective" or "real" primary deviation existed in the first place.*'[5] Furthermore, although the attributes ascribed to particular deviancies can be spurious, they will still shape the way in which the deviancy is handled by those who believe in these attributes. Any study of social deviancy must therefore ground itself in the understandings which prevail in a society. Deviancy is an outcome of a process of judgment and evaluation which distinguishes certain forms of behaviour as rule-breaking and attaches penalties to them. The context in which the rules emerge, are applied, and sanctions are inflicted is all-important:

Social groups create deviance by making the rules whose infraction constitutes deviance, and by applying those rules to particular people and
labelling them as outsiders . . . deviance is not a quality of the act the
person commits, but rather a consequence of the application by others of
rules and sanctions to an 'offender'. The deviant is one to whom that label
has been successfully applied; deviant behaviour is behaviour that people
so label.[6]

Becker's definition regards as problematic what many criminologists
have taken for granted. It does not assume in advance that crimes are
alone the proper study of the sociology of deviancy; that deviancy
can be construed as 'anti-social' behaviour; that it is statistically
infrequent activity; or that it is behaviour which flouts widely held
norms. Moreover, it does not prejudge the character of the causal
processes that can generate deviancy. Whilst it treats social rules as
an identifying system, it presupposes nothing else about the characteristics of those who may become deviant or the experiences which
they may share as a result of their having become deviant. It is thus a
definition of great potential fruitfulness: it assembles a wide range of
events together for examination and directs attention at their change-
ful and interdependent nature. Above all, it anchors them in a social
structure instead of viewing deviants as 'sociopathic' or 'psychopathic' individuals who develop in a social limbo. Deviancy is
everywhere and always the outcome of an interaction between rule-
makers, rule-enforcers and rule-breakers. As David Downes and I
have remarked elsewhere:

The result has been a momentous enlargement and enrichment of the
scope of criminology. The issues of defining and enforcing the criminal
law are now regarded as in themselves problematic, and not objectively
given. There has been a resultant loss of clarity about the kinds of question
we can legitimately ask about crime and delinquency, and a loss of
certainty about the ways in which we can evaluate the answers. But this
erstwhile clarity and certainty have been shown to have been in large part
spurious: which in turn may help account for the barrenness of a great
deal of orthodox criminology and penology.[7]

It is, of course, true that the definition proffered by Becker and
others does not constitute a clear guide to recognising deviant
phenomena. It works best in those settings which are characterised by
a well-articulated social structure; where the task of making authoritative moral rules is entrusted to a special body or set of bodies;
where the rules which they produce are concisely expressed; and
where there is substantial consensus about the nature of the moral
world. In all other cases there are considerable difficulties in deciding
what, amongst a great wealth of possibly critical groups and rules,
constitutes the definitive deviancy-defining reaction.

In the first place rules themselves are often ambiguous and conflicting.[8] The precise meaning of rules, their applicability in various contexts, and their competition with one another all promote uncertainty in delineating what is or is not deviant. Indeed, in many cases, deviancy is a very fluid and elusive phenomenon. It may be that this vagueness is not a reflection of the sociological scheme itself but a consequence of the blurred nature of the phenomenal world. Lofland states:

To be true to the character of his materials the sociologist must reflect ambiguity as well as more or less consensual public definitions. The point is here that there are likely, at any given time, to be acts and persons about which it is difficult to make a decision as to their deviance. . . . By being attentive to such conflict and ambiguity, it becomes possible to follow the dynamics of how items can come to be defined in terms of kinds of conflict other than deviance or can reach consensual normality (as well as how they can come to be defined as deviant).[9]

It is also possible that it is the boundaries of relatively marginal or novel behaviour that are blurred rather than those of activities which have become organised over time. Certain 'core' deviancies such as theft are well orchestrated, reactions to them are institutionalised and predictable, and understandings about them have become firmly established. Whilst the understandings and the reaction can be misinformed, most mundane instances of these deviancies are clearly recognisable. Even the conventions for ordering ambiguity may represent some guarantee that a deeper consensus exists about the marginal or the emergent:

Plural evaluation, shifting standards, and moral ambiguity may, and do, coexist with a phenomenal realm that is commonly sensed as deviant. The very meaning of pluralism, the very possibility of shift and ambiguity, depends on a wider consensus founded in common understandings, regarding the patently deviant nature of many nonetheless ordinary undertakings.[10]

As I shall argue, the outcome of such uncertainty may be a curiously fruitful one for the sociologist of deviancy. He tends to resort to those areas where particular problematic states are experienced not so much by the studied actors as by the sociologist himself. It is this sense of ambiguity which can prompt the sociologist into attaining understanding. It may be welcomed rather than deplored.

The definitive deviancy-generating reaction cannot simply be a matter of the criminal law because deviancy is taken to be a large class of which crime is but a sub-class. It cannot simply be an issue of immediate, effective power because many social aggregates (such as lynch mobs and the Ku Klux Klan) are able to enforce their

notions of propriety without transforming those whom they deplore
into what sociologists would call deviants. That is, the reaction itself
is held to be deviant, not that which is reacted against. The reaction
does not, it seems, have to be supported by legitimated authority
because the pluralist model of society espoused by Becker and
Lemert portrays the authority of rulers and rules as problematic.
Indeed, in Becker's analysis of the deviant occupation of the dance
hall musician,[11] or in Lemert's discussion of blindness,[12] no reference
is made to an authoritative reaction. The use of Becker's definition is
further complicated by the fact that competing perspectives can exist
in the same situation; each one emanating from a social group and
each one buttressed by threats of sanctions. The selection of any one
perspective as critical could be merely arbitrary. Resort to the subjective meanings of an action for the actors is not necessarily much
of a solution. People may conceive of themselves as immoral or
wayward although no discernible rule-making or rule-enforcement
may have occurred. Indeed, their self-definition may be built around
the responses of a generalised other* which is foreign to their society,
imaginary or anachronistic.

In sum, there are abundant cases which can be examined as socially
deviant but do not appear to share very much in common. The
grounds for analysing stuttering,[13] radicalism,[14] hippies,[15] nudism[16]
and stripping[17] as members of the same class of behaviours as
murder, rape and opiate addiction are not always obvious. It may
well be that, apart from a sociological preoccupation with the
Gothic,[18] the study of deviancy is distinguished by an approach
rather than by an area. A concern with the Gothic need not necessarily be purely whimsical. The sociologists of deviancy tend to
adhere to the methodological tenet that understanding is best
acquired when a balance is attained between two states. One state
is achieved when the interior world of a system of action can be
appreciated. The sociologist can so imbed himself in the commonsense meanings prevailing in a setting that he can more or less
faithfully reproduce them. The other, contrary state is that of social
distance which permits the sociologist to regard the commonsense
world as strange and unfamiliar. Thus Goffman writes:

In pursuit of their interests, parties of all kinds must deal with and through
individuals. . . . In these dealings, parties—or rather persons who manage
them—must orient to the capacities which these individuals are seen to

* The generalised other refers to the sense which an individual makes of the
attitudes of the organised social groups which constitute his significant environment. It is *generalised* because it does not refer to the qualities of specific, discrete
individuals but to the qualities of abstract or real groups. (See G. Mead, *Mind,
Self, and Society*, University of Chicago Press, Chicago, 1934, esp. pp. 154–5.)

have and to the conditions which bear upon their exercise, such as innate human propensities, culture-bound beliefs, social norms, the market value of labor, and so forth. To orient to these capacities is to come to conclusions . . . concerning them; and to come to these conclusions is to have assumptions about the fundamental nature of the sorts of persons dealt with. These assumptions about human nature, however, are not easy to uncover because they can be as deeply taken for granted by the student as by those he studies. And so an appeal is made to extraordinary situations wherein the student can stumble into awareness. For example, during periods of marked social change, when individuals acquire rights or lose them, attention is directed to properties of individuals which will soon become defined as simply human and taken for granted.[19]

There are few ready-made situations which facilitate such a stumbling into awareness, and it may be that the sociology of deviancy is unusually replete with them. It is in this sense that deviant occasions serve as test-beds for the generation of theory about social process. The taboo, the proscribed or the unusual all promote distancing experiences. But it is precisely this quality of the area that has denied unity to its study. The charms of the Gothic appear to have seduced some sociologists into mistaking a collection of diverse phenomena for a coherent field.

The difficulties attached to using Becker's conception proliferate as the societies which are analysed become simpler, more closely integrated and less dependent upon formal codes of rules. With decreasing social distance between a society's members, the tendency readily to impute deviant status to people may also decrease. Other things being equal, the existence of clearly articulated deviant subgroups cannot always be anticipated in a community which contains little structural differentiation. Becker's definition implies a routinisation and formalisation of deviancy-creating mechanisms and these may typify only a limited range of communities.

Yet it does not follow that these limitations clearly commend the rejection of Becker's perspective and the adoption of another. Any other formulation of deviancy encounters as many or more problems of application. For instance, a reliance upon ideas of social disorganisation precludes an examination of deviancy which is stabilised and orderly. Criminality is a routine, predictable feature of business organisation and the disorganisation stance would either ignore it or resort to palpably metaphysical arguments. Similarly, reference to statistical infrequency cannot account for the findings of self-reporting studies which demonstrate the very normality and frequency of many kinds of rule-breaking. A seemingly safe retreat into a reliance upon legal codes for criteria again hampers analysis; the law is simply one of a number of expressions of social control and the study of deviancy must encompass an understanding of how control is differentially applied to various problematic activities. It thus seems that competing attempts to define deviancy encounter complications no less often that the 'reactions' position. It is clear that problems abound most frequently when Becker's idea is employed in settings which are not covered by concise or formal rules and where there is no official institutional response. Whilst these cases are eminently worthy of analysis, I shall try to restrict my discussion to less ambiguous areas.

CONCEPTIONS OF DEVIANT ROLES

Deviant roles are social constructs which are parts of a society's organisation of beliefs and understandings about itself and the larger world. Whilst disruptive, problematic or bizarre behaviour would exist without these constructs, collective acts of interpretation give deviancy a peculiar clarity and concreteness of expression. In their joint efforts to understand and sustain social life, men designate certain phenomena as deviant and endow them with special properties. These designations serve to explain, separate and justify particular activities. They impose an order on what might otherwise be an inchoate world. In this chapter I shall examine the manner in which these acts of designation take place.

Only rarely, as is the case with some drug-induced experiences, will men have even the slightest claim to have had 'direct' confrontation with the reality of social life. 'Pure experience', if it does indeed exist, can never be communicated because the very act of description imposes a structure which makes it impure. Visions which approximate to 'pure experience' are regarded by the visionary as virtually incommunicable. Religious ecstasy, trance and hallucinated states are said to defy conventional patterns of classification and comprehension; they transcend the structures of everyday thought. As Irwin says of the drug LSD, it 'seems to break down, temporarily at least, one's categorization of the world . . .'[20] Other experiences are prearranged for us. They are pre-selected and pre-structured by groupings of categories and expectations which are socially 'given'. We enter a social world which is already organised and coherent in a way that most people accept as natural and unquestionable. On to a potentially bewildering range of stimuli are imposed shapes, formations and meanings which seem so obvious that alternative structures are not normally considered possible. Not only is a chair clearly a chair, it is also immediately understood what it is and what purposes it serves. Symbol and object are thus usually fused in the same perception. Life has a commonsense quality and an ability to be organised which permit prediction, concerted action and mutual understanding. Wilkins remarks, 'It is as though the human mind had a storage system linked to some classificatory and integrating device which was used for purposes of subjective prediction and regulation of behaviour. . . .'[21]

The very act of categorisation and comprehension imposes a simplicity on the objects which are typified. The grasping of an object necessarily entails that many of its details are distorted or ignored, that a coherence is detected or forced upon the object, and that the object is detached from its background and made discrete. The abundant complexities and contradictions that may characterise a deviant phenomenon can rarely be built into an easily manageable typification.* As Simmons argues:

The 'overcategorization' of objects seems to be a necessary and ubiquitous aspect of human thought processes—a necessary means of organizing the infinite detail and complexity of the 'outside' world. But such coding is necessarily a simplification of incoming stimuli; a *selective* simplification in which information is lost, and misinformation may be added.[22]

Whilst our activities continually test and revise the meanings of our immediate experience so that reality is always in a state of negotiation and rebuilding, most of our lives are dominated by assumptions which we can never test. The bulk of our knowledge of the world must be taken on trust and, for most of the time, it serves well enough. There are many groups and situations in society which we can never personally encounter but they nevertheless form a real background to our own actions. Most frequently, we assume the existence and characteristics of such deviants as skinheads, drug addicts and homosexuals although we may never have the time or inclination to explore the accuracy of the information we have about them.

We also require a stable background of understandings so that even minor revisions can be made. Some stable criteria and definitions must support our testing behaviour. Furthermore, symbol and object become progressively integrated over time so that a critical distance becomes more and more difficult to attain. 'As time goes on and experiences pile up, we make a greater and greater investment in our system of labels. So a conservative bias is built in.'[23] More important, the actions and statements of others can validate the commonsense and indisputable quality of our own notions. What others accept and take for granted acquires an objectivity and reality which are independent of our wills. Perspectives which we share with others can become increasingly anonymous and rooted in the natural order of things:

* By 'typification' I mean an intellectual reconstruction of a phenomenon which is employed both to describe it and to grasp it.

It is obvious that both idealizations, that of the interchangeability of standpoints and that of the congruency of relevances—together constituting the *general thesis of reciprocal perspectives*—are typifying constructs of thought which supersede the thought objects of my and my fellow-man's private experience. By the operation of these constructs of common-sense thinking it is assumed that the sector of the world taken for granted by me is also taken for granted by you, my individual fellow-man, even more, that it is taken for granted by 'Us'. But this 'We' does not merely include you and me but 'everyone who is one of us', i.e., everyone whose system of relevances is substantially (sufficiently) in conformity with yours and mine. Thus, the general thesis of reciprocal perspectives leads to the apprehension of objects and their aspects actually known by me and potentially known to you as everyone's knowledge. Such knowledge is conceived to be objective and anonymous, i.e., detached from and independent of my and my fellow-man's definition of the situation, our unique biographical circumstances and the actual and potential purposes at hand involved therein.[24]

Our ability to test information about objects in the social world diminishes as those objects become distant from us. Whilst we may doubt the validity of what we are told about those whom we know intimately, we have little opportunity to dispute contentions about those who are socially distant. Not only is opportunity lacking, incentive may also be weak. Berger claims that social knowledge is shaped by an 'imperative to triviality',[25] a need to reduce the strange and the problematic to the level of inconsequentiality and the taken-for-granted. If new events at the margins of our social world can be understood in terms of existing categories and can be made to appear familiar, it seems that we do not often wish to probe further. When disconcerting phenomena are thus trivialised, the desire for further exploration is generally curbed. If one can 'make sense' of an event, it will tend to provoke less discomfort. The sense which is made can be inaccurate or misleading, but triviality has been restored and life can be resumed. Highly relevant to Berger's concept is the distinction made by James[26] and Schutz between 'knowledge of acquaintance' and 'knowledge about': 'there are centres of explicit knowledge *of* what is aimed at; they are surrounded by a halo of knowledge *about* what seems to be sufficient'.[27] Schutz claims further that 'in the ordinary course of affairs it is sufficient to know something *about* the general type or style of events we may encounter in our life-world in order to manage or control them'.[28] That is, information about many objects can be minimal and not deliberately pursued so long as it serves to permit orderly social life. The more marginal the objects (and deviancy as we imagine it is very marginal for most of us at most times), the more will knowledge be knowledge *about*.

Another source of simplification stems from the *quality* of the

information which we possess about socially distant occurrences.
There is a vividness and immediacy about face-to-face relations which
is absent when we think about others who are not physically present.
Our ability to impose increasingly anonymous and general characteristics on people grows as they become socially removed from us:

The social reality of everyday life is . . . apprehended in a continuum of
typifications, which are progressively anonymous as they are removed from
the 'here and now' of the face-to-face situation. At one pole of the continuum are those others with whom I frequently and intensively interact
in face-to-face situations—my 'inner circle', as it were. At the other pole
are highly anonymous abstractions, which by their very nature can never
be available in face-to-face interaction.[29]

Furthermore, as Schutz remarks, the manner in which we recognise
one who is distant 'does not apprehend the unique person as he
exists within his living present. Instead it pictures him as always the
same and homogeneous, leaving out of account all the changes and
rough edges that go along with individuality'.[30] In a sense, then,
social distance dehumanises our typing of people. We are able to
describe them in a way that would seem peculiar were we to apply it
to our intimate acquaintances.* Social distance also increases the
facility and speed of typing processes:

A set of cultural rules exists for typing deviants. These rules are not
necessarily fully explicated; rather they are tacit, and therefore known
usually after the fact. One rule on typing, inferred from many observations,
may be summarised as the greater the social distance between the typer and
the person singled out for typing, the broader the type and the quicker
it may be applied.[31]

Most of us are prone to such dehumanising activity. There are at
least two main reasons for this. Many kinds of deviancy are at the
social margins and are territorially confined. Few of us are familiar
with drug-addicts, rapists, robbers or prostitutes in their deviant
roles. The very playing of these roles tends to locate such deviants in
social networks which are structurally removed from us. Furthermore, most of us have no wish to reduce this distance. Deviants who
are recognisable as rule-breakers can stigmatise those with whom
they associate. Closeness to deviancy can impugn our own moral
standing. This situation approximates closely to the relations which
Schutz claims exist between a stranger and foreign groups:

* Where social distance is combined with a poverty of information, it seems that
typifications are not only simplified but they also tend to express something of the
typifier's private fears and anxieties. Checks on social typing which are imposed
in face-to-face situations do not restrain impersonal typing. Typifications can
thus become very much the personal response of the definer.

. . . the ready-made picture of the foreign group subsisting within the stranger's home-group proves its inadequacy for the approaching stranger for the mere reason that it has not been formed with the aim of provoking a response from or a reaction of the foreign group. The knowledge which it offers serves merely as a handy scheme for interpreting the foreign group and not as a guide for interaction between the two groups. . . . Hence, this kind of knowledge is . . . insulated; it can be neither verified nor falsified by responses of the members of the foreign group.[32]

Physical boundaries also restrict access to deviant worlds. When deviancy is stabilised and concentrated in certain areas (such as Soho, Harlem, the Tenderloin or, earlier on, the Ratcliffe Highway and Five Points) possibilities of random and unintended confrontations with deviants are considerably reduced. At the symbolic level, too, prohibition and the embellishment of deviancy with significance place scarecrows around rule-breaking. In Matza's words, the result of a moral ban is 'to restrict and discourage access to the designated phenomenon at its invitational edge'.[33]

An interesting consequence of such dehumanisation is that we may transform our attitudes towards our acquaintance when we discover that they are deviant. Instead of feeling that the moral and social gulf that separates us from deviancy is diminished when we make such a discovery, we frequently impose this gulf between ourselves and our redefined acquaintance. The typifications that arise from generalisations about abstract others can be applied to those whom we know in face-to-face situations. As Duster remarks, 'When the discovery is made that an individual is a drug addict, the typical response is that, "I now know what there is to be known about that person".'[34] We may reconstruct our knowledge of him, search for consistencies, and place his action in a new context of meaning which estranges him from us. Kitsuse discovered that people reconstructed their images of individuals who were alleged to be homosexual:*

A general pattern revealed by the subjects' responses . . . is that when an individual's sexual 'normality' is called into question, by whatever form of evidence, the imputation of homosexuality is documented by *retrospective interpretations* of the deviant's behavior, a process by which the subject reinterprets the individual's past behavior in the light of the new information concerning his sexual deviance. This process is particularly evident in

---

* Of course the process of reformulating the significance of a biography in the light of new information is not necessarily uncompassionate. The provision of a master status which leads to reinterpretations of other statuses can sometimes bring about a decrease in social distance. Percy Cohen suggested to me that 'He never bothers to listen' can become 'I didn't realise that he was hard of hearing.' The point is, however, that there are dominant statuses, particularly deviant ones, whose ramifications are commonly supposed to extend to almost all behaviour and motives.

cases where the prior relationship between the subject and the alleged homosexual was more than a chance encounter or casual acquaintanceship. The subjects indicate that they reviewed their past interactions with the individuals in question, searching for nuances of behavior which might give further evidence of the alleged deviance. This retrospective reading generally provided the subjects with just such evidence to support the conclusion that 'this is what was going on all the time'.[35]

The imposition of social distance not only finds expression in changed attitudes, it also has physical consequences. Many deviants are subject to ostracism, segregation and, in some instances, to incarceration in prisons or mental hospitals. The discovery of deviancy may be so momentous that it results in a shunning of the one whose rule-breaking has become apparent. As Denzin remarks, 'We daily reaffirm our moralities and value structures by placing ourselves apart from others whom we regard as deviant.'[36] Rejection can, in turn, lead to the deviant's retreat from what are now painful and embarrassing relationships. As such reciprocal shunning develops and secondary deviation occurs, it becomes more and more possible to describe the deviant in impersonal and abstract terms. Wilkins has constructed a model of deviancy amplification to describe this process.[37] He argues that when a society receives misleading or simplified feedback about its deviant populations, it reacts in a way that makes those populations even more deviant. Further feedback generates a more agitated response which encourages even greater deviancy. The consolidation of stereotypes can engender a punitive stance which allows the deviant less and less freedom to play anything but a deviant role.

There are, of course, alternative outcomes. The rule-breaker may abstain from further deviancy. He may be able to neutralise the implications of his deviancy in certain situations: it may be 'forgotten' or transformed into something which does not conform to the larger stereotypes.[38] Definitions of the deviancy may even change so that the larger abstractions are revised. Some criminologists have been accused of 'softness' towards the deviant. Sir Richard Jackson, formerly Assistant Commissioner of Metropolitan Police, remarks, for instance:

For glossy magazines to print glamorized pictures of criminals; for journalists and sociologists to write articles making heroes out of petty crooks and brutal thugs; for radio and television producers to put out programmes which deride and attack the police while deliberately working up sympathy for thieves and murderers—such behaviour seems to me either irresponsible or malicious.[39]

Such accusations may well stem from those who still maintain the impersonal typifications and resent the reformed and personalised accounts of those who entertain close relations with rule-breakers.[40] Nevertheless, one of the characteristic fates of deviants is the experience of rejection.

In the case of deviants who break significant rules which are grounded in deep and widely held moral feelings, typifications are applied in Britain and America which are unusually complete. Deviancy is often viewed as a total moral state which reflects the substantial self, or essential inner nature, of the wrongdoer. Rule-breaking is not so much regarded as an ephemeral partial aspect of a person's self but an indication of his essence. A deviant role is not just another role in a varied repertoire; it is a critical and revealing guide to a deviant *personality*. Mary Douglas argues that such comprehensive attributions are made in societies which are marked by ritual poverty and that Protestantism is a ritually impoverishing religion. Transgressions in a society which is lavishly endowed with ritual can be treated as improper role-performances rather than as statements about the transgressor's substantial self. They can be redressed by correct ritual. In symbolically impoverished societies, however, deviancy is not a matter of external impropriety and the damage cannot be so easily repaired:

Where symbols are highly valued and ritualism strong, then the idea of sin involves specific, formal acts of wrong-doing; where ritualism is weak, the idea of sin does not focus on specific external actions, but on internal states of mind; rituals of purification will not be so much in evidence.[41]

Another strain in Protestant thinking tends to engender complete typifications. The rationalising propensity (described by Weber)

contributed . . . to the eventual official quantification of moral phenomena . . . it contributed the view of men and their actions as *absolute categories* (or absolute typifications). That is, rather than see men and their actions as the continuous, situation-bound, concrete persons we normally assume for our purposes of everyday interaction, it saw them as *discrete*, discontinuous phenomena that are independent of time and situations.[42]

The consequences, according to Duster, are profound:

This matter of one's total identity as morally good or evil has been viewed as having roots in a specific strain of Western thought, and more particularly, in the northern Protestant conception of the evil and immoral. Ranulf and Weber are among the observers who have noted that Roman Catholicism has a more wholistic [*sic*] integrated view of 'good and evil' in human action. The Roman Church has always acknowledged both the attainment of virtue and the existence of evil and sin in all men. . . . Men in Protestant nations are said to see men as either 'good, upstanding, righteous' members of the normal community, or as 'bad, evil and immoral'. Such men will typically ridicule the Catholic confessional as a futile exercise in momentary purgation, or at its worse, ephemeral truth overladen with a few layers of hypocrisy. The argument continues that the 'deviant' in Protestant nations is viewed in terms of his total evil or total deviance, and it follows that such a strong moralistic conception seeks total condemnation and total punishment.[43]

This Protestant theme in thinking on deviancy generates unusually well-rounded and coherent typifications.* When deviancy is thought to be intimately tied to matters of intention and character, it cannot be dismissed as nothing more than a facet of a more complex whole. The revelation that someone is deviant can bring about a total reformation of the significance of his past, present and future actions. Such a typifying trend reinforces the simplified processes of definition which occur when social distance intervenes between typifier and typified. The production of these elementary stereotypes furnishes a society with an easily intelligible pandemonium of folk devils. The pandemonium is an important part of the social structure as it is known to a society's members: 'social structure is the sum total of . . . typifications and of the recurrent patterns of interaction established by means of them. As such, social structure is an essential element of the reality of everyday life'.[44] Typifications of such deviants as the Teddy Boy, the Dope Fiend, the Tart and the Queen are considerably more than simple representations of social knowledge about roles. They have an important symbolic quality which

* I find these arguments cogent, but they should not be treated as more than interesting conjectures. Designations of deviancy cannot ever be attributed solely to religious sources or even to some of the wider thought systems of which religions are but members. Bureaucratisation and scale combine with complexity to make of society a network of relatively isolated social worlds. Industrialisation and the application of rationality tend to reinforce the social distance which separates deviants from nondeviants. Protestant societies underwent industrialisation much earlier than did Catholic societies, and it is likely that differences in typifying practices can be attributed to the social structures brought about by differences in industrialisation. It may be that, of the processes which were at work, the systematic use of 'rationality' was the most significant in structuring perceptions of deviancy (see M. Foucault, *Madness and Civilization*, Tavistock, London, 1967). Another difficulty prevents full acceptance of Douglas' and Duster's ideas. Research on the entire area of deviant typifications is novel. It is largely an American and, to a lesser extent, a British enterprise. Information from contemporary Catholic communities or from our Catholic past has not been explored and, in the absence of comparative data, assertions of the sort which I have quoted should be treated circumspectly. A final point is that absolute or integrated typifications lead to different systems of control, but the control in 'Protestant' and 'Catholic' cases may be equally severe. Indeed, in Catholic societies, control in many instances was more strenuously applied than in Protestant ones. The pursuit of witches, for example, was predominantly Catholic. It was also waged more severely in Catholic countries. It would be interesting to discover whether conceptions of witchcraft were systematically structured by the kinds of constraints that Douglas and Duster refer to.

colours them and makes them serviceable for social control. The emergence of folk devils imposes a form and meaning on our own actions; they enable us to recognise whom we should avoid and whose behaviour we should not emulate. They act as dramatic reminders of what roles are intolerable:

Because the range of human behavior is potentially so wide, social groups maintain boundaries in the sense that they try to limit the flow of behavior within their domain so that it circulates within a defined cultural territory. Boundaries, then, are an important point of reference for persons participating in any system. . . . For all its apparent abstractness, a social system is organized around the movements of persons joined together in regular social relations. The only material found in a system for making boundaries, then, is the behavior of its participants; and the kinds of behavior which best perform this function are often deviant, since they represent the most extreme variety of conduct to be found within the experience of the group.[45]

Typifications of deviancy thus serve an exemplary and educative purpose. They are caricatures of abhorrent behaviour which frequently stress the most unpleasant features of rule breaking. They are rarely attempts at compressing information in an accurate and dispassionate manner. According to Klapp, there are many such exemplary typifications which are organised around core elements in social control concerns. Not only are there pandemonia, there are also pantheons which stress the heroic and the commendable. Whilst many recurrent themes in drama focus on the villainous, others applaud the virtues of the altruistic, the brave or the patriotic:

The hero, villain and fool represent three dimensions of social control in our society. Heroes are praised, set up as models, and given a central part in dramas. Villains and fools are negative models, respectively, of evil to be feared and hated, and absurdity to be ridiculed. Heroes, villains and fools represent three directions of deviation: (1) better than, (2) dangerous to, and (3) falling short of, norms applied to group members or status occupants. These basic kinds of model are used by all societies to maintain the social system, especially to control persons, and put on significant dramas and rituals.[46]

The hero, the villain and the fool represent clusterings of *qualities* of typifications. In part, orderly social life is made possible by personalised and highly abstract depictions of aberrant role-styles. The reified deviants act as checks on proscribed impulses, warnings about the type of person we might become if we continue to find deviation attractive. It is plausible that much of the expensive drama and ritual which surround the apprehension and denunciation of the deviant are directed at maintaining the daemonic and isolated character of deviancy. Without these demonstrations, typifications would be weakened and social control would suffer correspondingly. When strongly supported laws are enforced, court procedures often seem to be devoted to unmasking the rule-breaker and placing him in his proper position in the pandemonium. Were it not for this unmasking and degradation, we might persist in assuming that his rule-breaking is unimportant and that it can be integrated with rule-observing. Deviancy's terrifying implications for the self, its power to mar, are publicised in what Tannenbaum calls the 'dramatisation of evil'.[47] Such dramatisation is not the ritual of a Catholic society which demands formal penance, but the ritual of exorcism and outcasting. It reveals the deviant as a wicked outsider who has lost his right to claim membership of the normal community:

The work of the denunciation effects the recasting of the objective character of the perceived other. The other person becomes in the eyes of his condemners literally a different and new person . . . the former identity stands as accidental; the new identity is the 'basic reality'. What he is now is what, 'after all', he was all along.[48]

Typifications are ways of organising the world so that it becomes knowable to its inhabitants. They map out social structure. More important, exemplary typifications fashion motives, perceptions and reactions. As Klapp argues:

A major function of types is providing the individual with self-images and corresponding motivation. I believe that social types provide the main motivational force for the individual to relate himself to the system— accounting for his mobility, seeking and finding a place, orientation toward one goal or career rather than another—even deviation. . . . From the outside, a person finds a more or less deliberate effort by society to mould him in accordance with certain types that may not be the same as he has chosen.[49]

Whilst the institutions of the state are armed with a pomp and authority which are peculiarly effective in confirming deviant typifications, other groups in society are engaged in a constant effort to change social types. If a group can manage to recast the character of its opponents, it can discredit and deny the legitimacy of their actions and perspectives. A great deal of political activity is organised around attempts to redefine elements of the social structure in a way which prompts favourable reactions. When political conflict becomes acute, the combatants may each try to cast the other in the role of deviant. In the case of the universities in the late 1960s, for instance, opponents tried to provide competing definitions of reality which would further their goals. Sir William Alexander, Secretary of the Association of Education Committees, typified militant students thus:

There is little doubt that there is deliberate organisation seeking to cause disruption and provoke displays of bad manners by university undergraduates. . . . One hears of people who seem to spend most of their time going from university to university to try to do a bit of rabble rousing.[50]

Sir William represented students as bad mannered and rabble rousers; not as they would themselves care to be defined, political activists seriously dedicated to bettering the cause of humanity. Their deviancy was a simple breach of the etiquette that civilised people should observe and nothing to do with political concerns. Undergraduates at the London School of Economics, on the other hand, portrayed the School's administrators as politically motivated men masked by a pretence of academic disinterest:

Any exercise whatever in the sociology of the LSE—rather sociology *at* the LSE—would be too dangerous for the reactionary oligarchy of bureaucrats, businessmen and professors who control the School. It would explode, instantly and irremediably, the ludicrous mystification that the LSE has been an 'impartial' and 'non-political' institution of learning, above all class interests. Any elementary research into the facts reveals that the exact opposite is true. The LSE has always had a political record that stands out a mile—to the right. This record is consistently, openly and rabidly reactionary—linked at every step to the most odious traditions of imperialism and racism.[51]

Typifications and counter-typifications are thus constantly bartered and publicised in an attempt to rebuild social reality. An important part of any complex society is the work of countless groups who are trying to cast others as deviant. As Douglas argues, 'To the extent . . . that each individual does want to construct a moral image of himself, he is necessarily committed to a competitive struggle to morally upgrade himself and morally downgrade others (not identified with himself).'[52] Very largely, the success of these groups depends on their access to institutions which confer power and authority on their efforts. I shall discuss this aspect of classifying processes in the next chapter.

The validity of typifications of deviants can be rarely tested by us. Even if we do know some deviants personally, there are many kinds of deviancy whose nature we have to take on trust. 'Most of what we "know" we have taken on the authority of others, and it is only as others continue to confirm this "knowledge" that it continues to be plausible to us.'[53] When social distance intervenes between us and those whom we type, when our contacts with deviant others are fleeting, and when association with deviant phenomena can confer stigma, a communication gap tends to develop. Most of our information about deviancy is not only second-hand, it is also transmitted to us by special agencies whose function it is to bridge this comforting gap:

> Intermediary communications systems have been established so that the direct contact which was essential in earlier times is not now required. . . . The insane, the criminal, and the deviant can now be isolated so that the normal members of the culture do not gain any experience of the non-normal. . . . Thus, apart from indirect experience derived from newspapers and other mass media, our modern culture has led to the isolation (and alienation) of deviant groups. The nature of the information obtained from direct experience and that obtained from mass media differs in both quality and type.[54]

Much of the work of constructing deviant social types is taken up by intermediary organisations. In many cases the operations of the press, radio and television are the only means by which information about deviancy is diffused. The way in which these media construe and report deviancy can thus be of the greatest importance in shaping the typifications made by a society's members and, in some instances, by its lawmakers and law-enforcers. Those who report news about deviancy must make a series of decisions: what deviancy is 'news-worthy' and ought to be reported; what significance should be attached to the deviancy; how deviancy and deviant events should be assessed and described; what causal sequences play themselves out in deviancy, and so on. As Quinney argues, 'Public conceptions of crime and delinquency are constructed on the basis of "news" presentations. Specific conceptions are shaped by what is considered to be news about the subject of crime.'[55] The sociology of deviancy-reporting is undeveloped, yet it is clear that reporters exercise con-tinual discretion in deciding what to report and how to report it. In what follows, I shall focus on newspapers alone although the other channels of public communication are obviously important. News-papers seem to be critically important disseminators of information about deviancy. In their study of the 'Seattle Windshield Pitting Epidemic' (see pp. 42–3 for a further account of the epidemic), for example, Medalia and Larsen remark, 'While radio is generally con-sidered the most adaptable and efficient mass medium for rapid coverage of the news, the windshield situation suggests that for certain kinds of information, the newspapers, without benefit of a head-start, are able to far outdistance the other media in giving a public its first remembered contact with the news'.[56]

Press discretion in reporting is an inevitable response to the wealth of data that *could* be discussed in newspapers. Courts and prisons are continually processing deviants and each processing episode is a potential subject for 'news'. Unless a newspaper is catering for a highly localised readership, it is unlikely to report the mundane and the usual episodes. What is newsworthy often tends to be the bizarre or the untoward. Park suggests that the metropolitan press offers 'a flight from reality' by its 'persistent search in the drab episodes of city life for the romantic and picturesque, its dramatic accounts of vice and crime. . . .'[57] What becomes news, therefore, is not necessarily what is most representative of a particular set of phenomena; rather, it is its very unrepresentativeness that will probably ensure that it will be reported. Only colourful or unusual events are thus likely to feature in any account of what happened on a particular occasion. Skinheads or train vandals are more likely to be recorded than petty delinquents, and much more likely than the normal rule-observing behaviour of most adolescents. The generation of exciting accounts about such deviant types is the task of the news reporter:

Newsmen define their job as producing a certain quantity of what is called 'news' every twenty four hours. This is to be produced *even though nothing much has happened.* News is a continuous challenge, and meeting this challenge is the newsman's job. He is rewarded for fulfilling this, his manifest function. A consequence of this focus on news as a central value is the shelving of strong interest in objectivity at the point of policy conflict. . . . Newsmen do talk about ethics, objectivity, and the relative worth of various papers, but not when there is news to get. (This is a variant of the process of 'displacement of goals', newsmen turning to 'getting news' rather than to seeking data which will enlighten and inform their readers.)[58]

It follows that the volume and quality of deviancy as it is known on the basis of press reports bear little relation to the character of deviancy as it is daily pursued by rule-breakers. Alterations in rates of rule-breaking and the types of rule-breaking that occur are inaccurately mirrored by newspapers. In one survey of Colorado papers, for example, Davis remarks, 'There is no consistent relationship between the amount of crime news in newspapers and the local crime rates. Semi-annual percentage changes in crime coverage were found to be at marked variance with Colorado crime trends, both for total crime and for selected types of crime.'[59]

The *manner* in which deviant affairs are reported is shaped by forces which impose a structure and simplicity on typifications. Crime reporters usually have little time to analyse events,[60] and they are not sociologists or disinterested observers of behaviour. 'They are not rewarded for analyzing the social structure, but for getting news.'[61] The process of recognising and assembling news is facilitated by symbols which signify the importance of certain events and help to explain those events. The detection of these symbols in a situation suggests that it deserves reporting:

Reporters undergo craft training which encourages the selection from an array of symbols those which best can be purveyed to the public as news. The reporter selects what he believes is the most pertinent, the most easily identified symbols. . . . Although there is at times almost universal agreement among reporters on the key symbol in a given news situation, the selection process has no direct relationship to the wants of the readers. Nor is the selection based on any evaluation of a symbol as being representative of a value system.[62]

When such use is made of easily recognised symbols, there is a tendency for crime reporting to become an act of *classifying* deviancy. In particular, it tends to place new forms of deviancy in old categories which have become associated with certain key symbols. The problematic qualities of new deviancies are reduced by their being subsumed under familiar labels. In this way, a subtle process of redefinition can be carried on. According to Cohen, press descriptions of the 'Mods and Rockers' clashes of the 1960s were subject to just such a process:

The process of spurious attribution is not, of course, random. The audience has already created stereotypes to draw upon and, as with racial stereotypes, there is a readily available composite image which the new picture can be grafted on to. The emergent composite draws heavily on folklore elements such as the Teddy Boys, the James Dean–Marlon Brando complex, West Side Gangs, etc.[63]

When a novel phenomenon shares symbols with familiar phenomena it is evaluated as 'newsworthy', but when it is described in terms of these symbols, its novelty is soon lost. In the case of the Teddy Boys, for example, early press descriptions typified the deviants as 'spivs', 'thugs' and 'coshboys'. Teddy Boys were defined as old deviants wearing new clothes. It was only when several spectacular incidents made the old symbols obviously unusable that the Teddy Boy was identified as a new deviant role.[64] What might have been of great significance in an old deviancy may be of considerably less important in a new one. Quite radical changes in rule-breaking behaviour can thus be neglected by a press which employs old symbols to typify them. Crime reporting may treat as highly salient what is, in fact, a peripheral facet of the behaviour. For example, the possession of long hair and the occupation of student status can signify, amongst other things, that one is a revolutionary militant or a quietist hippy. These deviant role-styles are organised around radically different world-views yet, to the press, the long-haired student is unambiguously the possessor of a single role. By focusing on immediately visible or dominant symbols, newspapers create a confused and confusing typification. Halloran, Elliott and

Murdock have illustrated how this selection of a dominant symbol by the press affected reporting of the anti-Vietnam war demonstration of the 27 October 1968. Newspapers had predicted that the demonstration would be extremely violent but it was actually relatively peaceful. Halloran *et al.* argue:

... events will be selected for news reporting in terms of their fit or consonance with pre-existing images and the news of the event will confirm earlier ideas. The more unclear the news item and the more uncertain or doubtful the newsman is in how to report it, the more likely it is to be reported within a general framework that has already been established.[65]

Before the demonstration, the 'pre-existing image' was that the event would be an unusually hostile clash between police and demonstrators. When the prediction was not confirmed, the image was *imposed* on reporting:

... when the definition of the event-as-news was contradicted by the fact that the majority of the participants marched peacefully to a rally in Hyde Park, the resulting discrepancy was resolved by emphasizing those incidents which confirmed the definition and playing down those aspects of the events which contradicted it. The event-as-news thus became a self-fulfilling prophecy.[66]

The symbolic structure into which the reporting was placed was provided by the Paris demonstrations of the same year. Those events which were congruent with this structure were given prominence, those which were not were under-valued:

In 'news' terms, the violent confrontation between police and students in the streets of Paris provided an ideal context within which to elaborate an image of the 27 October demonstration. It combined the optimum possibilities for the development of 'news values' within a framework which was familiar and still salient. However, this demand for a single, unambiguous, newsworthy image necessitated a concentration upon those aspects which were relatively non-specific to the situation and a corresponding neglect of those elements which were unique ... it is obvious ... that the image of the event-as-news, based as it was on a misleading parallel, nevertheless provided the context within which the coverage was elaborated and consequently any aspect which could not be assimilated to this framework was either ignored, given very little attention, or counterpointed.[67]

Another source of misleading typification is the tendency to make a description of deviancy coherent and simple. Deviant stereotypes are created which suggest that the rule-breaking is a homogeneous class of behaviour which is not particularly complicated to understand.[68] Ambiguities and nuances of meaning are frequently eliminated in the process of producing compact, intelligible descriptions.[69]

Order is made out of disorder and a structure is forced on confusion.[70] Fights between the Mods and Rockers, for instance, were described by a vocabulary which employed terms such as 'gang'; this was 'attributable less to conscious and malicious policy than to the fact that the "warring gang" is the easiest way for the ignorant observer to explain such a senseless and ambiguous crowd situation'.[71] Complex social phenomena are thus reduced to a simplistic form which can be presented as 'news'. In the attempt to 'make sense' of deviancy, several distortions are commonly introduced. Rule-breaking phenomena are not often treated as disorganised or without apparent purpose. Even more rarely are they treated as the results of wide-scale changes in the social structure. Instead, the potentially incomprehensible is given a structure by key symbols and designations, such as 'gang', 'hippy' and so on. Low level explanations are proffered to organise understanding of what cannot be seen as random events. One of the commonest explanatory devices is the personalisation of behaviour. In the case of disasters, Drabeck and Quarantelli argue:

. . . disasters can . . . evoke the worst in persons—a relentless search for scapegoats to blame for destruction and loss of life. This tendency to seek the cause in a *who*—rather than a *what*—is common after airplane crashes, fires, cave-ins, and other catastrophes not caused naturally. Personalizing blame in this way is not only a standard response, but well in harmony with the moral framework of American society. Sin and crime are, after all, matters of personal guilt, by traditional Western legal and theological definitions.[72]

When this kind of catastrophe can be blamed on the actions of specific people, disasters or events involving deviancy are even more prone to such attributions.[73] Riots are seldom described as occurring 'spontaneously', they are fomented by organised subversives. The disorders in the American Negro ghettos of the late 1960s were described by the press as the product of deliberate conspiracy, yet the Kerner Commission Report managed to find no evidence of such plotting.[74] More recently, riots in Ulster have been explained as the fruits of the sinister activities of particular groups.[75] These explanations deflect attention away from the more baffling analysis which social structural hypotheses would demand. Similarly, student 'sit-ins' are almost invariably the result of conspiracy.[76] Cohen refers to this quality of typifying deviants as 'cabalism':

In this theme, the behaviour which was to a large degree unorganized, spontaneous and situational, is seen as having been well planned in advance as part of some conspiratorial plot. . . . People who are reluctant to use the mental illness explanation can, by assuming conspiracy, remove some of the capriciousness from the situation.[77]

In many cases the imposition of organisation is not enough; deviant events are held to centre around the activities of one or two critical role-players. When deviancy is a group phenomenon, it is typically explained as the consequence of the machinations of leading figures. Interviews with members of the group furnish newspaper reporters with a 'King of the Teddy Boys', a 'Queen of the Hippies' or a 'Leader of the Squatters'.[78] For instance, a *Sunday Times* reporter was introduced to 'Sid Rawle, 24-year-old "digger" leader, son of an Exmoor shepherd and naïve but honest friend of the drop-outs and homeless . . .' when she described the occupation of 144 Piccadilly by hippies.[79] Similarly, a London *Evening Standard* reporter managed to interview 'the leader of the hippies' who were evicted from a house in Russell Square.[80] As Cohen remarks, 'Another highly effective technique of symbolization was the use of dramatized and ritualistic interviews with "representative" members of deviant groups.'[81] Halloran, Elliott and Murdock succinctly summarise this facet of news construction:

Concentration upon the negative aspects of a situation, particularly incidents of violence, provides the reader with a simple unambiguous image, while attention to 'personality' offers him opportunity to empathize with or project on to an identifiable person or group. These two 'angles' therefore constitute an optimum combination of novel emphases within a familiar framework with which to satisfy the readers' demands for interest and clear meanings. Moreover, the choice of these two 'news values' is reinforced by the fact that they are ideally suited to the situation of a journalist on a daily newspaper. For the actions and remarks of individuals, particularly in their negative aspects, are both more quickly reported and more easily explained than the total structure of the event.[82]

The way in which the press lends structure to events is unusually well illustrated by descriptions of 'pseudo-disasters'. Pseudo-disasters are perceived catastrophes which, in retrospect, can be seen to have been imaginary.[83] The 'Windshield Pitting Epidemic' in Seattle provides an example:

. . . the attention of a large number of Seattle residents became centered on reports of sudden and widespread damage to automobile windshields throughout the city, although for almost a month prior to the 14th [of April 1954] there had been intermittent accounts in Seattle papers of 'vandalism' to windshields in Pugest Sound communities north of Seattle. By the morning of the 16th newspapers estimated that more than 5,000 cars had been affected. . . . An exhaustive chemical and physical study of the situation, reported several months after the 'epidemic' had faded from the newspapers, confirmed what some had suspected all along: that damage to windshields, where it existed, was of the type incurred in the course of driving over a period of time rather than from some unusual attack or precipitation over the space of a few minutes or hours but that the sudden mass concern with windshields had brought this damage into view for many persons for the first time.[84]

Pseudo-disasters frequently stem from the refocusing of public and press attention on an area of events which had previously escaped notice. An interesting example in 1971 was that of the sudden attention awarded attacks by dogs, particularly Alsatians, on small children. Ambiguous or once unnoticed events become symptomatic of the disaster which has befallen a community.[85] In the case of sexual attacks on small children, for instance, Sutherland states that the apprehension of disaster gives rise to newspapers reporting 'daily on the progress of the case, and every real or imagined sex attack, from near and far, is given prominence'.[86] The creation of fear is as much a response to press reporting as to any alarming change in the 'disastrous' phenomenon itself: 'Fear is seldom or never related to statistical trends in sex crimes. . . . Ordinarily, from two to four spectacular sex crimes in a few weeks are sufficient to evoke the phrase "sex crime wave".'[87] When disasters or pseudo-disasters strike, a typical response is the attempt to make 'sense' of what has occurred. The calamity is interpreted at a fairly low level of sociological sophistication; often by reference to the actions of particular social groups.

One of the interesting consequences of press reporting is that the authority of newspaper accounts is almost invariably greater than the countering assertions proffered by deviants themselves. Quite frequently, deviants are poorly organised members of the least powerful social strata and their capacity to defend themselves is correspondingly limited.* Moreover, since deviancy is a discredited activity, the pronouncements of those who justify it are very often discredited. Attacks were made on the Wootton Committee Report[88] on marihuana use because the committee had alluded to evidence submitted by drug-takers.† Similarly, attempts to change the California State Legislature's policy on drugs were denied legitimacy because the attempts were made by groups identified with deviancy:

* There are, of course, exceptions: homosexuals, for instance, are not infrequently represented by defensive organisations.

† For example, Mr Callaghan, the Home Secretary, remarked at the time: 'I think it came as a surprise, if not a shock, to most people, when that notorious advertisement appeared in *The Times* in 1967, to find that there is a lobby in favour of legalizing cannabis. The house should recognize that this lobby exists, and my reading of the report is that the Wootton sub-committee was over influenced by this lobby. I had the impression . . . that those who were in favour of legalizing pot were all the time pushing the other members of the committee back, so that eventually these remarkable conclusions emerged that it would be wrong to legalize it but that the penalties should be reduced.' (Quoted in M. Schofield, *The Strange Case of Pot*, Penguin Books, Middlesex, 1971, p. 91.)

Legislators saw as supporters of the treatment-no-penalty approach the Friends (Quakers), American Civil Liberties Union, NAACP, California Democratic Council, and the social welfare people. . . . Wryly noting that 'the addict has no friends', some observed that not only were the anti-treatment forces much stronger than the pro-treatment ones, but that the latter—for example, the civil liberties groups—were themselves under fire for their 'subversive' activities or were decried for their attempts to break down law-enforcement in the state.[89]

These typifications may have the effect of blocking access to the political process. The views of those who favour the impotent are frequently typified as illegitimate. Thus, Bachrach and Baratz argue, 'Status-quo-oriented persons or groups may succeed in branding an issue as illegitimate, e.g. by arguing noisily and at length that the proposal is communistic, socialistic, reactionary.'[90] I shall argue in another chapter that there is a hierarchy of credibility which endows the statements of the powerful with authority. The consequence of such a hierarchy is that deviants who are typified, however inaccurately, may have little opportunity to pose an effective challenge to the way in which they are portrayed.[91] They may be presented with a critical choice: abandon the deviancy or the deviant role-style altogether; attempt to change the typification by refusing to conform to it; or become more like the typification. Whilst many deviants may abandon their deviancy when it is falsely presented, others may become so estranged by the manner in which they are depicted that they experience a sense of solidarity and outrage against the typifying world. The second alternative is unlikely to meet with much success; not only do hostile typifications lead to fairly radical changes in people's attitudes towards the deviant so that social distance is frequently imposed, but the deviant's attempts are not often effective. The final alternative, conforming to a stage in Wilkin's deviancy amplification sequence, makes the deviant even more deviant. The press can thus engender self-fulfilling prophecies. If the prophecies are taken seriously by law-making and law-enforcing agencies, deviancy amplification is even more likely.

One of the phases in the natural history of deviancy reporting is the emergence of a portrait of the deviant. When new deviant fashions arise, the press usually gives its readers a detailed description of the rule-breaker.[92] This description could serve as a detailed set of role-prescriptions for any neophyte deviant. The more marginal adherent of the fashion may even learn more about his role-requirements from the press than from contacts with core devotees. At the same time, readers who wish to avoid the deviants but are troubled by them will be provided with a ready typification to apply. Such portraits are rarely tentative or qualified; instead they suggest that any one who can be identified with the fashion must adhere to the press's version of its role-style. Very seldom will this version be contradicted by anyone with expertise about deviancy. Instead, it will remain for a long while as the *only* authoritative account of the new role-style. An interesting exception to this natural historical process occurred when the press attempted to define student militancy. Since the typifications were directed at universities, the work-place of those who generate authoritative descriptions of social reality, they *were* met with opposition. Shelston protested:

Far more serious, in terms of the influence they have on the public image of the university world, than the columnists' opportunist sniping are those articles and features which pretend to examine in some detail either individual events, or the protest phenomenon in general, and in doing so present an image of the university world which may satisfy the curiosity of the outsider but which has only limited relevance to that world as known to teachers and students.[93]

If such criticism can be levelled against a press for describing a world which is not so socially distant from middle-class reporters and readers, how much more pertinent it must be when applied to press commentary on drug addiction, 'gang violence', prostitution and so on. It is not the substantive inaccuracy which misinforms the public as much as the attribution of form, coherence and homogeneity to deviant groups. The following report is quoted at length because, while it is detailed, it does not entertain the assumption that such an amorphous and widespread fashion as the 'Skinhead' role-style is characterised by *some* ambiguity, *some* variation, or *some* gradation in degrees of conformity. Instead, the wearer of the Skinhead clothing is typified as invariably and unidirectionally deviant:

From London's Mile End looking westwards, and South of the river into Kennington, Camberwell and Peckham, for example, you can see what a sociologist would call a phenomenon and what an authoritarian would call hooliganism. Young working class boys, average age 15 to 17, dressed in a spare, inelegant style, but all dressed strictly the same, out in the streets, looking for fights, playing pintable, dancing to Blue-beat music, causing 'agro'. That's the skinhead term for aggravation, provocation, a state of mind where it doesn't feel good to go to bed without having had a good scrap.
 Skinhead style is rigidly conventional, among skinheads. It is a violent reaction against anything that looks like personality indulgence. What really maddens them and starts their shoulders rolling and fists punching, shadow boxing style, is anything 'flash'. Long hair is flash. . . . Flowers, frills, colours are anathema. Hippy is a dirty word. The skinheads dress in big boots, called Cherry Reds or Doctor Martin's, which are American. . . . They wear slimline braces which clip on to the top of Levi jeans, usually

rolled up a fraction. . . . They wear sleeveless V-neck pullovers and their hair is crew cut. They call themselves peanuts as well as skinheads.

Skinheads dance to bluebeat music, or rock-steady music of West Indian origin which is solid, punchy and a little soulful. Blues is equated with everything the skinheads are reacting against—longhairs and hippies —and as such is revolting. . . .

There is a radical difference between skinheads and the mod. For one thing skinheads are really poor kids on the lowest rung in society, who work all day. . . . Unlike mods they are totally unpretentious, unambitious; they do not stand for anything except part-time violence, or making the most of living around a tough and violent environment where there has never been any pretence of love or peace. . . .

Whether the skinheads go out looking for it or not, they're unlikely to go for a week without a fight. Groups from other areas get reputations, there are rumours that one gang defeated another, and then retaliation is called for. The skinheads have a hard image for the outside world—and between themselves—which they couldn't bear to lose.[94]

Fox displays little hesitation in preparing this recipe for a Skinhead role-style. For many people, this portrait is simply an accurate description of what all wearers of Skinhead clothing *are*. The etiquette of avoidance which marks social class relations in Britain, coupled with the fear inspired by what is construed as the unambiguously violent deviancy of *all* Skinheads, might guarantee that this typification will remain unchanged and influential. Fox has constructed a segment of social reality for hundreds of thousands of people (some of whom may well be embryo Skinheads). Skinheads have no champions to attack this typification. Instead, this is what Skinheads really are in the imagination of a substantial section of the British public.

Most deviancy reporting is, of course, prosaic and sparse in detail. It is usually only the exceptional case or the novel and perturbing deviant fashion that receives such lavish press attention. Moreover, I do not accept that my own idiosyncratic version of the interactionist theory of deviancy has 'the paradoxical consequence of inviting us to view the deviant as a passive nonentity who is responsible neither for his suffering nor its alleviation—who is more "sinned against than sinning".'[95] I have tried to argue that the press, as an intermediary agent of reality construction, distorts and simplifies images of the deviant. Whilst deviancy undoubtedly has its own internal logic of development (which can be substantially independent of the way in which it is interpreted) this logic is frequently misconstrued and mis-represented. Deviancies at the outer margins of society are very vulnerable to inaccurate typification and, as Cohen argues, 'One's view of deviance is second-hand . . . in mass society images arrive already processed and on the basis of those processed or coded images of the deviant, people react, become angry, formulate plans, make speeches. . . .'[96]

So far, I have described some of the ways in which people fashion their conceptions of deviancy. I have not yet discussed the ways in which other conceptual structures generate deviancy. If people organise the world in a systematic manner, it is reasonable to suppose that their classification schemes will influence one another. Some kinds of rule-breaking may be understood as the products of a formal order which is imposed on deviant and nondeviant phenomena alike. I shall outline four instances of such deviancy construction although there are undoubtedly many others.

DEVIANCY AND STRATIFICATION

In complex societies the distribution of deviant phenomena is closely linked to the distribution of power and life-chances. After all, so many beliefs and activities are affected by social class that it would be surprising if deviancy was not. Very largely, the connections between rule-breaking and enforcement can be explained in terms of the exercise of power in making and enforcing laws. These are issues which I shall pursue in other chapters.

A stratification system can also be viewed as a moral system: a major organisation of beliefs about the rights, duties and moral properties of the members of a society. As I shall argue elsewhere, when force is not the main means of defending a hierarchical and unequal society, the deprived must acknowledge the propriety of their deprivation. A system of control based on authority rests, in part, on a recognition of the *moral* right of the authoritative to make decisions. Thus, in a stable but unequal society class position is often identified with moral position—the higher one's position in a stratification order, the greater is one's moral worth. As Douglas argues,

the various categories of social status, especially those concerning success and failure, have themselves become morally meaningful categories . . . it is apparent that the categorical status of poor (and, even more, that of lower class) has as one of its (abstract) meanings that of being immoral, at least to the large middle-class groups. On the other hand, being well off, successful, and so on, means (in the abstract) being virtuous to these same groups.[97]

Such is certainly the finding which Centers made in his analysis of the subjective structures of social class. Whilst there may not be a strict British counterpart to the American 'lower class', a group which is ranked below the working class, Centers' observations are still pertinent:

A surprisingly large proportion of people appear to think of the lower class as a rather despicable group. Poor character and low morals, drink, crime, lack of ability, low intelligence, shiftlessness, laziness, lack of ambition or motivation, menial labor, etc., all indicate the disesteem in which this group is held. The middle and working classes differ little in their responses on the whole. For both of them the term lower class frequently connotes a despised or *declassé* group.[98]

If there is no major effective opposition to the validity of the scheme by which people are organised into social classes, it is likely that those who are the least successful will be assumed to possess immoral or unlovely characteristics. Even though a relatively stable class system, such as that which prevails in Britain, may sustain feelings of dignity and worth *within* each class, it is probable that there will be a progressive differentiation *between* the dignity and worth of the members of the various strata. The qualities which are peculiarly associated with the least privileged will be regarded as inferior or stigmatising. Even now, for example, it is not uncommon to talk of the 'better classes' or 'good family'. Behaviour which is insignificant in itself may well acquire meaning from the nature of the groups which display it. Thus deviancy may arise not because the deviant behaviour is a direct example of rule-breaking but because it is identified with 'the criminal classes' or 'lower orders'. Activity might become deviant only because it has been taken up by a despised group. As Duster argues:

... certain classes of persons in any society are more susceptible to being charged with moral inferiority than other classes of persons. The behavior in which persons indulge is often less important than the social category from which they come. In order to understand how certain acts get labeled over time, and how others get the deviance label lifted from them, it is necessary to take into account the conditions under which persons in the 'moral center' of society are publicly associated with a given behavior. Indeed, the thesis can be stated more categorically: when it is part of the public view that the predominant perpetrators of the act come from the moral center, that act cannot long remain 'immoral' or deviant; it can become deviant again only under circumstances where the public conception is that the 'morally susceptible' classes are those who are the primary indulgers.[99]

This tendency to distribute imputations of immorality unevenly throughout the social structure is reinforced by the making of laws which address themselves to certain groups alone. British laws seldom overtly discriminate between social classes, but they *are* enacted to control the 'morally susceptible' members of society as it is stratified by age. There are innumerable actions which identify the young as delinquent but which are perfectly legal when committed by adults.

Intercourse by or with a young girl, the buying of cigarettes, drinking alcohol in public houses and so on are activities which are denied most adolescents by law. In other societies, there are status-specific proscriptions which are related to estates, nationalities or 'race'. In South Africa, for instance, 'at least 50 per cent of the offences which bring Africans to the courts are statutory offences, things which, if done by a European, would not be "crimes"'.[100] Of course, South African law is less immediately tied to a conception of moral stratification than to the control of a disenfranchised population, but imputations of differential morality are very much integral to Afrikaaner thought.

So complete may the connection between stratification and morality become that certain groups may be turned into pariahs who are estranged from the normal moral community. Duster's thesis can be reversed: instead of a low status group conferring stigma on certain activities, certain activities can lead to the social isolation of a community. An instance is provided by the Swedish *tattare*: 'rogues and vagabonds' who were assumed to be a distinct group not of Swedish stock. The *tattare* were thought to be an alien element resident in Sweden, an element which was so immoral that some advocated that they should be sterilised. Ohlander, for example, urged:

Considered as a race the *tattare* are undoubtedly inferior to the Swedish stock. This may be proved by the fact that a relatively higher percentage of *tattare* are lodged in prisons, reformatories, homes for inebriates and similar institutions for criminal and vicious people.[101]

This assumption that the *tattare* are a genetically and ethnically discrete group is widespread in Sweden, yet, according to Heymowski, they were forced into isolation because of their association with stigmatised occupations. So intimately were the travellers identified with deviancy that the Swedish stratification system rejected them altogether:

It should be pointed out that the alien character of the traveller community has been emphasized both by the Swedish peasantry and by the travellers themselves who firmly believed . . . in their descent from Charles XII's Tartar soldiers. We may describe this as a myth, but we can hardly underestimate its importance and its social consequences. The resident population was inclined to look upon rootless vagrants and representatives of despised occupations as an alien element with whom it had practically nothing in common. . . . Regardless of the origin of different families forming today's traveller community they all show a predilection for certain occupations. These occupations were of decidedly low status and may be divided into two categories: (a) occupations implying an itinerant life (hawkery, peddling, itinerant glass- or iron-trade, rag-gathering . . .)

and (b) pariah occupations despised by society, although often combined with a resident life and with an almost official status (hangmanship, gelding, skinning . . .).[102]

The *tattare* are an extreme case of the relationship between deviancy and social distance. Their incumbency of ill-favoured roles promoted social distance between them and the Swedish peasantry; a social distance which became so extended that totally erroneous assumptions could be entertained about their nature and origins. The process of alienation culminated in typifications of the *tattare* as a group which was utterly foreign to Swedish society. Social distance inevitably separates those in the lowest strata from those who are able to make authoritative statements about morality and immorality. Not only are these groups likely to possess disparate perspectives, they are also likely to be misinformed about one another.

An interesting, domestic example of such links between stratification and attitudes towards deviancy is provided by the comments of Sir Richard Jackson, who was in turn a barrister, a member of the staff of the Director of Public Prosecutions, and Assistant Commissioner at Scotland Yard. Sir Richard was educated at Eton and at Trinity College, Cambridge. His typifications of crime and criminals were unambiguously condemnatory. Thus, 'The causes of crime are multiple and complex—a combination of greed and boredom, of resentment, arrogance, disrespect for property, of vanity and a lack of imagination or compassion.'[103] A sub-division of the category of professional criminals is made up of 'congenital layabouts, hopelessly weak and ill-disciplined characters . . .'[104] He deplores the 'substantial increase in public woolliness and sentimentality about criminals . . .'[105] Yet his autobiography is full of praise for his great-grandfather, Sir Thomas Turton:

In a book called *Reminiscences and Recollections*, by Captain Gronow, this great-grandfather of mine is said to have been highly regarded as a classical scholar by . . . the Headmaster of Eton, and by his schoolfellows 'as a determined poacher whose daring led him to exert his abilities in Windsor Park itself'. On one such occasion . . . he escaped by swimming the Thames with a hare in his teeth, leaving the royal keepers frustrated on the river-bank. I wish I could claim that it was a desire to emulate this feat which encouraged me to win the Junior and School swimming cups when I was at Eton; but, to be honest, I hadn't read Gronow's book in those days.[106]

His ancestor's deviancy and safe escape from the consequences of law-enforcement are just a schoolboy prank worthy of admiration, while criminals are socially distant aliens whose behaviour is a pathology caused by pathological conditions.

DEVIANCY AND ANOMALIES IN CLASSIFICATION SCHEMES

People attach value to their classification schemes as a way of making the world meaningful. When phenomena are clearly distinguished from one another, evaluations can be made, social life can become intelligible and projects planned. Between an individual and his environment there is a culturally structured 'pseudo-environment' which interprets and orders phenomena. The categories which men employ tend to affect how and what things can be perceived. In consequence, cultural categories are the social reality as it can be known to a society's population. Nevertheless, because no useful system of classification can ever be totally comprehensive, there must always be anomalous cases which do not clearly fit the scheme. These cases obtrude and threaten the viability of the world as it is understood by people. Mary Douglas states:

Culture, in the sense of the public, standardised values of a community, mediates the experience of individuals. It provides in advance some basic categories, a positive pattern in which ideas and values are tidily ordered. And above all, it has authority, since each is induced to assent because of the assent of others. But its public character makes its categories more rigid. . . . They cannot . . . easily be subject to revision. Yet they cannot ignore the challenge of aberrant forms. Any given system of classification must give rise to anomalies, and any given culture must confront events which seem to defy its assumptions. . . . [The problem of anomaly may be solved]: first, by settling for one or other interpretation, ambiguity is reduced. . . . Second, the existence of anomaly can be physically controlled. . . . Third, a rule of avoiding anomalous things affirms and strengthens the definitions to which they do not conform. . . . Fourth, anomalous events may be labelled dangerous.[107]

When a classification scheme centres on events or institutions which are regarded as of major social importance, anomaly can become intolerable. A number of anomalous phenomena may thus be subjected to avoidance patterns or social control. The anomalies are not so much abhorrent in themselves, but abhorrent because of their implications for the way in which reality is constructed. Some instances of deviancy may be understood as anomalies in this sense. They constitute threats to social order as it is interpreted by a population. This is one way of explaining why they are deviant, although other accounts may be offered to justify attempts to suppress the anomaly.*

* It may well be true that once an anomaly gives rise to deviancy, that deviancy will enjoy a longer life than the cultural inconsistencies which foster it. Deviancy may acquire a stability which persists after the threatened cultural pattern has itself changed.

Anomaly seems to explain certain forms of sexual deviancy in particular. Sexual attributes are neatly categorised in our society and are assumed to belong invariably to one or other of the sexes. Sexual identity and roles based upon it are of critical importance in the structuring of people's lives. When people appear to straddle sex roles, the result is very often hostility. Garfinkel has produced an extensive list of 'properties of "natural, normally sexed persons" as cultural objects'. He states:

From the standpoint of an adult member of our society, the perceived environment of 'normally sexed persons' is populated by two sexes and only two sexes, 'male' and 'female' . . . the population of normal persons is a morally dichotomized population. The question of its existence is decided as a matter of motivated compliance with this population as a legitimate order. It is not decided as a matter of biological, medical, urological, sociological . . . fact. . . . The adult member includes himself in this environment and counts himself as one or the other not only as a condition of his self-respect, but as a condition whereby the exercise of his rights to live without excessive risks and interference from others are routinely enforceable. . . . The members of the normal population, for him the *bona fide* members . . . , are essentially, originally, in the first place, always have been, and always will be, once and for all, in the final analysis, either 'male' or 'female'. . . . For normals, the presence in the environment of sexed objects has the feature of a 'natural matter of fact'. This naturalness carries along with it, as a constituent part of its meaning, the sense of its being right and correct; i.e., morally proper that it be that way.[108]

If Garfinkel's reconstruction of sexual typifications is sound,* some of the abhorrence expressed in Western societies about homosexuality and, frequently, about commercial prostitution becomes intelligible. The homosexual is a role-player who attempts to refute the conception that the world is dichotomised into discrete sexes with their peculiar sets of characteristics. He poses the possibility of a midway position which is neither fully male nor fully female, and, by so doing, threatens the classification scheme with an anomalous case. Garfinkel's contention that such a dichotomy is regarded as normally proper explains why homosexuality is defined as immoral. The prostitute is also an anomaly, but a rather less pronounced one. She represents a confusion of the attributes conventionally associated with sexual identities. She is not submissive but aggressive; she treats her sexuality as a means rather than an end; she is detached from her sexual performance rather than immersed in it; she is promiscuous rather than loyal to one partner; she is cold and calculating rather

* The recent court case of April Ashley certainly supports Garfinkel's observations. It was held by the court that sex is irrevocably fixed at birth and that no subsequent transformations can alter sexual identity. See, for example, *The Times*, 28 July 1970.

than warm and spontaneous, and so on. The prostitute's role-style contains many qualities which are normally regarded as masculine. She flouts the expectation that there is a clear division of labour and symbolisation between male and female roles.

Similarly, the hermaphrodite is a threatening anomaly. In an East African instance:

All concerned, from parents to physicians, are enjoined to discover which of the two natural sexes the intersexed person most appropriately is and then to help the ambiguous, incongruous and upsetting 'it' to become a partially acceptable 'him' or 'her'.[109]

Lofland amplifies this point in a slightly different fashion:

. . . serious ambiguity is an essential feature of . . . items defined as deviant. Persons defined as mentally ill are precisely so defined because of the havoc of ambiguity they inflict upon the interactional order of the everyday lives of those around them. . . . In the larger perspective of institutional orders, categories of persons who defy existing conceptions of possible and proper being serve to create ambiguity about that order. Homosexuals of both sexes serve to make ambiguous the institutionalized division between the sexes. Prostitutes make ambiguous the sexual benefits of the familial order.[110]

DEVIATION AND AFFIRMATION

Many classification schemes are also moral systems; things which are taken for granted are also assumed to be morally proper; things which are not taken for granted may be urged as moral. The affirmation of a particular moral principle necessarily places limits on correct behaviour and leads to the branding of the acts which fall outside those limits as immoral. The very act of defining an object or phenomenon defines what is *not* that phenomenon. The moral force of that definition is considerably strengthened if the things with which the defined phenomenon is contrasted are represented as wrong or bizarre. This is rather more than the simple assertion that moral principles and classification systems constitute sets of rules whose infringement is deviant. Such an assertion would be no more than a tautology. Rather, it seems that deviancy serves as a necessary reinforcement to moral categorisation; not merely a result but a buttress.* Following Durkheim, Douglas argues:

* cf. Marwick's summary of sociological accounts of witchcraft: '. . . the witch is depicted as the very antithesis of the social ideal, as the one who plays the villain in society's morality plays. So numerous and so revolting are the believed practices of witches that to accuse anyone of witchcraft is a condensed way of charging him with a long list of the foullest crimes. By graphically summing up all forms of deviance, such an accusation throws into sharper relief the positive moral precepts of the society to which the accused person belongs.' M. Marwick (Ed.), *Witchcraft and Sorcery*, Penguin Books, Middlesex, 1970, pp. 16–17.

. . . when we observe and analyze the moral communications in our everyday lives we find that the social meanings of either deviance (immorality) or respectability (morality) can be adequately understood only if reference, whether implicit or explicit, is made to the other, its opposite. As some Christian theologians have argued . . . without evil there would be no good, without Satan no God. The existence of Satan and his evil has not only been as necessary to Western man's way of thinking as God and his good but has at the same time been a necessary condition for adequately understanding the nature of God and his good. . . . In the same way, in our everyday lives morality and immorality, respectability and disreputability, the otherworldly and the this-worldly, the sacred and the secular—each term necessarily implies the existence of its opposite for its own meaning and, above all, for much of the force it exerts on our lives.[111]

A deviant thus lends colour and intensity to moral pronouncements and it is arguable that, without vivid typifications, moral principles would lack much of their effectiveness. Deliberate attempts are often made to manufacture graphic and personalised antitheses of authoritatively approved moral positions. This is particularly likely to happen when a state is engaged in the task of nation-building. When a state creates a new social structure, populated by an appropriately motivated kind of man, it also creates new, and emotionally charged, forms of deviancy. As Walzer argues, 'Before Puritans, Jacobins, or Bolsheviks attempt the creation of a new order, they must create new men. Repression and collective discipline are the typical methods of this creativity: the disordered world is interpreted as a world at war; enemies are discovered and attacked.'[112] Social constructions of the capitalist in Communist China and Russia, of the Jew in Nazi Germany, of the Communist in the America of the 1950s,[113] of the neo-colonialist in new African states[114] and of the whites by American Black Muslims,[115] are all examples of the demons created by those who furnish their populations with a new vision of heaven. In Nazi Germany, Shoham remarks:

. . . an authoritarian state where ambiguity could not be tolerated, the Jew was portrayed as the antithesis of the Teutonic Superman. The Jew, as stereotyped, was more than a contrasting antecedent to the Nazi superman, he was an essential part of the Nazi ideology. The thesis and the antithesis, the ideal and the negation, were generally voiced together.[116]

The link between deviancy and the enunciation of moral principles can be examined from another perspective. Many organisations are devoted to the activity of generating classification systems which describe aspects of the moral world. Although psychiatrists, sociologists, criminologists, lawyers and others are concerned with their occupational tasks they are, intentionally or unintentionally, refining our knowledge of the social and the moral. When a psychiatrist produces a typology of mental disorder he has not only offered a new intellectual conception but new possibilities of action. At one time, the manias, such as pyromania, kleptomania and monomania, dominated psychiatric thought. They also dominated the way in which deviant roles were construed and handled by those who had social control functions, such as the police or legislature. When the scheme based on the notion of mania changed, deviant roles also changed. In the case of the psychiatric profession, dominant models affect treatment and management policies. Psychiatrists organise their work and their work material around current typologies. Patients who do not clearly fit into these typologies upset the smooth running of psychiatric practice. Thus, Goffman argues:

An over-all title is given to the pathology, such as schizophrenia, psychopathic personality, etc., and this provides a new view of the patient's 'essential' character. When pressed, of course, some staff will allow that these syndrome titles are vague and doubtful, employed only to comply with hospital census regulations. But in practice these categories become magical ways of making a single unity out of the nature of the patient— an entity that is subject to psychiatric servicing.[117]

Quite naturally, psychiatric categories can become translated into a reality which patients and psychiatrists confront alike.[118] The categories may also be expressed in legislation,[119] in courtroom adjudications, in enforcement decisions, in penal administrations and in lay constructions of the deviant world. Even when psychiatric morphologists do not view their function as the active reshaping of the world, they may have just that effect. Academic work which is supposedly concerned only with the resolution of intellectual problems can have quite practical consequences. The affirmation of a particular interpretation of the world can thus shape the forms which deviancy is considered to assume and the responses which are made to those forms.

An excellent example of such intellectual work having the consequence of defining deviancy is provided by analytical jurisprudence. This discipline is largely concerned with a systematic logical resolution of legal problems on the basis of *a priori* propositions about the nature of law. It can be an instance of the legalism which I shall discuss in another chapter, a legalism which tends to make the law itself an end divorced from instrumental functions. According to Stone:

Modern analytical jurisprudence has its main point in facilitating our vision of the logical coherence of the several propositions and parts of a legal order and on fixing the definition of terms used and the presuppositions which will maximise such coherence.[120]

An intellectual project of this kind involves the consistent application of rationality to an axiomatic system so that confusions can be minimised and a refined clarity substituted for them. The constant introduction of refinement and coherence can lead to an ever-increasing proliferation of legal distinctions.* In a somewhat scathing manner, Arnold makes much of this possibility:

The scientific attitude is useful in order to study the folkways of the people and to determine what kind of formulas most appeal to them. However, this way of thinking violates the great idea that jurists must be 'sincere'. They must not be politicians, and they should not be permitted to advance theories for a purely practical purpose. Hence jurisprudence has been forced to supply the deficiencies of the rational process by applying more reason. Such conflicts always have had the effect of producing an enormous amount of argumentative literature. A practical result of this conflict . . . is the fact that twenty-five thousand cases pour from our appellate courts every year. This great literature follows from the idea that the inconsistencies of the reasoning process can always be cured by applying more reason. If the law gets complicated, the only way to simplify it is to add more law to it. Therefore the American Law Institute spent millions in producing a restatement of the fundamental principles of this mass of cases. However, this restatement was not intended to be a substitute for the cases but only to clarify them. It therefore becomes only an additional source of argument.[121]

Arnold makes perfectly clear the *quantitative* implications of jurisprudential reasoning. There are clearly qualitative implications as well. The multiplication of legal distinctions has a corresponding impact on the number of types of deviant role. As the law becomes more complicated and sensitive, so the organised response to rule-breaking becomes increasingly sophisticated. More and more minute details are employed to differentiate between kinds of rule-breaking. Moreover, as reason is progressively applied, so the world of deviancy as it is combated by legal and law-based institutions becomes subjected to a logical and clear structure. Such a structure, derived from a propositional logic, separates and treats rule-breaking phenomena in a way that can be quite foreign to everyday constructions of those phenomena. Events are distinguished and endowed with a meaning-structure by a system of interpretation which is far clearer, more explicit and more precise than that which is employed by most deviants, victims and laymen. Commonsense understandings may be

* Of course, jurisprudential reasoning is unlikely to represent an evolution into ever-growing rationality. Instead, following Lemert, it is probably more helpful to represent it as 'normal' legal reasoning within a fixed paradigm or conceptual system—progress being attained through paradigmatic revolutions in the manner described by Kunn. cf. E. M. Lemert, *Social Action and Legal Change*, Aldine, Chicago, 1970.

violated by the way in which analytical jurisprudence organises the world. Something of this tension has been described by Weyl:

The basic assumption of the strict alternative of true and false, character-istic for classical logic, leaves no room for bridging the abyss by 'perhaps' or 'possibly'. However, the major part of statements in our everyday life which have a vital meaning for us and our communicants are not of this rigorous nature. A given hue may be *more or less* gray instead of pure black or pure white. We may find it too arbitrary or even possible to set exact boundaries in a continuum.[122]

When a classical logic generates law, the result may be just as Weyl alleges. The incongruence between the perspectives on deviancy adopted by British lawyers and an Indian population was revealingly acute:

The common law proceeds on the basis of equality before the law while indigenous dispute-settling finds it unthinkable to separate the parties from their statuses and relations. The common law gives a clear-cut 'all or none' decision, while indigenous processes seek a face-saving solution agreeable to all parties; the common law deals with a single isolated offence or transaction, while the indigenous system sees this as arbitrarily leaving out the underlying dispute of which this may be one aspect; the common law has seemingly arbitrary rules of evidence, which do not permit what is well-known to be proved and that which is not can be proved; the common law then seems abrupt and overly decisive, distant, expensive, and arbit-rary.[123]

Since law is the form which authoritative deviancy-defining rules take, the unravelling and elucidating work performed by analytical jurisprudence is of critical importance. Yet this work serves goals which are not necessarily those sought by the population controlled by law. The conceptual processes which engender law are foreign to most members of a society. In consequence, legal institutions may be regarded as substantially autonomous sources of classification systems. They are responsible for bringing a logical order to deviancy which lacks this order in its pristine form. The modifications acted upon by legislators and law enforcers impose clarity, limits and relations upon deviant phenomena which necessarily affect the players of deviant roles. Yet, in many cases, the people who carry out this classification task tend to see themselves as primarily pursuing the advancement of knowledge, the training of thinkers, the simpli-fication of procedures or the rationalising of intellectual schemes. Many persons, institutions and processes may separate the academic criminologists or legal philosophers from the rule-breakers whom they influence. The autonomy is thus not only cognitive, it is also structural. As knowledge grows, so does the proliferation and complexity of deviant forms.

DEVIANCY AND 'RESIDUAL RULES'

The very acceptance of conventionally legitimated classification schemes is a test of one's eligibility for full, effective membership of society. The denial, whether by action or statement, of the validity or authority of the socially constructed world is a primal deviancy. So basic are these interpretative rules that violation of the norms which govern their use is, according to Scheff, virtually unthinkable:

> Most norm violations do not cause the violator to be labeled as mentally ill, but as ill-mannered, ignorant, sinful, criminal, or perhaps just harried, depending on the type of norm involved. There are innumerable norms, however, over which consensus is so complete that the members of a group appear to take them for granted. . . . A person who regularly violated these expectations probably would not be thought to be merely ill-bred, but as strange, bizarre, and frightening, because his behaviour violates the assumptive world of the group, the world that is construed to be the only one that is natural, decent, and possible. . . . The culture of the group provides a vocabulary of terms for categorizing many norm violators. . . . Each of these terms is derived from the type of norm broken, and, ultimately, from the type of behavior involved. After exhausting these categories, however, there is always a residue of the most diverse kinds of violations, for which the culture provides no explicit label. For example, although there is great cultural variation in what is defined as decent or real, each culture tends to reify its definition of decency and reality, and so provides no way of handling violations of its expectations in these areas. The typical norm governing decency or reality, therefore, literally 'goes without saying' and its violation is unthinkable for most of its members. For the convenience of the society in construing those instances of unnameable rule-breaking which are called to its attention, these violations may be lumped together into a residual category: witchcraft, spirit possession, or, in our own society, mental illness.[124]

The breaker of residual rules is thus the most alien deviant, one who rejects the world as it is known to commonsense. His perceived threat is even more profound than that posed by, say, the anomalous deviant. The deviant whose role or status is anomalous does no more than challenge the sense of a limited area of a society's system of interpretation. The residual rule-breaker is more diffuse in his threat and is more incomprehensible. A person who is assumed to be unbound by the most basic and natural understandings is not only an outsider, but is also capricious, random and unpredictable in his behaviour. He has lost many of his rights to be taken seriously as a fully human member of society. The witch or the possessed person is both human and inhuman; 'Witches are not entirely human. . . . A witch is a human being who incorporates a nonhuman power. . . . [Some myths say] that witches are possessed by spirits or devils, or that at night they forsake human form and turn into were-creatures.'[125] In the case of the mentally ill, Nunnally claims that the mass media portray 'both psychotics and neurotics . . . as relatively ignorant, dangerous, dirty, unkind, and unpredictable'.[126] Both kinds of deviant seem to possess a peculiar kind of power, the power to create disorder and anarchy.[127] Theirs is the most fundamental deviancy because they deny the validity of the orderly world and the way in which it can be understood. Furthermore, like the stranger described by Schutz, the residual rule-breaker (and other deviants as well) is vulnerable to the accusation of being disloyal and ungrateful. His offence is, however, probably far greater than the stranger's:

. . . very frequently the reproach of doubtful loyalty originates in the astonishment of the members of the in-group that the stranger does not accept the total of its cultural pattern as the natural and appropriate way of life and as the best of all possible solutions of any problem. The stranger is called ungrateful, since he refuses to acknowledge that the cultural pattern offered to him grants him shelter and protection.[128]

These brief descriptions are intended to do little more than suggest how integrally deviancy is tied to the ways in which a society systematises its beliefs about itself and the larger world. While many deviant roles are products of a general typifying and defining capacity of society, they are given form and solidity only in the behaviour of deviants themselves and those who are able to translate the definitions into effective action. In a sense, conceptions of deviancy are no more than the organising beliefs which guide the activities of people who sustain rule-breaking behaviour. They cannot be understood independently of a society's power structure and social groupings. These I shall discuss in the next chapters.

1. R. Quinney, *The Social Reality of Crime*, Little, Brown and Co, Boston, 1970, p. v.

2. R. Turner and S. J. Surace, 'Zootsuiters and Mexicans: Symbols in Crowd Behavior', *American Journal of Sociology*, vol. 62, no. 1, July 1956, pp. 14–20.

3. A. Schutz, 'Common-sense and Scientific Interpretation of Human Action', in M. Natanson (Ed.), *Alfred Schutz: Collected Papers*, vol. 1, Martinus Nijhoff, The Hague, 1967, pp. 5–6.

4. E. M. Lemert, *Social Pathology*, McGraw-Hill, New York, 1951, p. 76.

5. E. Freidson, *Profession of Medicine*, Dodd, Mead and Co., New York, 1970, p. 219.

6. H. S. Becker, *Outsiders*, Free Press, New York, 1963, p. 9.

7. D. M. Downes and P. E. Rock; 'Social Control and its Effect on Crime and Criminal Careers', paper delivered at the Fourth National Conference on Research and Teaching in Criminology, University of Cambridge, July 1970.

8. My argument draws on, but does not really reflect, a passage from M. Phillipson and M. Roche, 'Phenomenological Sociology and the Study of Deviance', in P. Rock and M. McIntosh (Ed.), *Deviance and Social Control*, Tavistock, London, forthcoming, pp. 22–4.

9. J. Lofland, *Deviance and Identity*, Prentice-Hall, New Jersey, 1969, p. 22.

10. D. Matza, *Becoming Deviant*, Prentice-Hall, New Jersey, 1969, p. 12.

11. H. S. Becker, 'The Culture of a Deviant Group: The Dance Musician' and 'Careers in a Deviant Occupational Group: The Dance Musician', in *Outsiders*, op. cit.

12. E. M. Lemert, 'Blindness and the Blind', in *Social Pathology*, McGraw-Hill, New York, 1951.

13. cf. E. Lemert, 'Stuttering Among the North Pacific Coastal Indians', in *Human Deviance, Social Problems and Social Control*, Prentice-Hall, New Jersey, 1967.

14. cf. E. Lemert, 'Radicalism and Radicals', in *Social Pathology*, McGraw-Hill, New York, 1951.

15. cf. J. Bingham, 'The Intelligent Square's Guide to Hippieland', in S. Dinitz, R. Dynes and A. Clarke (Ed.), *Deviance*, Oxford University Press, New York, 1969.

16. cf. M. S. Weinberg, 'Becoming a Nudist', in E. Rubington and M. S. Weinberg (Ed.), *Deviance*, Macmillan, New York, 1968.

17. cf. J. Skipper and C. McCaghy, 'Stripteasers: The Anatomy and Career Contingencies of a Deviant Occupation', *Social Problems*, Winter 1970, vol. 17, no. 3.

18. For an example of the Gothic, see articles in M. Truzzi (Ed.), *Sociology and Everyday Life*, Prentice-Hall, New Jersey, 1968.

19. E. Goffman, 'Expression Games', in *Strategic Interaction*, Blackwell, Oxford, 1970, pp. 3–4.

20. J. Irwin, *The Felon*, Prentice-Hall, New Jersey, 1970, pp. 21–2.

21. L. Wilkins, *Social Deviance*, Tavistock, London, 1964, p. 57.

22. J. L. Simmons, 'Public Stereotypes of Deviants', *Social Problems*, Fall 1965, vol. 13, no. 2, p. 225.

23. M. Douglas, *Purity and Danger*, Routledge & Kegan Paul, London, 1966, p. 36.

24. A. Schutz, op. cit., p. 12.

25. P. Berger, 'Sociology and Freedom—Is Sociology a Liberating Discipline', public lecture delivered at the London School of Economics, 16 June 1970.

26. W. James, *Psychology*, Henry Holt and Co., New York, 1890, vol. 1, pp. 221–2.

27. A. Schutz, 'The Stranger: An Essay in Social Psychology', *American Journal of Sociology*, May 1944, vol. 49, no. 6, p. 500.

28. ibid., p. 502.

29. P. Berger and T. Luckman, *The Social Construction of Reality*, Allen Lane, The Penguin Press, London, 1967, pp. 47–8.

30. A. Schutz, *The Phenomenology of the Social World*, Northwestern University Press, Chicago, 1967, p. 184.

31. E. Rubington and M. S. Weinberg, *Deviance*, op. cit., p. 10.

32. A. Schutz, 'The Stranger . . . ', op. cit., p. 503.

33. D. Matza, *Becoming Deviant*, op. cit., p. 147.

34. T. Duster, *The Legislation of Morality*, Free Press, New York, 1970, p. 68.

35. J. Kitsuse, 'Societal Reaction to Deviant Behavior', in H. Becker (Ed.), *The Other Side*, Free Press, New York, 1964, p. 96.

36. N. K. Denzin, 'Rules of Conduct and the Study of Deviant Behavior', in J. Douglas (Ed.), *Deviance and Respectability*, Basic Books, New York, 1970, p. 121.

37. L. Wilkins, op. cit.

38. cf. F. Davis, 'Deviance Disavowal: The Management of Strained Interaction', in H. S. Becker (Ed.), *The Other Side*, op. cit., pp. 119–37, and E. Goffman, *Stigma*, Prentice-Hall, New Jersey, 1963.

39. Sir R. Jackson, *Occupied with Crime*, Harrap, London, 1967, p. 134.

40. cf. L. Wilkins, op. cit., p. 69.

41. M. Douglas, *Natural Symbols*, Crescent Press, London, 1970, p. 8.

42. J. Douglas, *American Social Order*, Free Press, New York, 1971, pp. 58–9.

43. T. Duster, op. cit., pp. 90–1.

44. P. Berger and T. Luckman, op. cit., p. 48.

45. K. Erikson, *Notes on the Sociology of Deviance*, op. cit., p. 13.

46. Q. Klapp, *Heroes, Villains and Fools*, Prentice-Hall, New Jersey, 1962, pp. 16–17.

47. F. Tannenbaum, *Crime and the Community*, University of Columbia Press, New York, 1938, ch. 1.

48. H. Garfinkel, 'Conditions of Successful Degradation Ceremonies', *American Journal of Sociology*, March 1956, vol. 61, pp. 421–2.

49. O. Klapp, op. cit., p. 22.

50. Quoted in P. Rock and F. Heidensohn, 'New Reflections on Violence' D. A. Martin (Ed.), *Anarchy and Culture*, Routledge & Kegan Paul, London, 1969, p. 112.

51. Anon, 'Sociology of the L.S.E.', *Agitator*, undated, p. 1.

52. J. Douglas, 'Deviance and Respectability', in J. Douglas (Ed.), *Deviance and Respectability*, Basic Books, New York, 1970, p. 6.

53. P. Berger, *A Rumour of Angels*, Allen Lane, The Penguin Press, London, 1970, p. 19.

54. L. Wilkins, *Social Deviance*, op. cit., p. 63.

55. R. Quinney, *The Social Reality of Crime*, op. cit., p. 282.

56. N. Z. Medalia and O. N. Larsen, 'Diffusion and Belief in a Collective Delusion: The Seattle Windshield Pitting Epidemic', *American Sociological Review*, vol. 23, no. 2, pp. 182–3.

57. R. E. Park, 'The Natural History of the Newspaper', in R. E. Park, *On Social Control and Collective Behaviour*, University of Chicago Press, Chicago, 1967, p. 110.

58. W. Breed, 'Social Control in the Newsroom', *Social Forces*, May 1955, vol. 33, no. 4, p. 331.

59. F. J. Davis, 'Crime News in Colorado Newspapers', *American Journal of Sociology*, January 1952, vol. 57, no. 4, p. 330. For a comparable British study see R. Roshier, 'Crime and the Press: A Study of the Reporting of Crime in the English National Daily Press', Ph.D. Dissertation, University of London, 1971.

60. cf. W. Gieber, 'How the "Gatekeepers" View Local Civil Liberties News', *Journalism Quarterly*, Spring 1960, pp. 199–205, esp. p. 201.

61. W. Breed, 'Social Control in the Newsroom', op. cit., p. 331.

62. W. Gieber, op. cit., p. 204.

63. S. Cohen, 'Hooligans, Vandals and the Community', unpublished Ph.D. Dissertation, University of London, 1969, p. 466.

64. cf. P. Rock and S. Cohen, 'The Teddy Boy', in V. Bogdanor and R. Skidelsky, *The Age of Affluence*, Macmillan, London, 1970.

65. J. D. Halloran, P. Elliott and G. Murdock, *Demonstrations and Communications: A Case Study*, Penguin Books, Middlesex, 1970, p. 26.

66. ibid., p. 110.

67. ibid., pp. 140, 141.

68. For a discussion of the presentation of information about the mentally ill, see J. C. Nunnally, 'What the Mass Media Present', in T. J. Scheff (Ed.), *Mental Illness and Social Processes*, Harper and Row, New York, 1967.

69. cf. J. D. Halloran *et al.*, op. cit., esp. p. 26.

70. cf. L. Yablonsky, *The Violent Gang*, Free Press, New York, 1962, for a description of the way in which loosely structured 'near-groups' are often depicted as well-organised 'gangs'.

71. S. Cohen, op. cit., p. 467.

72. T. E. Drabeck and E. L. Quarantelli, 'Scapegoats, Villains, and Disasters,' in J. F. Short (Ed.), *Modern Criminals*, Aldine Press, Chicago, 1970, p. 161.

73. cf. J. Galtung and M. Ruge, 'The Structure of Foreign News', in J. Tunstall (Ed.), *Media Sociology*, Constable, London, 1970.

74. cf. *The Report of the National Advisory Commission on Civil Disorders*, Bantam Books, New York, 1968, and T. A. Knopf, 'Sniping: New Pattern of Violence?', *Trans-Action*, July/August 1968.

75. In the case of the 27 October demonstration, Halloran *et al.* describe the press-constructed image of the march as 'a potentially violent clash between police and demonstrators manipulated by small groups of extremists. . . .' This image was formed *before* the march, it was not later confirmed. J. D. Halloran *et al.*, op. cit., p. 109. This kind of description has a very long history. For its use in the description of eighteenth century riots, see G. Rude, 'The Motives of Popular Insurrection in Paris during the French Revolution', *Bulletin of the Institute of Historical Research*, 1953, vol. 26, pp. 53–74, and G. Rude, 'The Pre-Industrial Crowd', *Flinders Journal of History and Politics*, 1969, vol. 1.

76. cf. P. Rock and F. Heidensohn, 'New Reflections on Violence', op. cit.

77. S. Cohen, op. cit., p. 473.

78. cf. P. Rock and S. Cohen, op. cit.

79. *Sunday Times*, 21 September 1969.

80. London *Evening Standard*, 22 September 1969.

81. S. Cohen, op. cit., p. 454.

82. J. D. Halloran *et al.*, op. cit., p. 91.

83. cf. G. Baker and D. Chapman (Ed.), *Man and Society in Disaster*, Basic Books, New York, 1962, esp. the article by I. Cisin and W. Clarke, 'The Methodological Challenge of Disaster Research'.

84 N. Z. Medalia, 'Who Cries Wolf? The Reporters of Damage to Police in a Pseudo-Disaster', *Social Problems*, Winter 1959–60, vol. 7, no. 3, p. 233.

85. cf. D. M. Johnson, 'The Phantom Anesthetist of Matoon', *Journal of Abnormal and Social Psychology*, April 1945, vol. 40, pp. 175–86, and N. Jacobs, 'The Phantom Slasher of Taipei', *Social Problems*, Winter 1965, vol. 12, no. 5, pp. 318–28.

86. E. H. Sutherland, 'The Diffusion of Sexual Psychopath Laws', in W. J. Chambliss (Ed.), *Crime and the Legal Process*, McGraw-Hill, New York, 1969, p. 75.

87. ibid., p. 76.

88. Advisory Committee on Drug Dependence: Hallucinogens Subcommittee: *Cannabis*, Home Office, HMSO, London, 1968.

89. R. H. Blum and M. L. Funkhouser, 'Legislators on Social Scientists and a Social Issue: A Report and Commentary on Some Discussions with Lawmakers

about Drug Abuse', *Journal of Applied Behavioural Science*, 1965, vol. 1, pp. 99–100.

90. P. Bachrach and M. S. Baratz, *Power and Poverty*, Oxford University Press, New York, 1970, p. 59.

91. cf. D. Matza, *Becoming Deviant*, op. cit.

92. For a fuller discussion of this natural history, see P. Rock and S. Cohen, *The Teddy Boy*, op. cit.

93. A. Shelston, 'Students and the Press', in D. Martin (Ed.), op. cit., p. 100.

94. J. Fox, 'The Scapegoat Kids: Why the "Skinheads" are in for Trouble', *Sunday Times*, 21 September 1969.

95. A. Gouldner, 'The Sociologist as Partisan: Sociology and the Welfare State', *American Sociologist*, May 1968, p. 106.

96. S. Cohen, op. cit., p. 443.

97. J. Douglas, *Deviance and Respectability*, op. cit., pp. 6–7.

98. R. Centers, *The Psychology of the Social Classes*, Princeton University Press, New Jersey, 1949, p. 95.

99. T. Duster, op. cit., p. 247.

100. L. Marquard, *The Peoples and Policies of South Africa*, Oxford University Press, London, 1962, p. 130.

101. Quoted in A. Heymowski, *Swedish Travellers and their Ancestry*, Acta Universitatis Upsaliensis, Uppsala, 1969, p. 27.

102. A. Heymowski, op. cit., pp. 111–12.

103. Sir R. Jackson, *Occupied with Crime*, Harrap, London, 1967, p. 122.

104. ibid., p. 127.

105. ibid., p. 133.

106. ibid., p. 30.

107. M. Douglas, *Purity and Danger*, op. cit., pp. 38–9.

108. H. Garfinkel, *Studies in Ethnomethodology*, Prentice-Hall, New Jersey, 1967, pp. 122–3.

109. R. Edgerton, 'Pokot Intersexuality: An East African Example of the Resolution of Sexual Incongruity', *American Anthropologist*, 1964, vol. 66, p. 1290.

110. J. Lofland, *Deviance and Identity*, op. cit., p. 17.

111. J. Douglas (Ed.), *Deviance and Respectability*, Basic Books, New York, 1970, pp. 3–4.

112. M. Walzer, *The Revolution of the Saints*, Weidenfeld & Nicolson, London, 1966, p. 315.

113. cf. R. Rovere, *Senator Joe McCarthy*, Harcourt, Brace, New York, 1959.

114. cf. L. Mair, *New Nations*, Weidenfeld & Nicolson, London, 1963, esp. p. 126.

115. cf. E. Essien-Udom, *Black Nationalism*, University of Chicago Press, Chicago, 1962.

116. S. Shoham, *The Mark of Cain*, Oceana, Jerusalem, 1970, pp. 7–8.

117. E. Goffman, *Asylums*, Doubleday-Anchor, New York, 1961, pp. 374–5.

118. cf. T. J. Scheff, *Being Mentally Ill*, Weidenfeld & Nicolson, London, 1966, and M. Balint, *The Doctor, His Patient, and the Illness*, International Universities Press, New York, 1957, esp. p. 216.

119. cf. E. Sutherland, *The Diffusion of Sexual Psychopath Laws*, op. cit.

120. J. Stone, *Social Dimensions of Law and Justice*, Stevens and Sons, London, 1966, p. 7.

121. T. W. Arnold, *The Symbols of Government*, Harcourt, Brace and World, New York, 1962, p. 51.

122. H. Weyl, 'The Ghost of Modality', in M. Farber (Ed.), *Philosophical Essays*

in Memory of Edmund Husserl, Harvard University Press, Cambridge, 1940, p. 287.

123. M. Galanter, 'Hindu Law and the Development of the Modern Indian Legal System', 1964, Annual General Meeting of the American Political Science Association, p. 25.

124. T. J. Scheff, *Being Mentally Ill*, op. cit., pp. 31–2, 33–4.

125. P. Mayer, 'Witches', in M. Marwick (Ed.), *Witchcraft and Sorcery*, Penguin Books, Middlesex, 1970, p. 48.

126. J. C. Nunnally, op. cit., pp. 61–2.

127. cf. M. Douglas, *Purity and Danger*, op. cit.

128. A. Schutz, *The Stranger*, op. cit., p. 507.

2

THE EFFECTS OF DEVIANT ORGANISATION

Whilst I make much of the role of meanings in sociological analysis, there is a dangerous seed in the sociological tradition which is based on empathetic explanation. The use of concepts heavily dependent on ideas of meaning is a difficult enterprise. The very meaning of the term 'meaning' is elusive in the extreme, and the reproduction of subjective experience can never be fully validated. Above all, there is a constant straining towards solipsism or idealism—the viewing of the world as an object created by thought alone. The sociology of deviancy which emphasises definitional processes has been singled out for the charge of solipsism; it has been maintained that it constructs models of a society which receives form only when authority acts. Deviation becomes a projection of the mind of Leviathan. For instance, Akers states, 'One sometimes gets the impression from reading this literature that people go about minding their own business and then—"wham"—bad society comes along and slaps them with a stigmatized label'.[1] This charge makes two points: that official acts are regarded by the sociologists of deviancy as critical in delineating what and who are deviant, and that, without these acts, deviation would have no structure.

The first criticism may stem from a confusion between two distinct analytical areas; the area of 'normative ambiguity' where definitional processes elucidate the nature of socially problematic behaviour so that old norms are changed or new ones generated; and 'behavioural ambiguity' where the processes assess whether a person or incident is actually covered by proscriptive norms.[2] Even if this confusion did shape Akers' argument, some sociologists can be quite properly accused of adopting a unilateralist approach. Their work implies that there is no exchange between deviants but simply a unilinear flow of influence which the deviant is powerless to resist. Yet,

c

although the sociology of deviancy has its idealists, it would be a mistake to assume that it must always take a solipsist guise. It is possible to use a definitional perspective without arguing that deviants are instantaneously brought into being by single and cataclysmic acts of labelling or that properties of deviation are merely imputed.

Whilst complex societies tend to rely upon formal agencies for the articulation and enforcement of rules, the process of identifying and controlling deviation is diffused throughout the whole community. Social control is built into the very structure of language, role behaviour and interaction. Every morally proper action is bounded and defined by impropriety. Without such boundaries, it would be nebulous and ambiguous. As Douglas states, 'Deviance and respectability are necessarily linked together: each necessarily implies the other; each is a necessary condition for the existence of the other. . . .'[3] It is this dialectical tension that makes social life possible. In this sense deviation is an all-permeating phenomenon which lends force to any serious decision involving some detachment from routine activity. It is rarely an alien label which strikes the unprepared innocent from afar. The process of becoming deviant is a vastly more complex negotiation of identities and consequences which takes place in an endless series of mundane contexts.

All of us have toyed with forbidden experience and considered its possible effect on ourselves. Such toying is not simply reflective activity which has no implications for our identities. As Dewey remarks, 'The thing actually at stake in any serious deliberation is . . . what sort of person is one to become, what sort of self is in the making.'[4] Thus, instead of there being a great gulf between the labeller and the labelled, conceptions of deviancy are woven into the very fabric of everyday life and minutely affect behaviour which is not officially monitored. Toying of this sort can usually be satisfactorily described as a process of 'drift' rather than as a series of abrupt and fateful encounters with bad society.[5] Whilst official rituals lend clarity and authority to moral passages, there is abundant deviation which develops without any formal intervention by official agencies. Indeed, in many cases such intervention occurs only when informal control procedures have failed and the person is unofficially recognised as deviant. Until the evolution of deviancy is recognised as the creature of a host of petty interactions which communicate definitions of propriety and impropriety, empathetic sociology will continue to be misunderstood as the unilateralism which Akers describes.

The second major feature of the solipsist charge is that definitional sociology ignores the importance of deviant structures and development. It is with just these structures that the rest of this chapter will be concerned. I shall examine the ways in which the organisation of deviancy shapes the extent to which rule-breakers are identified and managed as deviant. The presentation of deviancy affects the manner in which typifications are formed, applied and confirmed. The social impact of visible and recognised deviancy is radically different from that wrought by invisible and unrecognised deviation. The impact is not only experienced by control agencies and by lay members of a society, it is felt by deviants themselves. The impact is, in one sense, nothing less than the basis upon which a society's knowledge of deviancy rests.

I change the social world every time I appear in it. The influence which I exert is differentially distributed along and over the contours of my surroundings. Within my immediate environment there is a zone which is more or less available for me to dominate. This 'manipulatory sphere' is 'the region open to my immediate inter-ference which I can modify either directly by movements of my body or with the help of artificial extensions of my body.... The manipula-tory zone is that portion of the outer world upon which I can actually act.'[6] Any activity within this zone transforms it, by restructuring its physical constitution. When, as is most often the case, the physical constitution is seen as significant, physical restructuring can be read as symbolic restructuring. A rearrangement of the parts of my mani-pulatory sphere is usually taken to signify changes in my intention and attitude towards the world.

I tend to mould this sphere until it conforms to my use. Not only do I order it so that it permits me to realise projects which I have within it, I also make of it a symbolic environment which is marked out in a meaningful way:

I anticipate that what is now in my manipulatory sphere will reenter it later and require my interference or will interfere with me. Therefore I have to be sure that I shall then find my bearings within it and come to terms with it as I can now while it is within my control. This presupposes that I shall be able to recognise those elements which I now find relevant in the world within my actual reach, especially within the manipulatory zone, and which . . . will prove relevant also when I return later on. I am, thus, *motivated* to single out and to *mark* certain objects. When I return I expect these marks to be useful as 'subjective reminders'. . . .[7]

Both inside and outside my manipulatory sphere there is an arena of others before whom I am either present or can impress the mark of my presence. In my activity I generate signs which reveal something of me. At the very least, I am part of the social environment of these others and thereby structure their world. 'Individuals, like other objects in this world, affect the surrounding environment in a manner congruent with their own actions and properties. Their mere presence produces signs and marks. Individuals, in brief, exude expressions.'[8]

Any person who is socially present before others is a field of expression for them to read. In his gestural style, posture, facial movements, positioning, overt movements, clothing and so on, he presents a range of signs which provide information about him, his past and his future.[9] People generate and respond to signs whether or not they are manifestly in interaction with one another.[10] Most people in even the loosest settings assess their fellow-beings before they are able to ignore them. Even what may appear to be total mutual disregard rests on the acceptance of others as unthreatening, predictable and safe enough to be placed in a position where they may be disregarded.

Coupled with nonverbal signs are more overt demonstrations of a person's intentions and thought. When linguistic utterances are interpreted through and besides the interpretations of the other indices, a more or less coherent portrait of the person is constructed. All these clues are taken to be in some way indicative of those states which are not susceptible to direct observation. They are evidence of honesty and dishonesty; truthfulness and untruthfulness, and so on. They are also generally regarded as indicative of a larger whole of which they are no more than parts. Collectively they are made up into a typification of the person which is qualitatively greater than their mere sum. They are treated as more than fragmentary and un-related—attempts are made to compound them into an integrated presentation. People are not viewed as simple agglomerates of discrete characteristics. Some factors are awarded a superior role in ordering the manner in which they are understood. People are 'really', basically and consistently nice, nasty or ordinary; not occasionally nice in some settings, occasionally nasty in others, and ordinary in yet others. There is an imputed core or essential person-ality which can and must be teased out from under the surface discrepancies. As Znaniecki argues:

. . . in every Western language there are hundreds of words denoting supposed traits of 'intelligence' and 'character'; and almost every such trait has, or had in the past, an axiological significance. . . . In naïve popular reflexion, such psychological traits are real qualities of a sub-stantial 'mind' or 'soul' whose existence is manifested by specific acts (including verbal statements) of the individual.[11]

Any life-history can be conceived of as an orderly sequence of events which are understood through the phenomenal presentation of expressions, signs and marks of the emergent personality. As I move through the world I leave behind me traces in the form of the impressions which I have made upon it. Traces may take the guise of recollections held of me by others; they may be concrete tokens in the shape of changes which I have wrought on the world; or they may be consciously compiled records. Assembled together in various ways, they present a range of different biographies of me—some creditable and others discreditable. These traces are indices which are employed to construct reputations, careers and typifications.

No one, not even the subject of the biography, can ever know in complete detail all the traces left behind by a person. At different points of time, in different areas of social space, and with different degrees of familiarity, others will interpret the signs deposited by an individual and make meaningful wholes out of them. In this task of imputing coherence and thematic unity to a portrait, the same signs will assume different relevances in different constructions. What one person sees as pivotal will be rejected by another as peripheral. Socially structured access to a person over time will determine how he is viewed. To take one example, bureaucratically compiled records can be juggled together to produce a number of different perspectives on a person:

. . . since individuals may accumulate records in several different locales, and since the records themselves may be transferred, records from various sources may be *combined* in myriad ways, often without the knowledge of the person whose fate they may be helping to determine. And since each of the pieces of the record may have been compiled with different ends in view, the composite picture provided by the record may bear little resemblance to the person it purports to describe.[12]

Traces are not read independently of some context and contexts are not self-evident either in their selection or their composition. Instead, what is regarded by one as an essentially meaningful environment of signs will be dismissed by another as meaningless. The significance of any one person will rest upon the place he occupies in other peoples' systems of relevance. A person's behaviour may be defined as normal by one, anomalous by another and pathological by a third. Critical in this range of definitions is the person's behaviour; the facet of himself which he is presenting to the other; the world of events assembled by the other as appropriately contextual; the significance attached to the facet and to the context; their juxtaposition; and, finally, their articulation with other behaviours and other contexts. As significant is the centrality of the person's behaviour to the other's system of relevance. Schutz has marked out the world of the actor in terms of a social cartography. He argues:

. . . the world seems to him at any given moment as stratified in different layers of relevance, each of them requiring a different degree of knowledge. To illustrate these strata of relevance we may—borrowing the term from cartography—speak of 'isohypses' or 'hypsographical contour lines of relevance', trying to suggest by this metaphor that we could show the distribution of the interests of an individual at a given moment with respect both to their intensity and to their scope by connecting elements of equal relevance to his acts. . . . Distinguishing . . . two kinds of knowledge, namely, *'knowledge of acquaintance'*, and *'knowledge about'*, we may say that, within the field covered by the contour lines of relevance, there are centers of explicit knowledge *of* what is aimed at; they are surrounded by a halo knowledge *about* what seems to be sufficient; next comes a region in which it will merely do 'to put one's trust'; the adjoining foothills are the home of unwarranted hopes and assumptions; between these areas, however, lie zones of complete ignorance.[13]

Such a cartography is critical in determining how a person, as a field of expression, will be understood by others. In particular, it is relevant to the activities of discreditable counterfeit role-players. Whilst the counterfeit may pass if he is an object which lies in the other's zone of ignorance or 'knowledge about', he will not manage to do so if he is the centre of explicit expertise. Thus it is vital to gauge who is making the interpretation, what is the structure of his system of relevances and what kind of knowledge he is utilising in his assessment of the counterfeit. The most ramshackle of fronts may 'pass' if the deviant is merely assigned to a background position of low importance. If, on cursory inspection, he appears other than deviant and is not then subject to knowing scrutiny, the more or less esoteric clues which might betray him will remain unnoticed or misunderstood. So long as deviation is relegated to the other's outer regions, passing may be a feasible accomplishment. Indeed, 'knowledge about' is often so ill-formed that it acts as an aid to the counterfeit. Popular stereotypes of, for instance, the homosexual are so misleading that many homosexuals can remain unmolested in their deviant roles.

The presentation of deviancy becomes much more complex when it is a group accomplishment. Many forms of deviation depend upon systems of joint action both within the deviant world and between that world and others. Numerous rule-breakers sustaining a system of exchange and support are necessarily more visible than solitary deviants. Furthermore, public exchange between them depends on artful management. Deviants may communicate by means of recognition signals which are not intended to be intelligible to conventional people. As Goffman remarks:

. . . there are important stigmas, such as the ones that prostitutes, thieves, homosexuals, beggars and drug addicts have, which require the individual to be carefully secret about his failing to one class of persons, the police, while systematically exposing himself to other classes of person, namely, clients, fellow-members, connections, fences, and the like.[14]

Thus, in any one social setting there can be multiple and coexisting worlds which are not apparent to all its members. Cooperative deviation rests on preventing the illicit worlds irrupting into the licit and vice versa. It is a difficult feat to control expressions which permit an appearance of conventionality before the nondeviant and an appearance of deviancy before the fellow deviant. A person may have to sustain plural identities in a single situation.

As the scale of joint deviant activity grows, so do problems of concealment and management. In some cases the problems are those experienced by the spy, traitor or impostor. They revolve around maintaining the semblance of an adequate level of commitment to the normal world; explaining other commitments which prevent full involvment in conventional activity; assembling traces which support this pretence of normality and destroying or disguising those which belie it; directing attention at those contexts which support the pretence and away from those which do not; and neutralising the risks which are presented by associations with potentially discrediting others. Supporting a system of links with the deviant and the non-deviant worlds simultaneously is a precarious enterprise. It demands a vigilance and a capacity to dissemble. The deviant must prepare two presentations of himself, each with a series of accounts and traces which are seemingly complete, and each of which is a convincing proof of his allegiance to one way of life. Of course, the strain and complexities of such an accomplishment may simply be excessive. The deviant may decisively opt for full commitment to one life-style. He may also reduce the burden by resigning himself to the penalties attendant on deviant status, mitigating them only by presenting the status in its most acceptable form. A 'strategy of those who pass is to present the signs of the stigmatized failing as signs of another attribute, one that is less significantly a stigma. Mental defectives . . . apparently sometimes try to pass as mental patients, the latter being the less of the two social evils.'[15] Lemert provides other examples:

In some Southern states Negroes have found relatively satisfactory status as Indians. Feigning lameness, blindness, and madness are historically old shrifts resorted to by paupers or professional beggars both to mitigate penalties and enhance rewards of their roles. It is possible to discover instances where psychotic persons and epileptics conceal their real status by passing themselves off as alcoholics. Moreover, there are cases where lepers have preferred to be publicly known as insane.[16]

There are still further solutions. The deviant can try to segregate his audiences so that he can perform properly, consistently and without strain in his deviant and nondeviant roles alike. He can create esoteric symbolic systems which are unknown to those who are uninitiated in the deviancy.[17] He can present accounts which explain his behaviour in terms of a conventionally satisfactory rhetoric.[18] He can implicate the knowing so that they too become discreditable. Nonetheless, he continually confronts a pivotal problem. If he is to live a reasonably agreeable life, he must not advertise those deviant aspects of himself which are, by definition, liable to sanction. His activities in the world lay out for others' inspection a field which reveals a great deal of him. It is only by constant attention to the appearance of that field that he can maintain dissonant identities. If he fails, not only will he be recognised for what he and a few others know him to be, he will also be penalised. This phenomenal field is structured, in part, by patterns of deviant organisation and, in turn, it generates possibilities of organisation.

MORAL AMBIGUITY

Ambiguity is one of the chief features of the manner in which deviancy is interpreted in everyday life. Unless some major crisis occurs or a clear revelation is made, few people engaged in deviant activity are transparently identifiable. Instead, morality and rules in everyday life are situationally problematic. That is, the meaning and applicability of deviancy-defining criteria are rarely established as general, inflexible and patent in their implications but rely on elaborate secondary interpretation. There is always some reservoir of ambiguity; some doubt about what rule should be invoked; what context it most exactly fits; and some challenge from other signs and understandings. As Bittner remarks:

If we consider that we must so order our practical affairs as not to run afoul of a very considerable variety of standards of judgement that are not fully compatible with each other, do not have a clear-cut hierarchy of primacy and are regarded as binding and enforceable only in the light of additional vaguely denied information; if we consider that for every maxim of conduct we can think of a situation to which it does not apply or in which it can be overruled by a superior maxim; if we consider that unmitigated adherence to principle is regarded as vice or at least folly; . . . then it is clear that all efforts to live by an internally consistent scheme of interpretation are necessarily doomed to fail.[19]

Not only are rules an undependable guide to the recognition of deviancy, interpretation of behaviour itself is difficult. The meaning of activity is not always obvious. It is precisely because people do not have 'unequivocally stable meanings'[20] that many deviancies remain unidentified. The vast bulk of rule-breaking behaviour in Britain, America and elsewhere simply does not come to the attention of agents of control.[21] In most instances it is improbable that deviancy will be met with sanctions of any sort. The whole work of recognising deviancy is ineptly performed by lay members of society. There is too little clarity and too much contradictory information to permit the ready comprehension of all the behaviour that is daily enacted before us. It is for this very reason that much organised effort is devoted to the task of imposing clarity upon the moral properties of behaviour:

Durkheim long ago argued that deviance serves the function of allowing society to make clear to all its members just what the norms and boundaries of societies are. . . . This argument assumes that the meanings are not really unclear or uncertain, but, rather, that they simply must be used so that they can be dramatized and reinforced. Actually, I think the dramatization, the conflict, the anxiety, and . . . the confusion, can all best be explained as being due to the problematic nature of the meanings. As Cohen and other jurists have argued, 'the law is always uncertain until a decision is made'. . . . Through their struggle with the relevant 'facts', 'moral and legal questions', and so forth, the members of society must construct specific meanings for this situation which will be accepted by themselves and other members. By constructing a socially plausible or acceptable meaning for this specific situation, they are making the meaning of things a little less problematic. . . . And the *ritualized* aspects of these encounters—the use of the magical paraphernalia and formulae of the society—was originally intended to gain acceptance for the constructed meaning. . . .[22]

The courts and other agencies act as institutionalised attempts to dispel ambiguity. It is still problematic what effects the pronouncements of these organisations do, in fact, have upon a society's members' understanding of deviancy. Nevertheless, the authoritative casting of people and events into distinct categories represents a strenuous endeavour to make the practical business of making moral judgments somewhat less difficult. This endeavour is shaped by bureaucratic imperatives, by a need to justify consequential decision-making and by a conception of the agency as educator. In its management of the social world, a defining agency violates the immensely complicated interplay of deviant, nondeviant and ambiguous phenomena: 'All control agencies in effect become responsible for drawing clearer lines than in fact exist either in everyday life or in the processes by which people were originally led into their services. . . . Both professionalism and bureaucratization objectify deviance and reify diagnostic categories.'[23]

Thus a twofold process is at work in the defining process of control agencies; not only does it reduce ambiguity and make the moral world simpler, it also makes moral actors discrete and clearly distinguishable. In their pristine, official form, these social types are then disseminated through the press, television and other media and, where they intersect usefully with lay maps of the world, become modified and adapted to everyday purposes. It seems to be the case that such modified types are rather more unresponsive to change than descriptions which emerge out of professional work. At the least, they constitute ideas in the area about which a society's members have knowledge; they do not represent specific foci of concern or expertise.

To the extent that lay and expert typifications are generalised, simplified, relatively 'anonymous' and abstract, there will always be some difficulty in readily applying them to people whom we know well and see every day. In the first place, without clear revelation of deviancy, many deviant acts are so ambiguous that they can always be construed as indicative of familiar and nondeviant states. Commenting upon the initial reactions of wives to what was subsequently defined as their husbands' mental illness, it was observed:

Once the behavior is organized as problem, it tends also to be interpreted as some particular kind of problem. More often than not, however, the husband's difficulties are not seen initially as manifestations of mental illness or even as emotional problems. Early interpretations often tend to be organized around physical difficulties or 'character' problems. To a very marked degree, these orientations grow out of the wives' long-standing appraisals of their husbands as weak and ineffective or physically sick men.[24]

Rather than resort to deviant typifications, innocuous explanations are proffered. Such explanations are more likely to be consonant with the hitherto nondeviant biography of the strangely acting individual than with the attribution of deviancy. If deviant behaviour is seen as discontinuous with everyday life, it is not likely to be immediately associated with what can be constructed as a reasonably coherent biography. Furthermore, a generalised typification is unlikely to capture the whole range of possible modes of deviant action. Instead, its restricted focus will tend to lend prominence to certain features of the deviation and ignore others. Certain typifications are too inflexible to accommodate variation, so that many kinds of deviation simply escape recognition. The 'masculine', 'normal' seeming homosexual, the physician drug-addict[25] or the wealthy thief all enjoy a measure of protection from vulgar or simplistic social typing procedures.

Ironically, it may be precisely because of the generalised and limited applicability of the types that social control agents have to intervene in critical defining situations. It is only their expertise that can unravel the difficulties surrounding the comprehension of problematic behaviour. When rule-breakers are immersed in networks of relationships, their ambiguous behaviour may successfully evade identification. As Denzin remarks:

... the greater the involvement in a relational social structure, the lower the probability of deviance ascription by members of social control agencies. That is, when we observe what by public standards would be an act of deviance, we predict that labeling will not occur if the potential deviant is highly involved in a relational network.[26]

If, however, the typifications of agents percolate through into the network, confusion and familiarity may be dispelled:

... the potential deviant may bring his actions to the eyes of influential outsiders, and their perceptions are then fed back into the relationship. Social workers, physicians, close friends ... and even legal authorities may take on such a role. The veracity of their definitions may lead the other relational members to view the potential deviant's actions in a new light. They may attempt to foster changes on his part, and if he is unsuccessful in validating his actions, ascriptions of deviance may appear *within* the relationship. Under these circumstances, the moral order of the relationship is challenged, and unless changes occur, a public deviant is created.[27]

THE 'EPOCHÉ' OF THE NATURAL ATTITUDE AND ITS SUSPENSION

In nonproblematic, everyday situations it is likely that the expressions which a person exudes, the marks he leaves, the symbolic field which he creates around him, and the communications he makes, are not routinely treated with too much suspicion. It is only when something which is strikingly anomalous appears, or when some eventful decision is to be made, that the world of signs produced by others suddenly seems counterfeit. There is an implied property of social order that the world is taken on trust, that the world as it appears to be is the world as it 'really is'. Schutz calls this stance the '*epoché* of the natural attitude', meaning, by 'natural attitude', the trusting and 'unscientific' perspective adopted by Everyman in his dealings with the world:

Phenomenology has taught us the concept of phenomenological *epoché*, the suspension of our belief in the reality of the world as a device to overcome the natural attitude. . . . The suggestion may be ventured that man within the natural attitude also uses a specific *epoché*. . . . He does not suspend belief in the outer world and its objects, but on the contrary, he suspends doubt in its existence. What he puts in brackets is the doubt that the world and its objects might be otherwise than it appears to him. We . . . call this *epoché* the *epoché of the natural attitude*.[28]

This 'willing suspension of disbelief' in the protestations and appearances of others is of critical importance. It allows for the possibility of deception, of the discreditable or deviant passing for what they are not.[29] It is a characteristic of certain groups in society that they are partially freed from the *epoché* of the natural attitude described by Schutz. Instead of taking the world of moral appearances on trust and imputing normality to ambiguous events, the emancipated practise a systematic distrust. According to the particular perspective they adopt, surface appearances hide clusters of pathological symptoms which, in turn, are signs of deviant personality. Of course, the typical freedom of these groups represents not so much a total distancing as a movement in perspectives towards a novel natural attitude. Criminals and deviants are prime candidates for the experiencing of such a movement. In many cases their view of the world has undergone a systematic shift so that what most people, in their natural attitude, take to be a society of honest people fringed by marginal deviants is, in fact, the very opposite.[30] Hartung states:

The delinquent's use of this rationalization [the condemnation of the the condemners] is facilitated by newspaper reports of widespread crookedness on the part of retail grocery store operators, establishments such as watch and jewelry repair, radio and television service and repair, automobile garages and the like. These assist the adolescent in accepting the rationalization 'Everyone has his own racket'. This reaches its finest flowering among (1) the young narcotics addict who claims that everyone is an 'operator' who is always shooting the angles . . . (2) the convict's ideal of the 'real man', who knows that there are only two kinds of people: the 'suckers' who work, and the 'smart guys' who 'skim it off the top'; and (3) the honest policeman who believes that 'everyone has larceny in his heart'.[31]

A constant confrontation with deviant phenomena, an existential commitment to deviancy, and a way of life that revolves around discovering the discreditable in others are all likely to lead to a reversal of the natural attitude. When deviancy is made highly salient, it can become treated as a basic, underlying property of social life. Events which might seem to contradict this view are either thrust out to the margins of apprehension or dismissed as misleading. Professional experts dealing in areas of 'social pathology' claim a competence to know better than the sufferer what the contours of his pathology are 'really like'.[32] They, like the criminal, tend to be liberated from the natural attitude. The policeman, the social worker, the judge and the psychiatrist acquire novel definitions of the world in which the socially problematic is of paramount importance. The transformation of 'knowledge about' deviancy into 'knowledge of' deviancy can generate a degree of cynicism about commonly accepted protestations concerning motives, behaviour and relationships. Inattention to surface appearance can produce deviant significances in almost any context. Schwartz and Stanton describe how the hospital psychiatrist, freed from the natural attitude, saw his junior colleague's statements as evidence of a 'deeper reality'. 'Many psychiatrists seemed to pride themselves on ignoring the face value of what their colleagues said to them, focusing instead on what they believed to be "really going on" . . . information was frequently lost . . . particularly when a junior staff member protested to a senior about certain aspects of the hospital; the protest was likely to be interpreted as transference rebellion.'[33]

Another mark of this detachment is an organised stance of suspicion towards the world. When a policeman is on patrol, for instance, it would be professionally naïve of him to accept on trust what he observes. Instead, he adopts a position from which everything appears potentially deviant:

From the front seat of a moving patrol car, street life in a typical Negro ghetto is perceived as an uninterrupted sequence of suspicious scenes. Every well dressed man or woman standing aimlessly on the street during hours when most people are at work is carefully scrutinized for signs of an illegal source of income; every boy wearing boots, black pants, long hair, and a club jacket is viewed as potentially responsible for some item on the list of muggings, broken windows, and petty thefts that still remain to be cleared; and every hostile glance directed at the passing patrolman is read as a sign of possible guilt.[34]

This organised working of the shifted natural attitude sensitises the social control agent to potential indices of deviancy. He is expert not only at manufacturing working definitions of rule-breaking, but also at ordering perception to identify the rule-breaker. Partly because recognition of the deviant by one who adopts the natural attitude is no easy task, the agent is structurally and territorially placed to be in key definitional situations:

It would appear dubiously facilitative to rely completely on everyday citizens for imputations of pivotal deviance. They appear too ready to code potentially 'deviant' emissions as simple variants of normality. Immersed in conventional pursuits, the man on the street has too little time or interest to be a fully effective coder, except, perhaps, during periods of 'crackdown' on some form of deviance. In all of social life, a high probability for the occurrence of a set of activities is best ensured by giving a set of Others some interest in, and payoff for, performing them. . . . As the number of *imputational specialists* increases in a society, it is likely that the number of people imputed as deviant will also increase. . . . The growing army of social workers, psychologists, psychiatrists, police, etc., constitutes a stratum with a precise interest in ensuring a flow of persons defined as deviant. The training undergone by such specialists creates a stratum whose aim it is to discover 'out there' in the empirical world those sorts of people they have been trained to see.[35]

The deviant thus lives in a world which is populated by the knowing, the unknowing and the too-knowing. With the too-knowing, an increase in deviousness may enable some degree of social invisibility to be attained. Yet certain forms of deviancy, those which involve permanent and immoveable organisations or props for instance, simply cannot depend on social invisibility. They are forced to attempt to gain some state of accommodation with the too-knowing. For the others, those who need not obtrude too conspicuously, a range of contingencies affects how vulnerable they will be to observation. I shall discuss these contingencies later.

There is one other major way in which the *epoché* of the natural attitude can prove undependable. The natural attitude rests on the 'world' having some predictability, order and intelligibility. It also depends on a substantial congruence of shared perspectives between a person and others significant to him. The fabric of this basis can be easily upset by the untoward and, in time of crisis, the natural attitude may be thrown into suspense.[36]

When such a suspension occurs, the person may find himself detached from the kinds of understandings that had hitherto constituted his world. They are no longer taken for granted but become visible. As Garfinkel remarks,

the operations that one would have to perform in order to multiply the senseless features of perceived environments; to produce and sustain bewilderment . . . ; to produce the socially structured affects of anxiety, shame, guilt . . . ; and to produce disorganized interaction should tell us something about how the structures of everyday activities are ordinarily and routinely produced and maintained.[37]

The world of challenged appearances may then permit a reorganisation in which inferences about the moral properties of actors are consciously made for perhaps the first time. Instead of deviation appearing familiar, it may suddenly seem suspect, problematic and unfamiliar. Unless the deviant (who is himself likely to be disoriented) can produce a good account of himself, he becomes vulnerable to discrediting. The deviant who has too much to hide may find himself exposed in an unprepared state.

In the work of collective adjustment which typically succeeds a crisis, 'transactions proceed in a halting, tentative manner. Those who act do so with caution. . . . They watch one another carefully for any hint of new patterns of adjustment.'[38] What were once background and unnoticed activities become phenomena to be watched with some interest and care. Those who are fully committed to the ostensible definitions of the situation espoused by a group may have a difficult enough task in renegotiating a satisfactory set of meanings which can govern action. Those who are not so committed experience a double difficulty.

In time of crisis, furthermore, the very existence of the problematically strange may be given an important place in the causal scheme which interprets how the crisis arose.[39] Instead of being comfortably accommodated, the deviant in an exposed position may receive abundant attention. Disorienting events may be attributed to his influence. He may be required to adopt the role of witch or its counterpart—the mentally ill, the conspirator, the polluter—if he is a member of a relatively cohesive system of relations:

> If witchcraft sharpens definition where roles are ill defined, we would expect it to be absent when there is no call for clear definition. . . . We would expect anthropomorphic ideas of power to dominate where humans press closely upon one another. And if these intensive social relations are well defined, we would expect anthropomorphism of the cosmos to be regulative, to uphold the moral and social codes by just ancestral wrath; whereas, if intensive social interaction is ill defined, we would expect a witchcraft-dominated cosmos.[40]

According to Douglas, witches and their equivalents are to be found at powerful centres of social 'disorganisation'. In crisis, roles become poorly defined and networks lose their clear structure. Presumably it is precisely then that anthropomorphic groups will be sensitive to the real or assumed existence of certain kinds of deviants who are alleged to have disruptive capacities.

MELDING AND NORMALISATION

At other times, when awareness *is* structured by the *epoché* of the natural attitude,[41] few forms of deviancy are immediately recognisable. Unless the deviant advertises himself, conforms to a popular typification, is an instance of striking anomaly, or cannot disguise transparent rule-breaking, his rule-breaking must be pushed into a salient position before it is acknowledged.[42] If, as Jack Douglas, Bittner and Lofland argue, imputations of deviancy are inhibited by the confusions and ambiguities surrounding the application of commonsense morality, additional information must be advanced to facilitate their production. One source of such information is the sheer sense of the appropriateness of things which tends to pervade perceptions of settings. When phenomena seem out of place or anomalous, they may then become eligible for classification as deviant. Instead of melding into a context of implied relationships and meanings which lend ambiguity (as well as a certain clarity) to a person's intentions and character, the person who is 'out of place' may be thought to have no 'good' reason for being where he is. The normal range of accounts which can be offered for his behaviour is not available to cast doubt on his possible deviancy. Whilst a normal set of intentions can be attributed to someone in place, special motives can characterise one who is not. For instance, 'in Chicago, an individual in the uniform of a hobo can loll "on the stem", but once off this preserve, he is required to look as if he were intent on getting to some business destination'.[43] The apparent aimlessness of the hobo is seen as innocuous when he is 'in place', but it becomes sinister when he is not. Similarly, a Negro youth in the white urban areas of America is regarded as being nefariously engaged.[44]

Deviancy is likely to be socially invisible when, to the unwary, it seems to be a natural part of some conventional setting. Some deviancies represent little more than a modified version of conventional behaviour and can be correspondingly disguised. The forger's apparatus can be transformed into legitimate printing equipment; the abortionist's theatre can become an orthodox operating room; the pornographer's studio can be put to legal use, and so on. As Cavan argues about more mundane deviancies:

The taken-for-granted character of the standing behavior patterns of any setting may . . . become a matter of practical interest to those who wish to exploit them, to use them in a way that is neither routine nor proper but nonetheless possible. Those who are willing to comply more or less with what is expected of them within the setting may at the same time be able to engage in other activities that are inappropriate. Stenographic pools that provide young women with a setting for earning a living may also provide lesbians with an opportunity to enjoy surreptitiously the presence of a bevy of female co-workers as well. Similarly, knowledge of what might be called the 'form' of conduct required in a given setting may permit one to engage in behavior that is inappropriate in the setting by masking it in a shape that is appropriate.[45]

A more interesting case of melding is that where, instead of deviant behaviour assuming nondeviant forms, the conventional context itself is transformed into one which permits deviancy *as* normal and routine behaviour. That is, deviancy itself becomes the standard, taken-for-granted substance and form of acts within the setting. There are many sanctioned occasions which are bounded and inconsequential enough to allow people to behave in what would otherwise be regarded as an impermissible fashion. These occasions are often legitimated by their place in the established social calendar of society; they are supported by a tradition and by a displacement of criteria whereby they become standards of conduct in themselves. Access to these deviant settings is so open that it is not possible to typify their members as deviant personalities; the occasions are limited in time and space and are not thereby consequential for either the participants or major social arrangements; and, finally, they are predictable and contained. Instances of such changed contexts are certain places on Guy Fawkes' Night, New Year's Eve, Election Night, Boat Race Night, the time of a Students' Rag, Mardi Gras, Carnival and the Stag Party. So conventionalised are these social occasions that a special licence to be deviant is afforded their participants.[46] As the Opies state:

For as long as history has been recorded special wildness and exuberance has been tolerated, if not exactly encouraged, at certain festivals of the year; and if we want to see in the present day how the great mass of the people enjoyed themselves in past times, the best practices we can look at are the juvenile fooling on the first of April and the first of May, the disorder of mischief nights, and the guising at Hallowe'en.[47]

Special deviant contexts permit a moral escape from the everyday self; in them, the situational deviant can respectably claim exemption from the obligations and rights pertaining to his normal self. He becomes 'not himself'. So changed can these contexts become that the person entering Trafalgar Square on New Year's Eve or Hampstead Heath on Guy Fawkes' Night cannot fully claim the conventional protection afforded one who is abroad in a public place. His rights are diminished. Of course, the licence in these settings is never absolute. Yet there is a substantial shift in the nature of what is publicly accepted and rejected. Social control effort is slighter and is chiefly devoted to restricting the deviancy to its accepted temporal and geographical place.

These settings provide ample opportunity for the expression of deviancy. The drinker, the violent and the sexually adventurous may discover that many of the normal constraints on their roles are absent. Instead, their behaviour is not significantly differentiated from surrounding activity and, more important, it acquires a totally altered meaning. Imputations of deviancy are neutralised by the assumption that the behaviour is not at all a reflection of the core or real self of the deviant. Altered contexts thus provide possibilities of deviancy becoming unobtrusive. Such contexts are not confined to major periods of licence. There are abundant minor occasions which

are woven into social life. Marriage, attainment of the age of majority, the ending of important examinations and the wake all serve the
same function in diluted fashion. Similarly, places are unequally
regulated by expectations of propriety. Any complex area can be split
up into subareas which are differentially patrolled by social control
agents; and which are governed by different conceptions of correct
conduct. As Wirth argues:[48]

Each urban area has its own external characteristics in the form of build-
ings, institutions, and general appearance, but each has its own moral code.
A population seeks an area in which its members can be gratified with the
least amount of interference.

The dominant social context can change both from place to place
and from time to time. The sentimental and moral order of a Soho
undergoes regular, cyclical alterations every twenty-four hours.
Permissible conduct in the Soho of an early afternoon is radically
different from that of the same area in the late evening. A final
instance of transformation is that wrought by the influence of certain
social groups who have acquired effective hegemony over an area. In
this case the context has been changed in an irregular and uncon-
ventional manner. Political demonstrations or large crowds may
usurp the power of social control agents to impose their definitions
on a situation. Usurpations of this nature can introduce radically
new notions of public decorum. In some instances, the public nature
of a public place has been challenged. People who enter that place do
so 'at their own risk'. A person who visits Grosvenor Square at
certain times is not supposed to expect an uneventful passage along
the streets. The fundamental aim of police action here seems to be to
confine a dangerous transformation of the meaning of space to as
small an area as possible. Within the boundaries of the confined
area, there may be little attempt to enforce conventional codes of
behaviour. Indeed, so long as containment is possible, licence is often
extended to deviant or transiently deviant persons. Many new modes
of social action seem to strain towards the attainment of such a contained state of tacitly condoned deviation. Confrontations between
university authorities and students, demonstrators and the police,
tend to become conventionalised forms of encounter which are
governed by new rules.[49]

SHIELDING PATTERNS

Whilst many secondary deviants possess the skills which permit
passing, they depend upon organisations or props which are obtrusive
and discrediting. The addict's equipment, the offertory box thief's

bamboo stick, or the burglar's tools are examples of minor props. The offices, records and plant of the bootlegger are major items which require some disguising. In much the same way, certain deviant actions can be unambiguously visible signs which alert the knowing. What is at stake is the issue of social visibility. No matter how astute they may be, certain deviants play roles which cannot easily be mistaken for conventional activity. The organisation of their behaviour and the absence of melding possibilities render the rule-breaking clearly identifiable.

Physical and behavioural proofs of rule-breaking are likely to be given when the deviancy involves large numbers of people, incursions into public areas, encounters with nondeviants and elaborate preparation. When such phenomena cannot be conventionally accounted for, rule-breaking may be simply presented in its naked form. Alternatively, potential discreditors' attention may be distracted away from the damaging signs.[50] Many forms of such obtrusive deviancy are made possible only by darkness, crowds or a high degree of dexterity and mobility on the part of the deviant. Yet most deviants who depend on sizeable props are at risk and must rely on police connivance, geographical seclusion, an attrition of their resources or a high arrest rate.

The most important way of coping with easily identifiable phenomena is physically to shield them. Deviants who have privileged access to hidden places and whose deviancy can be confined to such places are relatively invulnerable. These rule-breakers who do not require frequent transactions with an anonymous public, geographical mobility or large-scale settings can be protected by conventional shields against the outsider's gaze:

. . . central practical boundaries are such mundane things as walls, doors, window shades, and locks. But in modern society few of these are made to withstand a concerted effort by a group of men to breach them. . . . Yet these fragile doors and windows effectively prevent police or private citizens from interfering with our sleep, our classrooms, our toolbenches, or our bars. . . . This is because a door is a legal entity of great importance: legitimate concerted social efforts to break down a door may only take place on legally defined occasions. . . . The legal defence of doors and walls and windows means that small social systems which have legal possession of a place can maintain *continuous, discretionary* control over who crosses their boundaries. And this discretion may be enforced against agents of the state unless they have legal cause to penetrate the system or are invited in.[51]

Providing some minimum of attention is given to the external appearance of these boundaries, activities within them can be relatively freely conducted. In these cases the organisation of deviancy as a field of expression poses few problems because of the segregation of audiences. Conventions surround mobile boundaries too. Clothing or motorcars can provide useful shields. Taxicabs, for instance, have been often employed by prostitutes as usefully shielded sites. In the case of clothing, Victorian women were generously provided with body shields:

... stolen objects could be handily tucked into shawls, mantles and muffs, and the great bell-shaped skirt made an excellent hiding place for all but the largest and heaviest things. Skirts of the period frequently had a pocket, usually on the right side and opening under a flounce. Among professional thieves this was modified so that the opening led into a huge pouch sometimes extending all round into a sort of double petticoat. .... Finally, the sheer size of the crinolined, shawled, puff-sleeved woman could make her a useful screen for thieves working in public places.[52]

Social institutions can provide shields of a different sort. Schools, offices, factories and other establishments serve as relatively segregated areas of activity which are not normally patrolled by official enforcement agents. Whilst retaining something of a public character they do, at the same time, open up quite different possibilities of exposing deviancy. Recognition of deviancy in a school by a teacher may have a very different outcome from recognition of deviancy by a policeman in a public space.[53] Apprehension of an employee by an employer may again have different consequences.[54] Such complex organisations rest upon internally generated systems of control which, whilst ultimately relying on the coercive power of the state, effectively usurp the state's sanctioning functions. The defence of the institution's autonomy from external interference may lead to treatment of the deviant as someone peculiarly the concern of the organisation. Qualities of 'anonymous' and 'impartial' rule-enforcement are typically lacking in such organisations. Instead, the deviant is managed in a way more conformable with a system of distributive justice based on the known and special character of the rule-breaker.

Deviancy in such settings is generally regulated by criteria which are different in focus from those envisaged by law-makers. The meanings of deviancy tend to undergo a systematic shift when they are interpreted through perspectives derived from particular institutional experience and goals. Such renegotiated meanings can shield some deviancies and obscure others altogether. While they may not produce complete re-evaluation, they may change the significance of certain forms of rule-breaking.[55] Certain kinds of deviancy may, indeed, become so normalised that they are no longer managed *as* deviant. Cavan describes this species of deviancy as 'normal trouble', 'improper activities that are frequent enough to be simply shrugged off or ignored'.[56] She cites 'a variety of self-indulgent and otherwise improper acts' in public drinking-places as instances of normal trouble, arguing, 'What goes on in the bar is localized in time and space, and one need not anticipate being held accountable for one's conduct at some later time or in some other setting. . . . As a result, behavior which is either permissible or constitutes no more than normal trouble encompasses a broad range of activities that are often open to sanction in other, more serious public settings.'[57] All institutions tend to normalise some troubles so that they change meaning and become part of the routine, informal world of the organisation.[58] Such behaviour can become controlled by the deviants themselves so that unnoticed normal trouble does not change into abnormal deviancy requiring strenuous regulation. In the case of pilfering by Newfoundland dockers, for instance, the idea of 'working the boat' denotes what and how much can be purloined from ships:

The application of this concept . . . tends to institutionalise pilferage—to grant it the status of a recognised and regularly occurring activity and, therefore, to grant it some degree of acceptance as a normal part of life. . . . It also provides a formula which in every case fixes an unequivocal limit beyond which pilferage, no longer seen as laudatory, is instead perceived as a danger to one's workmates. If men go above the value of the boat it is thought they are likely to attract official intervention. Such behaviour, if persisted in, could easily involve a man in sanctions applied by his co-workers.[59]

This kind of process of normalisation can occur in other, more complex ways. When deviancy is defined by structurally distant groups, and when it is inadequately monitored by official agencies, there is always the possibility that it may receive local redefinition and thereby become conventionalised. Layers of intermediary groupings between deviants and enforcers can provide substantial buttresses against control. The meanings of the rule-breaking behaviour can change from area to area of society and, in some parts, can become nothing less than legitimations of that behaviour. A prime example is that of classical banditry, an activity typically found in peasant societies which lack a widespread system of effective control and communication. According to Hobsbawm, the cultural ideal of the bandit was one who was restrained in his use of violence, did not victimise the poor and was engaged in a struggle to redress the wrongs inflicted by a society gone awry. 'His role is that of the champion, the righter of wrongs, the bringer of justice and social equity. His relation with the peasants is that of total solidarity and identity.'[60] Consequently:

Since the social bandit is not a criminal, he has no difficulty in rejoining his community as a respected member when he ceases to be an outlaw. . . .

Indeed, he may never actually leave it . . . he is likely to operate within the territory of his village or kinfolk, being maintained by them as a matter of family duty as well as common sense. . . . In remote and inaccessible areas, where the agents of authority enter only on occasional forays, the bandit may actually live in the village, unless word should come that the police are on the way. . . . Indeed, in the real back country, where law and government leave only the faintest trace, the bandit may be not only tolerated and protected, but a leading member of the community.[61]

In effect, then, deviancy can become socially invisible because the qualities which justified and justify its proscription are not recognised by those who have immediate dealings with its rule-breakers. Instead, there is a range of social groupings intervening between those who break the rules and those who not only are responsible for identifying rule-breaking but for taking action about it. The behaviour can meld into what is locally acceptable so that, according to an area's commonsense definitions of what is reprehensible, it no longer *is* deviant or even noteworthy. The fruits of the competition between ethnic groups in the Chicago of the 1920s illustrate this well. Ethnic solidarity and a degree of isolation from the outside world led to a transformation of official understandings about deviancy. The organised criminal was not always regarded as a deviant by local standards; he was, instead, a hero, a benefactor, an astute politician or a source of aid. Not all complex deviancy is entirely visible to any one outside audience. It may well be that the benign facet of the deviant behaviour and its normality will acquire the greatest salience. As Landesco argues, 'What needs to be appreciated is the element of the genuine popularity of the gangster, home-grown in the neighbourhood gang, idealized in the morality of the neighbourhood'.[62] He further states:

Four leading sentiments color the morality of the stockyards; family solidarity, revolutionary labor heroism, patriotic national heroism, and unconditional mutual aid without hesitant criticism or question against any danger. . . . As for the law, it is believed to be often an ally of the exploiter or the tool of the enemy gang. The 'racketeer' is an example of success under grim conditions. He retains his popularity because he is loyal to the neighborhood's morals. In industrial relations, as in bootlegging, or 'racketeering', he promotes the interests of himself and his fellows 'by every means, in any manner'.[63]

Such local reinterpretation inevitably imposes important restraints on a deviant's ability to act freely. Whilst he may retain a measure of local support through coercion or strenuous attempts to claim legitimacy, his chief bulwark is based on an elaborate system of exchange and reciprocity between himself and his neighbours. The maintenance of this system limits his capacity to act as a visible predator on others in his vicinity. That he may do so in fact does not alter the nature of the restraint.

Practical shielding does not depend solely upon exchanges which are grounded in deviant role-systems. Deviants play deviant and nondeviant roles alike and, in many cohesive and relatively segregated social worlds, they may be assessed by the complex information which stems from transactions based on both types of role. That is, discreditable qualities may be neutralised by creditable ones with the outcome that the deviant is not thought to be 'really' deviant. The demonology of deviant types provided by society simply does not permit the ready stigmatisation of one who is known in the fullness of all his possible major roles. Of course, such neutralisation usually occurs only when the evaluating nondeviant members of the closed society are rather divorced from the larger society and are forced into frequent interaction with the known deviants. An instance of such a segregated world is the American Black ghetto. Hannerz, in his description of a Washington ghetto, remarks:

A curious case of . . . straddling [of life-styles] is that of some households in the Winston Street neighborhood which are well established in illegal businesses—bootlegging and the numbers game. Except for these means of income, the households seem to lead mainstreamer lives [that is, based on conventional life-styles prevalent in the world outside the ghetto]. Their houses are well-kept, the families keep largely to themselves, although they are friendly with their neighbors and well-liked by most people. . . . Other people are aware of the incongruity between on the one hand the respectable front and the mainstreamer life, on the other hand the kind of business they engage in. As one mainstreamer neighbor said about one of the men involved: 'Of course Jimmy Thompson is a crook, but he is a good man.'[64]

For many deviants such assimilation is not viable. The forced interaction and closure of the ghetto contrast with the isolated networks and fluidity of boundaries which characterise most social worlds. Unavoidable proximity to deviancy which does not overtly victimise the nondeviants can generate a shield. In the case of such deviancy, a number of qualities must exist before it is shielded. I have already mentioned closure and systems of exchange. As important is the nature of the victim and the manner in which the deviancy is revealed.

When the victim is the social world itself, a shielded deviancy must be normalised so that it permits stabilisation and does not threaten the world. More potent is the selection of foreign victims. When the world is not itself victimised, there is an increased likelihood that it will not regard the deviant unfavourably. Such is the case with banditry. Every social group bases its morality upon some comparison of the eligibilities of potential victims. This hierarchy of victims

will delineate how legitimate an attack upon a person or group might
be. When that hierarchy is respected by the deviants themselves, the
concurrence of ideas can contribute towards acceptance of the rule-
breaker. A victim becomes more and more legitimate as he grows
structurally distant from the group. A member of one's own family, a
neighbour or a friend are the least permissible targets of predatory
attack. More permissible are strangers or members of despised
groups. Most permissible are large, impersonal bureaucracies:

[A] reason why crimes against large organizations are more acceptable
to the public than are other categories of crime may be that our system
of ethics lacks rules which specifically apply to relationships between
individuals and large organizations. All major historical religions originated in small communities, in which obligations concerned relatives,
friends, and neighbors. From these static and personal communities a set
of personal ethical norms developed; responsibility to great impersonal
structures did not exist. Today, when large-scale organizations dominate
our lives, men may be ethically unprepared to cope with the problem of the
relationship between the individual and the corporation.[65]

A growing anonymity of victims can enable the deviant's activity
to become increasingly legitimate from a local perspective. Yet, not
only is the nature of the victim significant, the nature of the victimisa-
tion is also important. Those deviancies which are built up of a host
of small actions may receive acceptance and undergo subtle distortions. A multitude of minor events can appear substantially less
disturbing and consequential than one or two major actions. Thus
the craft criminal who routinises his activity by engaging in a long
series of small thefts may be more readily accommodated than the
'project' thief[66] who undertakes major enterprises at infrequent
intervals. Similarly, the organised or entrepreneurial criminal whose
work entails innumerable petty market exchanges may be treated as
less of a deviant. Since it is the individual exchange that is typically
witnessed by a member of a social world, the importance of the whole
enterprise can be minimised. It was the cumulative nature of organised criminal activity that the President's Crime Commission felt
constrained to impress upon its readership:

It is organized crime's accumulation of money, not the individual transactions by which the money is accumulated, that has a great and threatening
impact on America. A quarter in a jukebox means nothing and results in
nothing. But millions of quarters in thousands of jukeboxes can provide a
motive for murder and the means to commit murder with impunity.[67]

It is because very few nondeviants can ever gain a complete over-
view of such deviant organisations that distortions can emerge. At
best, nondeviants can acquire only a segmental perspective. Some

part of the deviancy will be in focus, others out of
completely invisible. When the salient facet is not dis
or when it emphasises only a very partial attribute, th
receive a fundamentally different identification tha
would endow it with. When, as is often the case, the
presented with all the trappings of a market situation, t
the whole may be simply neutralised. Negotiations of th
the public face of complex deviancy can lead to radical n   ....
tions of its significance. Such negotiations undoubtedly characterise
the manner in which a great many kinds of deviancy are understood.
Prostitution, for instance, is treated as an exotic activity indulged in
by sexually rapacious women. The homosexual is regarded as
effeminate and affected in his mannerisms.

The knowing are not exempt from this process of acquiring segmental and negotiated perspectives. The police, courts and other
agencies are dominated by the practical contingencies of decision-
making which create a collaboratively constructed penumbra of
meaning around deviant areas. In their everyday work, members of
such agencies are necessarily constrained to order their work material
into manageable categories. These categories may just as frequently
emanate from organisational beliefs and imperatives as from any sort
of detached evaluation of the material's properties. In their dealings
with deviants, these categories assume an importance which structures both the agent's actions and the deviant's reactions. To the
extent that these interactions become orderly, they will realise and
confirm the operating validity of the categories. According to
Sudnow, these categories are 'shorthand reference terms for knowledge of the social structure and its criminal events upon which the
task of practically organizing . . . work . . . is premised'.[68] The application of these categories can have the effect of self-fulfilling prophecies.
To the extent that agents are more powerful than deviants and are
able to reward them, it is their understanding of the world that will
generally prevail. Marihuana use in London provides an illustration.
Young maintains that 'the marihuana user and the marihuana seller
are not fixed roles in the culture. At one time a person may sell
marihuana, at another time he may be buying it.'[69] The police
entrusted with the task of enforcing the drugs laws, however, are
convinced that the two roles are occupied by entirely different kinds
of person. The marihuana user is frequently a victim of the predatory
pusher. Their chief enforcement object is to inhibit the activity of the
pusher:

The individual found in possession of marijuana is often . . . ignored by
the police. They are after the real enemy, the drug-pusher. In order to get

him they are willing to negotiate with the individual found in possession. . . . If [the individual] tells the truth [in court] and says that he smokes marijuana because he likes it . . . he will receive a severe sentence. If, on the other hand, he plays the court's game and conforms to their stereotype—say, he claims that he had got into bad company, that somebody (the pusher) offered to sell him the stuff, so he thought he would try it out, that he knows he was foolish and won't do it again—the courts will let him off lightly.[70]

Such protestations in court and before the police confirm the official stance that the drug-taking world is polarised into discrete types. Thus the person who has dealings with the organised criminal; the observer of the prostitute's behaviour; the police and the courts all have a limited and distorting access to deviant phenomena. Their access will, on the one hand, restrict the kinds of behaviour which they are able to recognise as clearly deviant and, on the other, affect the inference which they can make about the meaning of both the segment and the larger whole (if any is acknowledged) which is not revealed.

DEVIANTS WHO CANNOT PASS

Other deviants cannot or will not pass. Of crucial importance in the maintenance of social invisibility or social shielding is the sheer competence of the deviant, his competence to organise symbols, props, events and accounts in a manner likely to produce successful passing. Some deviants are relatively incapable of passing. The mentally ill may not dissemble properly; the drug addict may find it impossible to present himself as normal for long periods without recourse to drugs; the alcoholic will similarly require drink in order to sustain prolonged performances. Removal of props can, in the latter cases, lead to an inevitable disclosure. Taylor provides another example. He suggests that 'sexual interaction is a complicated game to play'. Seduction, for instance, is based upon a complicated sequence of moves and responses which, when improperly performed can lead to numerous penalties being inflicted on the inept. Taylor further argues:

The less intelligent individual may not only have difficulty learning the sequence, but more than this, he may by virtue of exclusion from various social groups have less opportunity to practice it. It may be, therefore, that the low intelligence groups are over-represented among sex-offenders not because of their freedom from inhibition . . . but rather because they lack the knowledge of how to conform to their moral precepts which may be just as exacting, if not more so, than those held by others more socially skilled than themselves.[71]

A more interesting case is that of the structural or
tion of the deviant world. Unless extreme secondar
been embarked on, most deviants are able to pass i
between deviant and nondeviant roles. After all, most
rules in very few of their roles. It may well be that, to a
purposes, most of the time and in most settings, the very
tion of a person as deviant is not particularly illuminati

Some secondary deviants, however, may become p   ....ively
dislocated from the conventional world. They are treated by their
significant others as substantially deviant. They organise their world
by symbols and conventions which are subculturally deviant in
origin. So estranged may they become from the conventional world
that it becomes foreign to them. Activities within it can involve all
the intricacies of prediction and understanding required of a stranger
in a society which is not his own. The core ghetto inhabitant or the
subcultural criminal may, in polar cases, simply lack the competence
to pass. Maurer describes this polar instance well:

The big-time confidence men are flexible and are equally at home in their
own subculture or in the dominant culture—in fact they are able to
simulate behavior within the dominant culture to a high degree of perfection. On the other hand, a criminal subculture like that of the Gypsies
touches the dominant culture so slightly that for all practical purposes it is
completely outside.[72]

He continues his analysis by examining pickpockets:

Most successful pickpockets are careful to avoid argot in their general
conversation and rigorously eliminate it when they are being observed by
anyone not on the *rackets*. However, their general speech is usually heavily
loaded with slang, much of it only recently delivered from its argot sources.
. . . Some, notably, among the lower levels, think, speak, and live in the
argot, and are unable to avoid it even if they so desire; without it they
would be inarticulate, and it is doubtful that they have any real awareness
of language outside the argot levels. To pickpockets of this class, standard
English is virtually a foreign language.[73]

Of course, this dislocation is almost never total. The subcultural
criminal subscribes to the greater part of the understandings which
pervade conventional culture. However, the surface world of appearances is ordered around critical tokens and procedures which may
not be easily feigned by him. Just as a conventional member would
find it difficult to pass as a competent pickpocket before other pickpockets, so the reverse may be true. (There may however be cases
where dislocation is so great that what the knowing would recognise

deviant signs are simply not understood by most conventional members. In this case, the subcultural deviant may pass as 'strange', 'uncouth' or 'eccentric' rather than as a deviant.)

Dislocation is likely to occur whenever the territorial segregation of a group is enforced or accepted for long periods of time. Idiosyncratic modes of thought are likely to develop within social groups substantially cut off from other groups. Increasingly, the gaps between them may make effective dissembling impossible. Similarly, the social organisation of criminal or deviant worlds can lead to dislocation. Certain styles of deviance originated in the fairly distant past and then, through craft training and symbolic differentiation between insiders and outsiders, became fossilised and closed. They are examples of cultural lag which are preserved because of their continued usefulness. What may once have been virtually indistinguishable from the modes of conduct and expression prevalent in the wider society can become progressively eccentric. Maurer, for instance, claims 'the argot of the thieving professions is very old, with reference to that of the pickpockets (in English) appearing in print in the 16th century, although it must be much older than that'.[74] What must have been, in the sixteenth century, a relatively insignificant series of differentials can, by the twentieth, become extremely revealing. Because craft crime (the confidence trick, pickpocketing and so on) has many professional qualities in the form of closed entry, apprenticeship and the acquisition of technical terminology, the accepted craft criminal must often be a dislocated figure. Presumably much the same process will characterise organised crime in the future. What is now a system which closely resembles the bureaucratic organisation of conventional business may eventually become so specialised and petrified that it will also provide stigmata.

An instrumental system of technical terms and recognition symbols can become a means of differentiating and awarding roles and statuses. When the argot and concepts prevalent in a deviant world become essential for delineating its structure, they become relatively impervious to change.[75] The accounts and 'vocabularies of motive'[76] made available by the argot can become tantamount to an ideological system. When these dislocating events occur, the deviant group may resemble a religious sect which is a 'social unit, seeking to enforce behaviour on those who accept belief, and seeking every occasion to draw the faithful apart from the rest of society and into the company of each other'.[77] Such a system is reinforced by the dangers presented by too frequent an exposure to conventional society. In consequence, the craft criminal tends to minimise associations with potentially discrediting settings. The professional thief, for instance, 'lives largely in a world of his own and is rather completely isolated from general society. The majority of them do not care to contact society except professionally.'[78]

The subcultural deviant who lacks the competence to pass can adopt a few strategies to reduce the risks presented by his rule-breaking. He may, as in America, subvert the knowing by corrupting social control agents.[79] Apparently, it is commonplace for professional criminals to neutralise the police and the courts by means of a 'fix', a systematically applied process of bribery. He may also rely on the protection afforded by areas and social scenes which are peculiarly his own. The network of rookeries in Georgian and Victorian London afforded the craft criminal escape routes and anonymity. Victorian pickpockets, for instance, 'clustered around the railway terminuses and the great wholesale food markets, which were thronged with well-to-do people and also conveniently near the slums into which a thief could disappear. . . . Whether in London, Liverpool, Manchester or Birmingham the gonoph was a creature of poor, crowded districts. . . . He liked to be near some friendly slum.'[80]

DEVIANTS WHO WILL NOT PASS

There are abundant deviants who, for functional or expressive reasons, need to communicate their deviancy to a wide audience composed of nondeviants, fellow-deviants and potential deviants. I shall discuss three major examples of overtly public deviancy—behaviour which is open to inspection by a whole assembly of others. The expressive, politicised and entrepreneurial deviant represent different facets of intentionally identifiable rule-breaking.

Expressive deviation

Any one kind of deviancy may take more than one form; any deviant role may have more than one role-style. The homosexual may be an expressive deviant (the Queen); a politicised deviant (the Gay Liberation Front member); an entrepreneurial deviant (the Hustler); what I shall call a coercive deviant (in closed, single sex institutions at least); or a covert deviant (the closet Queen). Similarly, the drug user may be expressive (at one time the Cat, now the Head); politicised (a Head Liberation Front member); entrepreneurial (the Hustler or pusher); or covert.[81]

In part, the assumption of a particular role-style is shaped by the deviant's practical power. The deviant, and all others who share the same deviant status, clearly lack effective *collective* power because they are unable to resist the attribution of deviancy itself. Yet any deviant has some control over the features of his social world. All rule-breakers experience problems posed by issues of organisation, collaboration, competition, isolation, social control, stigmatisation and the like. The way in which these issues can be managed is an expression of the deviant's command over men and resources. The wealthy drug-user or homosexual has many fewer problems of exposure than his poorer fellows. He is relatively capable of safely arranging his world so that its risks are reduced. He need not 'hustle' in order to sustain his deviancy; he does not always have to venture out into public areas in the search for sexual partners or drugs; and he can consume deviant goods or services behind shielding walls and doors. He has the greatest opportunity to remain covert if he so chooses; he does not have to affect an entrepreneurial role-style; and self-advertisement as a politicised or expressive deviant is not, as it may sometimes be, a necessary consequence of high visibility.

Expressive deviation is one possible mode of rule-breaking and it seems to arise as a response either to symbolic impoverishment; to the formation of segregated social worlds; or to the intersection of symbolic systems. It usually takes the form of a comprehensive life-style which permeates all or most of a person's behaviour and symbolism. Rule-breaking which is 'simply' a way of being in the world, not oriented to specific but diffuse goals, would be untenable were it hidden on public occasions. Without public appearances, indeed, the deviancy would not exist because it is intrinsic to appearance itself.

It can manifest itself when, in what is defined as a symbolically weakened universe, there is an attempt to carve out of existing materials a viable and satisfying identity. The lack of firm symbolism and systems of thought which permit people to anchor themselves in well-structured identities may lead to what Klapp calls the 'collective search for identity':

> . . . there is a disturbance of symbolic balance—a loss of nondiscursive symbolism—behind the identity problem of modern times . . . if man is a symbolic animal, then when things go wrong with him, it is likely that his symbols will also go wrong. . . . A society fails to supply adequate identity when symbols are disturbed to the extent that they no longer give reliable reference points . . . by which people can locate themselves socially, realize themselves sentimentally, and declare (to self and others) who they are. We now live in a world in which catastrophic changes are occurring in reference symbols . . . [There is] a need for a socially confirmed concept of self . . . ; fullness of sentiments, including mystiques; and centering or devotion, so that a person's life is focused on a point where he recognizes some highest value. . . .[82]

Rapid social change can generate *anomie*, loss of potency of identity-confirming symbolism, and a state of detachment from existing symbolism.[83] When the authority of a status-allocating system wanes, there may be attempts to reshape the world so that new points of anchorage and significance are established. It could be argued, for instance, that the millennial movements of Europe and New Guinea were prompted, in part, by massive collapses of a once effective symbolism.[84] The previously 'objective' world of understanding is rendered almost wholly subjective and the expressive deviant feels both enabled and required to renegotiate the meaning of his surrounding social terrain. The world is seen as contrived and artificial, the *epoché* of the natural attitude is thrown into suspense, and new efforts are made to replace it by something more real and substantial. This stance presumably underpins the hippy's identification of Anglo-American society as 'plastic',[85] and the student radical's conception of society as alienated and its members as manipulated. Young asserts about the former case:

. . . hippies argue that a great deal of modern man's activities are mere games which the participants play whilst all the time feeling alienated from the sequence of action: they are actors in a play which does not express their own inner feelings.[86]

When these collapses of symbolism occur, they do so unevenly throughout society. Some groups are more vulnerable or detached than others. Youth in Western society is a prime candidate for expressive deviation. Middle class young are relatively heavily dependent upon the broad framework of a society's symbolism. In contrast to certain working class and upper class groups, they do not generate their own localised and responsive symbolism. At particular phases in the life cycle, the young of the middle class are thrown into a situation which can distance them from the natural attitude:

In one sense, youth in general and students in particular are in a favorable position to experiment with identities. Adolescence . . . is an amorphous period, its rules undefined, and its incumbents regarded as persons passing through a transitional phase. Precisely because of its anomic and temporary character, this period affords youth unusual opportunities to try out personal styles and social themes.[87]

Segregated social worlds develop peculiar symbolic systems which are responses both to their own particular conditions and to the problems of coping with the larger universe. Whenever social boundaries divide up areas of social life so that there are discontinuities in social interaction, there is the probability that idiosyncratic modes of thought and behaviour will grow. Networks of relations serve as communication channels for the generation of culture.[88] Relatively frequent interaction between insiders, common problems and joint action will engender life-styles which can, over time, become quite different from those existing elsewhere. Whilst these life-styles may be thought by the members of the larger social universe to be strange or contrived, members of the particular world that gave them birth will consider them natural and entirely intelligible. The more disconnected is the world, the more likely is it that the life-styles will be sharply differentiated. Fashions and conventions predominant in the world will not be influential outside it, just as modes prevalent outside may not percolate in. When the life-styles are represented and embellished by special symbolism, as they almost invariably are, the grounds for expressive deviation are laid. In particular, the expressive activity of a world is likely to become deviant when the world is discredited, low in the moral hierarchy of a society or already implicated in other deviancies.

The forms of expressive deviation are given a particular clarity when they are in some opposition to foreign life-styles. Members of some discredited social worlds are not able to gain legitimate access to the trappings of role-styles and status positions valued in the larger society. The denial of identity-creating materials can stimulate the local manufacture of substitute or alternative matter. The authority of reference others in the world outside the boundaries is challenged. In its place, new reference others are selected who are in a position to validate the existential claims of the disprivileged. While I would not support their use of the concept 'social disorganization', Cloward and Ohlin describe the roots of the conflict subculture in a useful fashion:

To the extent that conflict activity—'bopping', street-fighting 'rumbling' and the like—is tolerated, it represents an alternative means by which adolescents in many relatively disorganized urban areas may acquire status. Those who excel in the manipulation of violence may acquire 'rep' within the group to which they belong and respect from other adolescent groups in the vicinity and from the adult world.[89]

Similarly, an extinct role-style, that of the 'cat', was formed around the deprivations experienced by the American ghetto inhabitant:

. . . the cat as a social type is the personal counterpart of an expressive social movement. The context for such a movement must include the broader community, which, by its policies of social segregation and discrimination, has withheld from individuals of the colored population the opportunity to achieve or to identify with status positions in the larger society. The social type of the cat is an expression of one possible type of adaptation to such blocking and frustration, in which a segment of the population turns in upon itself and attempts to develop within itself criteria for the achievement of social status and the rudiments of a satis-factory social life. Within his own isolated social world the cat attempts to give form and purpose to dispositions derived from but denied an outlet within the dominant social order.[90]

Finally, expressive deviation can represent a confluence of two cultural traditions, one expressive and the other deviant. This confluence represents the grafting on of deviant styles to such expressive endeavours as literary composition, [91] or musical creation. Members of jazz or pop music worlds, artists and the like may fashion such deviancies as drug-taking into behavioural styles which reflect the expressive components of their other activities. A unitary life-style can be forged out of diverse strands so that a once covert deviancy becomes proclaimed as a liberating or enlightening agency.

Without publicity, expressive deviation is emasculated as a means of conferring identity. The cat, for instance, was nothing if his behaviour was not public:

The cat seeks through a harmonious combination of charm, ingratiating speech, dress, music, the proper dedication to his 'kick', and unrestrained generosity to make of his day-to-day life itself a gracious work of art. Everything is to be pleasant and everything he does and values is to contribute to a cultivated aesthetic approach to living.[92]

Expressive deviation rests upon a new evaluation of styles of being and consequently represents a divorce from behavioural modes prevalent in the larger world. Deference to these modes can be identified as disloyalty to deviant perspectives. Thus expressive deviancy which is linked to a real or alleged reappraisal of the meaning of everyday symbols, behaviour and props is even more necessarily public. Hippies who claim that the conventional world is plastic would regard self-conscious and deliberate dissembling by a hippy as a betrayal of the deviant role-style. Just as moral or proper behaviour is bounded by the improper, so is impropriety defined by propriety. The vitality and structure of Bohemianism, the Beat World, and so on are derived from their constant state of opposition to that which is not Bohemian or Beat.[93] Expressive deviancy is organised to some extent in order to confront the nondeviant world. Without confrontation, it would wither. Whilst the 'straight' world is not always intended to be the deviants' public, lack of a straight response would lead to emasculation.

The expressive role-player advertises his deviancy. Such attention as he does receive often contains the seed of his own demise. Many expressive deviancies are more than eccentric life-styles. They revolve around criminal props. The Bohemian, the cat and the hippy, for instance, were involved in illegal drug use. Much of the *frisson* experienced in the open deviancy was derived from the implications of the hidden rule-breaking. Additional qualities were lent by

D

confrontations with the police in the case of the beatnik, hippy and
cat. The confrontations generated feelings of excitement and an added
sense of solidarity. In the drug-taking world, the 'bust' is a focal
concern. Thus Ciardi remarks of the 'beats':

The Beat Generation has marihuana and the ritual of dodging the 'narcos'
—the narcotics squad. The need to be illegal in some way is a simple
enough need to thumb one's nose at society. The need to make a ritual of
the illegality is as juvenile as the basic gesture itself. Let four Beats gather
in a desert to fire up some marihuana and at least two of them will mention
the narcos and look carefully in all directions before they bring the stuff
out of hiding. It is exactly the ritual of four high school pals about to
sneak a smoke in the boys' room.[94]

Thus, whilst one facet of the deviancy was ostentatiously displayed,
the other was concealed. The risks encountered in the latter coloured
the former. The revelation of the one pointed to the existence of the
other. This is perhaps why the cat died and the hippy, at least in
America, sought refuge in areas relatively free of police surveillance.

Not only does expressive deviancy tend to be sustained by confrontation and opposition, it also has isolating qualities which
reinforce the role-style's cooperative and communal basis. Carey
describes the appearance of the Berkeley marihuana user thus:

There was general recognition by community members that straight
people were upset or offended by what they considered flouting of conventional middle-class norms in dress styles. . . . Whatever value the distinctive style of dress and demeanor may have in flouting community
norms, it has one inevitable result—it isolates the head from conventional
people. The story of increasing involvement in the drug scene is character-
istically one of increasing estrangement from straight friends. . . . Wearing
certain kinds of clothing and action in certain ways are part and parcel of
being a certain kind of person. It emphasizes the values put on spontan-
eity, authenticity, and lack of regard for social proprieties. . . . To act
straight is regarded as a betrayal to friends who are involved in the drug
scene and to the open values represented by the scene itself. The clothing
and behavior function as side bets in two ways: they isolate the head from
conventional society and severely attenuate any relationship with that
world of persons in it; and they symbolize a certain set of values the head
espouses. . . .[95]

Expressive deviancy offers the conventional world few problems
of recognition. While there may be difficulties in interpreting the
meaning of the behaviour and symbolism, the deviant proclaims himself. Furthermore, since the deviant typically believes that his universe
of meaning is superior to the mundane understandings of the larger
society, there is a substantial element of proselytisation. Often
recruited from the middle class, the expressive deviant extends his

symbolism into art, literature and music. In elaborate expositions of the significance of this symbolism, his representatives articulate those features which facilitate recognition. The prolific productions of the Bohemians, beats, cats and others continually foist the allegedly distinctive nature of their fashions upon a wider world (which, very frequently, takes up their symbolism and puts it to its own uses). In more prosaic ways, too, the expressive deviant reminds others of his special character:

In face-to-face interaction expressive disclaimers occur in some form. One form is the 'put on'. It can be used in the sense of deliberately misleading a person into a false encounter and suddenly pulling the rug out from under him, but it is also used in the sense of provoking telling reactions. How a person reacts to a girl with a vintage 1940's hat on her head says something about himself. If he reacts by trying to label (e.g. beatnik) he has tipped his hand. If he doesn't notice, this is an expression of blindness to detail.[96]

Expressive deviancy prompts organised response. It is an overt or covert attempt to provoke debate about the validity of current typifications and practices. In its confrontation with what it conceives to be orthodoxy, the deviancy is obtrusive and highly visible. Unlike most other forms of rule-breaking, the distinctive qualities of the deviant life-style are deliberately magnified and posed in a challenging manner. Such deviancy frequently attracts attention, and social control effort tends to be deployed in its management. Unlike the instrumental and covert deviant who tries to establish an uneventful accommodation with social control agencies, the expressive deviant attracts vigorous enforcement. The hippies frequenting Piccadilly Circus and Hyde Park were penalised far more severely because of their assumption of overt deviant roles. Demeanour, so important a facet of police–deviant interaction, is transformed into an affront to police authority. The rule-breaker who observes the tacit conventions of unobtrusive deviant–nondeviant and deviant–control agent behaviour escapes many of the sanctions awarded a hostile role-style. Something of the animosity generated by expressive deviation is conveyed by the Chief Constable of Lancashire. He remarked:

The 1960s . . . was the decade of man's first probe into space—the moon landings—filling the front pages of our daily nationals as a change from the sex habits and antics of pop stars. The decade of drugs, protest marchers, students in revolt, a lowering of moral standards, nudity, simulated sex and obscenity as a feature of the culture of the theatre of the 1960s, and against all this background, we the police, have had to try and enforce a code of conduct to which too many in our society apparently do not wish to conform.[97]

Expressive deviancy necessarily revolves around communication, whether the communication is intended primarily for fellow-deviants or not. In collaboration or opposition, the deviant trades in symbols which are freely negotiable. He may maintain an esoteric system of understandings (based on Zen, the I Ching or the Tibetan Book of the Dead) but he is constantly thrown into some form of contact with the world. At the very least, he may frequently have to give an account of his distinctive symbolism.

The deviant tries to use appearance as a tool of transformation and must come into a viable relationship with the everyday. Expressive deviation focuses as much on audiences outside its own boundaries as those within it. Even the desire to shock necessitates an appreciation of what is commonly conceived as shocking. Relatively lacking in symbolic self-sufficiency, expressive deviancy is in a state of constant dialogue with stances alien to itself. Parkinson remarks of the Beat world-view, 'It would be easy to multiply points of comparison: the grey flannel suit and the existentialist costume, the smiling religious purveyor of togetherness and the egotism of Christ-as-beatnik, ranch house and pad, cocktails and marijuana.'[98] The thematic core of expressive deviation is shaped by a dialectical opposition to a typification of mass culture; by so doing it is couched in much the same language as mass culture. The evolution of a separate language would turn the deviancy completely in on itself and prevent it being fully expressive—absence of common understandings would incapacitate it as communicating activity. Thus, whilst misinterpretations of the activity can abound, it is brought into full view without deviousness.

Politicised deviation

The same necessary involvement with common semiotic systems is characteristic of another form of public deviancy. Deviancy which takes a political form (or political activity which takes a deviant guise)[99] shares with expressive deviation the dilemmas of concealment and revelation, of esoteric and exoteric communication, of expansion and contraction. Politicised deviancy is deliberately organised to persuade, convert or force others into redefining important sectors of the world.* As such, it is often difficult to distinguish it from certain forms of expressive deviation. Indeed, the boundaries between the two are far from distinct. It is the case with many deviancies that they shift from an expressive to a politicised stance when they acquire a more aggressive posture towards the world. Rather than assert the validity of a particular life-style, they seek to work fundamental

* I am not here concerned with those politicised deviants who resort to covert, guerrilla or similar actions.

changes in the way in which that style is recognised and ordered in society. Expressive deviation becomes politicised when it concerns itself with the boundaries between itself and other behaviours, and when it seeks to assert its superiority to or equality with behaviours which are conventionally regarded as more moral or desirable. In its extreme form, the deviancy challenges the very bases of ordering and evaluation that prevail in the larger society. Authoritative systems of classification are denied legitimacy and alternatives are urged. On the other hand, politicised deviation can become expressive when it becomes no more than a life-style or a series of poses. Some sociologists, for instance, have distinguished between the existential process of becoming a revolutionary and the fateful activity of making revolution. When the deviant undergoes personal changes alone and retreats from more consequential encounters with powerful social groups, he may be held to have become expressive.

Some of the preconditions of politicised deviation are similar to those entailed in the generation of expressive deviation. Stigmatised groups such as Blacks in Anglo-American society, homosexuals or drug-takers must feel some divorce from the *epoché* of the natural attitude. If they adopted the natural attitude, their self-regard would be coloured by guilt or shame. The shamefulness or unworthiness of what is regarded as their substance would only engender acceptance of a lowly position were there not a major detachment from prevailing definitions. Integral to this suspension of the natural attitude is a rejection of the existing structures of authoritative classifying and definitional work. As Haug and Sussman argue, in America politicised deviation has been accompanied by a withdrawal of legitimacy from professional groupings:[100]

The situation . . . is that professional knowledge, service, autonomy, and organizational authority is being challenged at various levels of society and among widely diverse groups. Students . . . deny the expertise and good will of their educators, while they demand an end to administration and faculty power to meddle in their private lives. Poverty group members, arguing that they know more about their community needs, problems, and solutions than the professional social workers and are more concerned, have organized for a voice in welfare benefits and their distribution. Cutting across social class lines, the blacks confront professors, teachers, and social workers with their demands for more adequate services while hospital patients organize to hold professional control over their lives in bounds.[101]

Concomitant with the process of estrangement is an attempt to reorder the world so that what are treated as 'authentic' classes of persons emerge. The 'real' structure of the world is revealed and the old clusterings of allegedly significant attributes are discarded.

Possessing a black skin, homosexual propensities or femininity is given a new meaning. Instead of occupying a particular, stigmatised place in a major hierarchy, the emerging politicised deviant sees himself as allied to new constellations of others. An essential part of politicisation is the formation of 'consciousness', and deliberate efforts are engineered to foster it. Discussing the formation of the American Women's Liberation Front, Stone recalls:

The women's liberation movement . . . for two years . . . functioned pretty much in what might be called an underground manner. Although there were occasional, small symbolic actions, the participants spent most of the time in simply getting together to discuss the oppression they felt as women. This was a prerequisite to launching the movement, because the ideas being put forward were so new and so controversial that it was necessary for women to first discuss them and gain confidence in their correctness. For this reason, one of the most characteristic forms the women's liberation movement has taken so far has been the small, consciousness-raising groups. On such questions as consciousness-raising . . . we can learn . . . from the rise of black nationalism. Women, like black people, are discriminated against on the basis of their physical characteristics. Both are said to be innately inferior. . . . And in both cases, there is a need to establish confidence and group solidarity, and to understand that the source of the oppression lies with the system and not with any innate failings.[102]

Accompanying such shifts in understanding, and prompting them, is a sense of relative deprivation and impotence. The manner in which privilege, power and rewards are distributed is perceived as inequitable. In contrast to the proper place which the group should occupy, there is a belief that there is gross and remediable injustice. It is this recognition that affairs can be changed, coupled with a conviction that they will remain unchanged unless action is embarked on, that produces the political thrust of the deviant. What might start out as a form of primary politicised deviation, the initial act of handling political affairs in an unorthodox manner such as the sit-in, the freedom ride, the occupation of a building, can become transformed into secondary deviation. Confrontations with social control agents, a growing investment of self and resources in an activist lifestyle, the closing of options, and the recognition by self and others of one's political identity lead to the generation of the fully fledged politicised deviant. Retrospective comprehension of the identity-changing processes involved can lead to a deliberately structured initiation sequence whereby secondary deviation is the subject of coaching. Experienced deviants engineer situations whereby the neophyte can undergo the existential changes produced by an experience of police violence, stigmatisation or role-closure. This critical stage in the moral career of the politicised deviant is typically regarded as educative and enlightening.[103] Chomsky recalls how he himself underwent this process at a Washington demonstration:

We found a place not yet blocked by the demonstrators, and walked up to the line of troops standing a few feet away from the building. Dellinger suggested that those of us who had not yet spoken at the rally talk directly to the soldiers. . . . From this point on, my impressions are rather fragmentary. Monsignor Rice spoke, and I followed. As I was speaking, the line of soldiers advanced, moving past me—a rather odd experience. I don't recall just what I was saying . . . but I do remember feeling that the way I was putting it seemed silly and irrelevant . . . another line of soldiers emerged from somewhere, this time in a tightly massed formation, rifles in hand, and moving slowly forward. We sat down . . . I had no intention of taking part in any act of civil disobedience, until that moment. But when that grotesque organism began slowly advancing . . . it became obvious that one could not permit the thing to dictate what one was going to do.[104]

Out of such encounters, politicised deviation can grow and become transformed both by interaction and by autonomous development. What may have been at one time conceived of as an unthinkable strategy becomes a next and inevitable step in a culminating process. Mature politicised deviants do not emerge out of some social limbo, but are nursed by a succession of responses to situations of their own and others' making.

I shall restrict my discussion to deviancy which has become politicised in a conscious and recognised fashion by its members. Otherwise, analysis can become metaphysical. Definitional complexities are produced by the fact that it is often moot whether crimes or deviances have a political basis. If political activity is taken to be concerned with the distribution of the ends and means of power in a social order, many forms of deviation are clearly political in effect.

Accordingly, some writers urge a kind of romanticism which views all criminals as primitive innocents who are engaged in inarticulate political conflict with institutional authority.* If the extravagant romantic is ignored, politicised deviancy may be defined as that activity which is regarded as expressly political by its participants. The rule-breaking activity may be shoplifting, arson or violent demonstration. It is the significances that the rule-breaker and, to a

* An example of such a position is the following: 'Most court cases are political cases. Many people get screwed for shop-lifting from supermarkets, nicking expensive cars, and other activities designed to transfer the bread from the rich, the banks and the businesses to the dispossessed people of the world. These actions involve the socialist goal of the redistribution of the wealth. The fact that it is illegal is a recommendation of its effectiveness.' (Agitprop Collective *et al.*, *Bust Book: The People* v. *Regina*, Action Books, London, 1970, p. 51.)

lesser extent the rule-enforcer, attach to the behaviour that are important. Otherwise one is forced to resort to a fanciful Zen cate-chism which poses such questions as, 'If the conflict of a thousand American Negroes with the police constitutes a political event, what does a solitary Black delinquent's encounters with the police represent?'

I shall concern myself with those aspects of politicised deviancy which render it a field of expression visible to the world. Most politicised deviants can be clearly recognised by outsiders because they are involved in public attempts to renegotiate the significance of ascribed or achieved stigmata. Typically, the prime audience of these attempts is the world of fellow-deviants. There is an internal debate designed to reformulate the meaning of the stigmata to the deviants themselves. Thus, the Gay Liberation Front addresses homosexuals by stating:

Gay people can be slandered by all the media, public institutions, organ-ized religions, and every part of the establishment. The hatred of society can be internalized in a self-hatred which poisons every aspect of an individual's relations with himself and others. The adolescence of a gay person . . . Have you ever had to laugh at a joke ridiculing what you are?[105]

Similarly, Essien-Udom argues that what are conceived to be black supremacist themes in the ideology of the Black Muslims

. . . are aimed at purging lower-class Negroes of their inferiority complex. The 'real' rather than the 'ostensible' enemy of the Nation of Islam or of the Negro masses in general, is not the white people *per se*, but the Negro himself—his subculture, his image of himself and of his 'place' in society, his attitude toward white people, and his idealization of all that is white. From the point of view of all black nationalists, the Negro can never be really free until he has purged from his mind all notions of white superiority and Negro inferiority and thus ceases to despise himself and his group.[106]

The stigmatised are rarely immersed only in their own social worlds. They are members of multiple worlds. If their stigma is widely regarded as a sign of inferiority, they are themselves likely to feel that they have been legitimately degraded. As Goffman states,

The standards [the stigmatised person] has incorporated from the wider society equip him to be intimately alive to what others see as his failing, inevitably causing him, if only for moments, to agree that he does indeed fall short of what he really ought to be. Shame becomes a central possi-bility, arising from the individual's perception of one of his own attributes as being a defiling thing to posses . . .[107]

Attempts to mask the stigma, to produce a creditable account of a discreditable failing, to avoid shaming incidents, and to distance the deviant from himself as stigmatised object, are all standard modes of coping with an acknowledged fault. Even the secondary deviant tends to develop an argot which is suggestive of self-contempt. Addicts refer to themselves and others as 'dope fiends' and to their heroin as 'shit'; American Negroes familiarly call each other 'niggers'; and homosexuals (surely ironically) label themselves 'gay', the female companions of males 'hagfags', and so on. The politicised deviant partly represents one who responds to organised stigmatisation by counter-stigmatisation and redefinition. He is simultaneously involved in a dialogue with himself (or his generalised other) and with the reified society which degrades him.

Such a deviant role-style chiefly revolves around efforts to neutralise shaming responses. Rather than succumb to shame, the deviant tries to discredit the shamers and their perspective. He thereby embarks on a rhetorical debate whose goals are considerably more specific than those of the expressive rule-breaker. Appearance becomes an instrumental phenomenon, not an 'end in itself'.* In the matter of authoritative classifications, there is an attempt to reclassify the deviant so that he is morally upgraded and aligned with worthy groups. According to the Gay Liberation Front, the homosexual is naturally allied to other oppressed groups. Its sponsor 'is an association of gay men and women who as revolutionary socialists see their liberation linked to the class struggle'.[108] The American Black militant seeks affinity with the Arab, the African or the working class rather than with 'respectable' groups in white society.

There is also an important terminological debate which substitutes honourable labels for dishonourable ones. 'In New York City, GLF picketed *The Village Voice*, a liberal weekly newspaper, for printing derogatory articles about Gays while refusing to permit the word "gay" to be used in the bulletin board section of the paper. . . . The *San Francisco Examiner*, a reactionary paper, was picketed for referring to "semi-males", "deviates", and "flexi-wrists".'[109] Similarly, Karenga claims 'the *Negro* is made and manufactured in America'.[110] Symbols and words which have had a long tradition of

---

* Thus, the decision to make an occasion explicitly political in its implications is often pragmatic. Rather than impose the deviant's definitions on every encounter, the politicised deviant is selective in his choice of settings which would be enhanced by publicising his perspective. In discussing courtroom strategies, for instance, Agitprop Collective argues, 'You or the collective will have to work out which approach is best for your case. The four main alternatives—conventional defence, political-legal defence, self-defence and getting a "deal"—all entail a number of political and personal considerations. You'll want to consider your chances of beating the rap altogether, your likely sentence if you're convicted, how well your case can be used politically, the strengths and needs of the struggle and your relation to it . . .'. (*The Bust Book*, p. 58.)

provoking shame are discarded and replaced by others with more
dignified connotations. All this is part of a collective endeavour to
reformulate the world. It is not so much spontaneously generated
from within the deviant world as created by countering specific
typifications proffered by powerful nondeviants. The authoritative
image of the deviant is turned on its head. The Black Muslims'
eschatology and cosmology[111] inverted the beliefs of the white
world; the homosexual becomes the sexually liberated; the drug taker
becomes the only awake person in a universe of Gurdjeffian
sleepers.[112] It is as if the politicised deviant were defending his status
in a point-by-point debate with an anonymous representative of
Leviathan. Curiously, some of the features of the crude typification
employed by Leviathan are accepted—even when they are the most
ill-informed. Eldridge Cleaver, for instance, approvingly builds a
model of social structure around the alleged white belief in massive
Black sexual potency.[113]

Politicised deviancy furthers this dialogue by attempting to
regenerate the stigmatised. The deviant answers shaming typifications
and processes by publicly proclaiming himself; by adopting a dignified role-style; and by counter-assertions. The homosexuals who sign
letters, march, picket and publish, advertise their association with a
stigma that can easily be hidden. The emergence from concealment is
often accompanied by an aggressive role-style and the adoption of
distinctive signs. The naming and clothing assumed by the Black
Muslims; the badges of the Gay Liberation Front; and the uniform
of the Black Panthers signify a determined effort to impress deviancy
upon the world. Consider Cleaver's description of his first encounter
with the Black Panthers:

Suddenly the room fell silent. The crackling undercurrent that for weeks
had made it impossible to get one's point across when one had the floor
was gone; there was only the sound of the lock clicking as the front door
opened, and then the soft shuffle of feet moving quietly toward the circle.
. . . From the tension showing on the faces of the people before me, I
thought the cops were invading the meeting, but there was a deep female
gleam leaping out of one of the women's eyes that no cop who ever lived
could elicit. I recognized that gleam out of the recesses of my soul, even
though I had never seen it before in my life: the total admiration of a black
woman for a black man. I spun round in my seat and saw the most
beautiful sight I had ever seen: four black men wearing black berets,
powder blue shirts, black leather jackets, black trousers, shiny black shoes
—and each with a gun![114]

Cleaver's account reflects the excitement of Bobby Seale's exclama-
tion, 'niggers with guns!'[115] The foisting of deviancy upon an audience accustomed to the successful workings of shame is intended to

provoke a crisis which will culminate in a redefinition of the proscribed behaviour. Parading homosexuals, groups of women who
confess to having undergone illegal abortions[116] and others share
with the expressive deviant a desire to have dealings with the mundane
world in terms of symbols intelligible to it. In their quest for an
expanded membership and amenable publics, they are forced to
trade in readily recognised signs. Thus, there are likely to be relatively
few problems in identifying the politicised deviant. His behaviour is
more or less artfully designed to be readily understood. He may be
misinterpreted, but that is not the intention of the deviant. An excellent example of such intention is given by the Yippies. Abbie Hoffman, describing the initial act of labelling the Yippies, stated:

Anita said . . . that although 'Yippie' would be understood by our generation, that straight newspapers like the *New York Times* and the U.S.
Government and the courts and everything wouldn't take it seriously
unless it had a kind of formal name, so she came up with the name of the
'Youth International Party'. She said that we could play a lot of jokes on
the concept of party because everybody would think that we were this
huge international conspiracy, but that in actuality we were a party that
you had fun at.[117]

Hoffman illustrates the dichotomised publics which the politicised
deviant faces; the public of the world which is to be changed, and the
public of the initiated. In the resolution of an expressive system
which can satisfactorily address itself to both worlds, a distinctive set
of symbols and significant events emerges.

Another kind of communication system can develop between the
politicised deviant and the larger society. When efforts to persuade
or educate are aborted, some measure of conflict may ensue. The
conflict is more intense than that which would naturally grow out of
relationships between a nonpoliticised deviant and social control
agency. There is an aggressive thrust in politicised deviancy, and a
major threat to the agency's authority, which lends an added
animosity. When compared with organised crime, for instance, the
conflict latent in the deviancy becomes more apparent. Thus Maas
states that Valachi, the Mafia defector, maintained:

In 1948 Frank Costello, while still acting boss of the Luciano Family,
ordered its membership to stay out of dope. . . . The canny Costello had
two reasons for the edict. One was his realization that there were rackets
and rackets; bootlegging and gambling, for instance, enjoyed wide public
acceptance or, at worst, indifference, while heroin not only was giving
organized crime a relative black eye, but also was spurring law enforcement efforts against it in other areas. Much more important, however, was
the dogged harassment of the Bureau of Narcotics. The Cosa Nostra

despised—and feared—it, and for the bureau's part, the first feeling was mutual.[118]

A similar avoidance of violence is displayed by the craft or professional criminal.[119] In one sense, such a criminal is a conservative who deplores the changes that might upset the stable relations he has established with control agents, colleagues, customers, competitors and victims. By contrast, a deviancy which takes a political stance is not characterised by a quest for smooth, unobtrusive activity. The politicised deviant searches for change which can be measured by significant benchmarks. There is an expectation of process and progress which can be easily thwarted. Additionally, there is a sensitivity to real or imputed attempts at stigmatisation which can result in confrontation rather than retreat. If Wilkin's deviancy amplification system has an analytical place, it must be in the study of politicised deviation. It is here that an escalation of antagonisms will be encouraged.[120] The deviant, attempting to promote change, acts in the streets and other public arenas and defines the opposing world as an entity with whom compromise is undesirable. Conflict tends to create its own 'language' which, in this case, can be a heightened form of the deviants' rhetoric. The language of conflict is a peculiar mode of sociation which demands the evolution of gestures comprehensible to the contestants:

If . . . a fight simply aims at annihilation, it does approach the marginal case of assassination in which the admixture of unifying elements is almost zero. If, however, there is any consideration, any limit to violence, there already exists a socializing factor, even though only as the qualification of violence. Kant says that every war in which the belligerents do not impose some restrictions in the use of possible means upon one another, necessarily . . . becomes a war of extermination. It is almost inevitable that an element of commonness injects itself into . . . enmity once the stage of open violence yields to another relationship, even though this new relation may contain a completely undiminished sum of animosity between the two parties. . . . One *unites* in order to fight, and one fights under the mutually recognized control of norms and rules.[121]

Within any but the most extreme conflict, therefore, there is a strain towards conventionalisation and the establishment of a system of common understandings. The relevant sectors of the other participant and the signs that are taken to provide information about these sectors are transformed in a conflict situation. New facets of the parties are revealed and others are subdued. There is an urgency about conflict which prompts anxious attention being paid to the nature of the opponent. It is through this emergent set of understandings that the politicised deviant may become known to social control agents and to the world at large. Certainly, as he becomes eventful and problematic, so he becomes worthy of fresh analysis.* It is when such conflicts occur that social change on a larger scale may ensue. The politicised deviant may challenge the *epoché* of the natural attitude simply because he cannot, on occasion, be taken for granted. As Berger and Luckman argue:

The institutional order . . . is continually threatened by the presence of realities that are meaningful in *its* terms. The legitimation of the institutional order is . . . faced with the ongoing necessity of keeping chaos at bay. *All* social reality is precarious. *All* societies are constructed in the face of chaos. The constant possibility of anomic terror is actualized whenever the legitimations that obscure the precariousness are threatened or collapse.[122]

The emergence of new expressions of deviation that do not respond to shame or guilt-provoking reactions can generate just such a threat to legitimations.[123] Unless the deviants are readily controllable, there is always the possibility that some shift in the boundaries of respectability and disreputability will occur. Changes in dominant conceptions of sexual propriety, valid modes of political activity, and the relations between stigmatised ethnic groups and others all seem to have been stimulated by politicised deviation. Of course, the shift may not necessarily be in the direction sought by the deviants themselves, but, at the very least, they are capable of producing 'trouble' at the margins and thereby challenges to their erstwhile taken-for-granted authority.

Some politicised deviants manufacture trouble in very much the same way as ethnomethodologists such as Garfinkel advocate.[124] They attempt, by confrontation or Dadaist techniques, to create situations in which commonsense understandings of the world are no longer tenable. The expressive deviant's 'put on' and the politicised deviant's confrontation are fundamentally similar in their attempts to challenge the natural attitude. The Yippie, Hoffman, illustrates the use of Dadaism as a trouble-provoking device: 'When we were arrested they asked us what we were doing. We said it was to measure the Pentagon and we wanted a permit to raise it 300 feet in the air, and they said "How about 10?". So we said "OK". And they threw us out of the Pentagon and we went back to New York and had a press conference, told them what it was about.'[125] Levitating the Pentagon, throwing money on the floor of the Stock Exchange to initiate a revealing and undignified scramble, nominating a pig for president are all potentially troublesome.

---

* Consider, for example, the plethora of books that have emerged in the last few years about black power and student militancy.

While not all politicised deviants conform to the description which I have offered, it is clear that there is a thrust towards self-advertisement, embarkation into relations with the larger world which are mediated through deviant rather than nondeviant roles, and the use of intelligible symbolism in many versions of such deviation. There is a deeper commitment to the validity of deviancy as a life-style which, with expressive deviation, denies the possibility of integrating deviant roles with a wide range of nondeviant activities.

Entrepreneurial deviation

There are at least three other minor instances of necessarily public deviation. The first is that of the forcible imposition of recognition marks upon the deviant: branding or mutilation, for example, or special regulations governing what deviants (such as prostitutes) should wear.[126] The marks, devised by nondeviant agents and intelligible to the world at large, single out the deviant as a person set apart for a peculiar position in society.

Another instance is that of secondary deviation which has developed in a manner which is comprehensible to wider society. Some kinds of secondary deviation entail an increase in deviousness, greater adeptness at concealment, and the evolution of highly esoteric communication symbols. Thus some of the marks of secondary deviation can be recognised only by the knowing. Signs of the deviant activity may simply pass unnoticed by most people. The marihuana user, for instance, may discover that he can pass for normal although he is 'high'.[127] There are other secondary deviations, however, which develop in ways that everyday knowledge can identify. Some homosexuals affect the Queen role which closely resembles the widespread typification of the person with a mincing gait and effeminate manner. Similarly, certain forms of alcoholism may take a familiar role-style. Some of these secondary deviations are adopted by naïve deviants who voluntarily or involuntarily assume gestural styles regarded as appropriate by the everyday world.[128] The alcoholic may not need subcultural exposure before he becomes embedded in a dominant deviant role. Other styles are acquired through status-coaching[129] conducted by authoritative figures in the nondeviant world. Even the subcultural secondary deviant builds upon typifications that are in public use, if only to reject them. After all, in most of their roles and in a major portion of their life, secondary deviants are not 'deviant' at all.

The third minor instance is that of the coercive deviant. Rule-breakers who have instrumental encounters with the public may create knowing victims. They depend upon being able to force others into the victim role. The very revelation of self as a particular kind of feared deviant may be sufficient to induce compliance. In the coercive encounters of robbery or burglary, the deviant does not make himself promiscuously known. Instead, he transforms himself in discrete and brief episodes, working transformations which convey his intentions and his likely behaviour if those intentions are thwarted. As Einstadter remarks, 'Robbery is an open, direct, face-to-face encounter coupled with a non-disguised coercive demand; there is no stealth or furtiveness as with a thief but a confrontation of unabashed power.'[130] Whenever deviancy is centred on a role which involves coercive dealings with nondeviants, there is a high probability that it will be expressed in an intelligible and identifiable form.

The final major instance of overt deviation which I shall consider is that of entrepreneurial or organised crime. Such crime and deviation may be crudely typified as 'rational' business activity in illegal or deviant areas. While a number of the fronts upon which he operates involve no exchange between himself and the nondeviant world, the entrepreneurial deviant frequently provides goods and services to the conventional public:

. . . the criminal as such is wholly predatory, whereas the underworld offers something in return to the respectable members of society. Thus, for example, burglars are lawbreakers who, if they could be abolished miraculously, would not be missed; but bootleggers, panderers, fixers, and many racketeers have a social function and perform services for which there is some kind of public demand.[131]

There are abundant disreputable markets in which deviant entrepreneurs encounter the public. In America, to a much greater extent than in Britain, there are exchanges centring on gambling, pornography, drugs, prostitution and so on. Rationing, shortages and proscriptions of activities lay the basis of illegal entrepreneurship. Although there are relatively few criminal markets in Britain, there are many that are disreputable. Prostitution, for instance, is not illegal *per se*, but the business of prostitution is subject to informal and formal controls which transform it into a clandestine enterprise. Entry into the profession of prostitution, and use of a prostitute's services, both carry a stigmatising potential.

Entrepreneurial deviation is, in a sense, a mirror image of legal business activity. It demands many of the same bureaucratic or organisational structures, risk-taking (although it can be substantially modified), cultivation of markets, acquisition of particular specialist talents, and so on. The explanation of such deviancy is generally couched in terms of a nonproblematic rationality. It is conventionally assumed that whilst the nonrational or the irrational requires elaborate discussion, the rational does not.

THE PROSTITUTE

Some deviant entrepreneurs cater for fellow-deviants who are relatively well-versed in gestures of secrecy. There are sets of explicit and implicit understandings about how business should be transacted; how negotiations should be initiated, and so on. Furthermore, in many cases, there are reputations to preserve. Rather than dealing with an anonymous public, the entrepreneur who caters for the deviant world knows and is known and is thereby enmeshed in a net of obligations and commitments which distinguish a face-to-face community.[132]

Others are not afforded the relative protection of such guarded exchanges. They are instead thrown into confrontation with innumerable untried people who can reward or sanction them. The deviant entrepreneur who serves the conventional community faces abundant risks. In my brief discussion of one instance of such entrepreneurship, I shall focus on problems of self-advertisement where the self that is advertised is illegal or degraded.

The streetwalking prostitute who existed before the 1959 Street Offences Act provides an instance of the entrepreneurial deviant whose occupational self was organised around widely understood episodes of display as an outsider. Almost all prostitutes are constrained, for greater or lesser periods of time, to confront an anonymous consuming public, parts of which will manifest themselves as clients. When she enters the market as a commodity, she has little ability to predict who will become a client, who will become a policeman and who will not effectively be in the marketplace at all. In consequence, her display episodes are risky. In the hierarchy of prostitution, the most highly rewarded and esteemed are the call-girls who do not have to be on view before an untried audience. A prostitute, who had been arrested by someone who had represented himself as a client, remarked:

. . . this time I'm going to stay out. I just got to. Johns with references from now on, references. They'll have to have good, damn good ones, too. And a small number of steadies. None of this street stuff, not even if I'm starving. They come by someone I know, pal, or they don't come.[133]

Clients can come from a wide variety of the public's subworlds and may, indeed, be total foreigners. Before she can effectively solicit custom, the prostitute must acquire some minimal knowledge of what passes for useful signs of her role. Ambiguity about whether she is available, whether she is to receive money for the sexual transaction and what services she will perform must all be dispelled unless she is to be at risk. Since prostitution can be profitable only if it is based on a rapid sequence of smoothly conducted transactions, communication must evolve which can dissipate confusions and neatly terminate each episode. Details of typical episodes become stabilised over time. A London street-walker reflected:

There is a routine of approach, performance and farewell. . . . Even the smallest action—the call to a cab, the switching on of a light, the pocketing of money, is duplicated time and time again. The same small talk, the same phrases are repeated, with only slight variations for the differing types of client, who behave with equally monotonous uniformity, within their type.[134]

The prostitute must manage a reasonably complicated impression when soliciting. Her scope is clearly restricted. First, she must be readily identifiable as an approachable prostitute. Behaviour in public places is governed by an enforceable set of understandings about how strangers can legitimately treat one another.[135] Decorum dictates that public areas cannot be regarded as the settings for excessively private gatherings; that people who are unknown to one another cannot freely enter into interaction; that they will not become the objects of keen interest; and that people will be generally free from molestation. These tacit rules are applied with special force to women, a group which is defined as particularly vulnerable. The prostitute blatantly upsets this sense of order. She transforms public spaces by redefining them as markets in which advances from strangers will be accepted. The consequences of mistakenly assuming a woman to be a prostitute are, at the very least, embarrassing. Unless she demonstrates that such consequences will not flow from overtures made to her, the prostitute will be protected by assumptions that are inappropriate to her role. Her management of impressions must thus depend on a somewhat exaggerated gestural and symbolic display. She must visibly emphasise the differences between herself and conventional women who are not safely approachable. The London prostitute, quoted above, related how differently she handled herself on and off the market:

I slow down to walking pace and am no longer outstanding in the crowd, despite the slacks. Thank God so many women are wearing them these days. It is pleasant to be dressed as one likes and not be obtrusive, not to attract stares and comment until the appointed time. Then the slacks must be worn with a different air, bold and flaunting. The walk must become a swing, a flirt of the hips, an invitation, instead of this steady pad-pad through the crowds.[136]

Some streets and areas were so frequently defined by prostitutes as marketplaces that their definition became the dominant one for a great many people. The system of proprieties regulating public

behaviour was slightly displaced in these territories. Doubts about
the meaning of a woman's presence there were fewer than in other
places:

> . . . mutual recognition is the reason for the man's frequently making
> the first approach, and, though he may be the first of the two to speak, his
> doing so may hardly be termed solicitation. A man who goes up to one of
> several girls standing along Euston Road late at night and asks 'Are you a
> naughty girl?' may reasonably expect an affimative answer. . . . A tradi-
> tion of place and behaviour has grown up whereby a man, seeing a woman
> loitering in a certain street, may assume that she is a prostitute. The posi-
> tion is so well defined in some places that the girl feels that merely by
> standing she is doing enough.[137]

The exploitation of such overt and widely appreciated significances
considerably reduces the problems associated with a prostitute's
successful self-advertisement. So radically may a combination of
place and time alter the meaning of a setting that conventional women
cannot rely on normal understandings for their protection. When the
Street Offences Act made public soliciting more difficult, prostitutes
were forced to generate a new system of equally blatant symbols.
Without such a system, rapid and numerous market exchanges
would have ceased:

> The Street Offences Act of 1959 cleared the girls off the London streets
> overnight, as it had been meant to. They went indoors into the pubs and
> clubs, and on to the telephone. Some put up fluorescent red bell-pushes;
> some hustled by standing at open doors and windows. So much as a nose
> or a finger in the air space of the street was illegal. Some advertised in
> the press, and many in shop windows. One put up a neon sign saying:
> 'French Lessons'.[138]

Yet the revelation of a prostitute was rarely total. Although men
seeking prostitutes were particularly sensitive to those signs which
indicated which women were on the market, the signs were so exoteric
that a prostitute could always confer stigma on her clients. She had to
acquire the skill to translate effortlessly a fairly transparent situation
into one which was innocuous. She must also have had to convey just
enough ambiguity to lay her symbolism open to more than one
interpretation. More important, she must have had the ability to
quickly redefine herself as one who was not 'after all' a prostitute. She
must be able to exercise some minimal discretion in her selection of
clients. Unwelcome potential clients need to have their understanding
of the situation rapidly and smoothly transformed so that doubts
enter about whether the woman was a prostitute after all. Thus the
streetwalker's self-presentation had to be fluid enough to permit some
ambiguity and the possibility of convincing shifts.

Nevertheless, the prostitute was an easily identifiable social object and was thus open to control by the police and other agencies. She could not present herself on a market before the public and escape the attention of those entrusted with law enforcement. In consequence, almost all prostitution rests upon some system of tacit reciprocity between the police and the deviant. The reciprocity may rest upon the prostitute offering bribes,[139] or it may rest upon more diffuse understandings. The prostitute may, for example, be allowed to play a deviant role provided she does not upset an authoritatively approved sense of social order. The places which she is permitted to change into overt markets might be territorially confined (the Storyville district of New Orleans, for instance); and, within those territories, she must lay herself open to constant supervision. A former Chief Constable of Liverpool described his police force's policy governing brothels:

For many years in Liverpool the practice of the police had been to at once institute proceedings against immoral houses, when it was known that (1) young girls were allowed in the house; (2) robberies took place in the house; (3) they were of notoriously bad character, or a public nuisance; (4) they were opened in a street hitherto free of such houses; or (5) two or more inhabitants complained and were willing to provide evidence to substantiate their complaint. There were necessarily, in a town like Liverpool, many of such houses in existence, but they were generally located in special streets. They were '*known* to the Police', who did not as a rule take action against them, for it was felt that any action taken would not result in decreasing the number of such houses, but only driving them into neighbourhoods unaffected by the evil, and where (so far as any chance of prosecution was concerned) they would be '*unknown* to the Police'.[140]

Another possible consequence of the prostitute's self-advertisement and her visibility to the police was a practice of token, routine control which did not pretend to be just or prompted by real concern. It constituted, instead, a means of 'beating the bounds' of deviancy; a ritual confirmation of the proscribed contours of the behaviour:

Between them the police and the prostitutes have come to what might almost be termed a happy concurrence to make the law into a working, though pointless, compromise. They are both fairly tolerant of what they regard as an irritation in their nightly routine . . . there appears to have arisen a system whereby prostitutes are charged at fairly frequent intervals roughly in proportion to their persistence in soliciting, rarely more than once or twice a month, usually once every two or three months.[141]

The expressive, politicised, coercive and entrepreneurial deviants deliberately proclaim themselves with characteristic consequences for their relations with control agents and nondeviants. They attempt, in the main, to reduce the ambiguities surrounding the identities which they are presenting to the world. Of course, their communication of information is censored and selective. There are facets of every deviant that would never be voluntarily conveyed to others. Yet, as far as simple recognition is concerned, these deviants turn themselves into social objects which are unequivocally stigmatised or subject to sanction. The stigmata may be treated as an unavoidable opportunity cost of the deviancy; as a sign of welcome differentiation; as part of a process of conflict and polarisation; or as a resource to be exploited. In their transactions with the nondeviant world, these deviants are engaged in a constant series of reformulations both of their role and of the symbols which proclaim it. Like the courts, they attempt to reduce what is essentially a multifaceted and complex set of meanings to one dominant and all-pervasive significance. They share with the courts an interest in the establishment of a discrete and immediately apprehended deviant identity.

The recognition of most instances of deviancy is inhibited by the ambiguity which surrounds not only our understanding of the intention and meaning of activity, but also our application of deviancy-defining rules. It seems, moreover, that deviancy (which is, typically, disguised or hidden activity) is taken for conventional behaviour in many cases. Certainly, the identification of deviant 'personality', if not deviant acts, is not the most likely first response of the unknowing to covert rule-breaking. It is only when the *epoché* of the natural attitude is challenged that such identification can take place. The challenge may emanate from crisis or from the rude thrusting of deviancy before others. Other deviancies are knowable even when the *epoché* is not challenged. Coercive, entrepreneurial, expressive or undisguisable deviation presents itself as recognisable rule-breaking. In all cases, the perspective on deviancy acquired by the sophisticated or the recently aware will inevitably be segmental and negotiated. This perspective will be part of the larger work which goes on in the construction of a society's members' understanding of rule-breaking. This construction will, in turn, feed back both into the identifying operations available to the members and into their formal and informal control responses. Such responses are in their turns agents in the formation of deviancy. It is clear, then, that the organisation of known deviancy is but part of a large and complex system of actions and interactions.

1. R. L. Akers, 'Problems in the Sociology of Deviance: Social Definitions and Behavior', *Social Forces*, June 1968, vol. 46, no. 4, p. 463.

2. This passage paraphrases the argument of D. Bordua, 'Recent Trends: Deviant Behavior and Social Control', *Annals of the American Academy of Political and Social Science*, January 1967, vol. 57, no. 4, pp. 149–63.

3. J. Douglas, 'Deviance and Respectability', J. Douglas (Ed.), *Deviance and Respectability*, Basic Books, New York, 1970, p. 3.

4. J. Dewey, *Human Nature and Conduct*, H. Holt, New York, 1922, pp. 216–17.

5. cf. D. Matza, *Delinquency and Drift*, John Wiley, New York, 1966.

6. A. Schutz, 'Symbol, Reality, and Society', in M. Natanson (Ed.), *Alfred Schutz: Collected Papers*, vol. 1, Martinus Nijhoff, The Hague, 1967, vol. 1, p. 307.

7. ibid., pp. 308–9.

8. E. Goffman, 'Expression Games', in *Strategic Interaction*, Blackwell, Oxford, 1970, pp. 4–5.

9. cf. T. Shibutani, *Improvised News*, Bobbs-Merrill, Indianapolis, 1966, p. 19.

10. cf. E. Goffman, *The Presentation of Self in Everyday Life*, Doubleday, New York, 1959.

11. F. Znaniecki, *The Social Role of the Man of Knowledge*, Harper Torchbooks, New York, 1968, p. 16.

12. S. Wheeler, Introduction to *On Record: Files and Dossiers in American Life*, Russell Sage Foundation, New York, 1969, p. 5.

13. A. Schutz, 'The Stranger', in M. Natanson (Ed.), op. cit., vol. 2, p. 93.

14. E. Goffman, *Stigma*, Prentice-Hall, New Jersey, p. 73.

15. ibid., p. 94.

16. E. Lemert, *Social Pathology*, McGraw-Hill, New York, 1951, p. 95.

17. cf. L. Humphries, *Tearoom Trade*, Duckworth, London, 1970.

18. cf. M. Scott and S. Lyman, 'Accounts, Deviance, and Social Order', in J. Douglas (Ed.), *Deviance and Respectability*, op. cit.

19. E. Bittner, 'Radicalism and the Organization of Radical Movements', *American Sociological Review*, December 1963, vol. 28, no. 6, p. 934.

20. ibid., p. 930.

21. cf. F. Murphy et al., 'The Incidence of Hidden Delinquency', *American Journal of Orthopsychiatry*, October 1946, vol. 16, no. 4; A. Gibson, 'Self-Reported Delinquency Among Schoolboys', *British Journal of Social and Clinical Psychology*, 1967, vol. 6; W. Belson, 'The Extent of Stealing by Some London Boys', *Advancement of Science*, December 1968, vol. 25, no. 124.

22. J. Douglas, 'Deviance and Order in a Pluralist Society', in J. McKinney and E. Tiryakian (Ed.), *Theoretical Sociology*, Appleton-Century-Crofts, New York, 1970, p. 378.

23. E. Freidson, 'Disability as Social Deviance', in E. Rubington and M. Weinberg (Ed.), *Deviance*, Macmillan, New York, 1968, p. 118.

24. M. Yarrow, C. Schwartz et al., 'The Psychological Meaning of Mental Illness in the Family', in E. Rubington and M. S. Weinberg (Ed.), op. cit., p. 36.

25. cf. C. Winick, 'Physician Narcotic Addicts', in H. S. Becker (Ed.), *The Other Side*, Free Press, New York, 1964, pp. 261–80.

26. N. Denzin, 'Rules of Conduct and the Study of Deviant Behavior', in J. Douglas (Ed.), *Deviance and Respectability*, op. cit., p. 148.

27. ibid., pp. 146–7.

28. A. Schutz, 'On Multiple Realities', in M. Natanson (Ed.), op. cit., vol. 1, p. 229.

29. cf. E. Goffman, *Stigma*, op. cit.

30. cf. T. Parker and R. Allerton, *The Courage of His Convictions*, Hutchinson, London, 1962, pp. 102–3.

31. F. Hartung, 'A Vocabulary of Motives for Law Violations', in D. Cressey and D. Ward (Ed.), *Delinquency, Crime and Social Process*, Harper and Row, New York, 1969, p. 469.

32. cf. M. Haug and M. Sussman, 'Professional Autonomy and the Revolt of the Client', *Social Problems*, Fall 1969, vol. 17, no. 2.

33. Quoted in A. Strauss, *Mirrors and Masks*, Free Press, Illinois, 1959, p. 54.

34. C. Werthman and I. Piliavin, 'Gang Members and the Police', in D. Bordua (Ed.), *The Police*, Wiley, New York, 1967, p. 56.

35. J. Lofland, *Deviance and Identity*, Prentice-Hall, New Jersey, 1969, p. 136.

36. cf. P. McHugh, *Defining the Situation*, Bobbs-Merrill, Indianapolis, 1968.

37. H. Garfinkel, *Studies in Ethnomethodology*, Prentice-Hall, New Jersey, 1967, pp. 37–8.

38. T. Shibutani, *Improvised News*, op. cit., p. 174.

39. cf. N. Cohn, *Warrant for Genocide*, Penguin Books, Middlesex, 1970.

40. M. Douglas, *Witchcraft Confessions and Accusations*, Tavistock, London, 1970, p. xxx.

41. For an extensive and sophisticated treatment of the general issue of awareness in social settings, see B. Glaser and A. Strauss, *Awareness of Dying*, Weidenfeld & Nicolson, London, 1966.

42. For a larger examination of the conventionalisation of criminality and deviancy, cf. H. Becker, 'Conventional Crime', in H. Becker, *Sociological Work*, Allen Lane, The Penguin Press, London, 1971.

43. E. Goffman, *Behavior in Public Places*, Free Press, New York, 1963, p. 57.

44. cf. C. Werthman and I. Piliavin, 'Gang Members and the Police', op. cit.

45. S. Cavan, *Liquor License*, Aldine, Chicago, 1966, p. 4.

46. cf. P. Rock and F. Heidensohn, 'New Reflections on Violence', in D. Martin (Ed.), *Anarchy and Culture*, Routledge & Kegan Paul, London, 1969.

47. I. and P. Opie, *The Lore and Language of Schoolchildren*, Oxford University Press, London, 1959, p. 232.

48. L. Wirth, *The Ghetto*, University of Chicago Press, Chicago, 1928, pp. 285–6.

49. For an interesting discussion of the way in which such conventionalised deviancy can emerge, see T. Smith, 'Conventionalization and Control', *American Journal of Sociology*, September 1968, vol. 74, no. 2.

50. cf. the operations of the stall in the case of the pickpocket in D. Maurer, *Whiz Mob*, College and University Press, New Haven, 1964.

51. A. Stinchcombe, 'The Behavior of Police in Public and Private Places', in E. Rubington and M. Weinberg, *Deviance*, Macmillan, New York, 1968, p. 147.

52. K. Chesney, *The Victorian Underworld*, Temple Smith, London, 1970, p. 134.

53. cf. A. Cicourel and J. Kitsuse, *The Educational Decision-Makers*, Bobbs-Merrill, Indianapolis, 1963.

54. cf. J. Martin, *Offenders as Employees*, Macmillan, London, 1962.

55. cf. D. Chapman, *Sociology and the Stereotype of the Criminal*, Tavistock, London, 1968.

56. S. Cavan, op. cit., p. 18.

57. ibid., p. 67.

58. In the case of employment patterns in a Negro ghetto, for instance, Liebow has shown how employers and employees tacitly negotiate wage levels on the basis of the theft potential of the jobs. cf. E. Liebow, *Tally's Corner*, Little Brown & Co, Boston, 1967.

59. G. Mars, 'Industrial Pilferage—Two Case Studies', paper delivered at 1971 Annual Conference of the British Sociological Association, pp. 26, 27.

60. E. Hobsbawm, *Bandits*, Weidenfeld & Nicolson, London, 1969, p. 35.

61. ibid., pp. 39–40.

62. J. Landesco, *Organized Crime in Chicago*, University of Chicago Press, Chicago, 1968, p. 169.

63. ibid., p. 178.

64. U. Hannerz, *Soulside: Inquiries into Ghetto Culture and Community*, Columbia University Press, New York, 1969, pp. 57–8.

65. E. Smigel and H. Ross, *Crimes Against Bureaucracy*, Van Nostrand Rheinhold, New York, 1970, p. 7.

66. cf. M. McIntosh, 'Changes in the Organization of Thieving', in S. Cohen (Ed.), *Images of Deviance*, Penguin Books, Middlesex, 1971.

67. President's Commission on Law Enforcement and Administration of Justice, *Task Force Report on Organized Crime*, US Government Printing Office, Washington, 1967, p. 2.

68. D. Sudnow, 'Normal Crimes', in W. J. Chambliss (Ed.), *Crime and the Legal Process*, McGraw-Hill, New York, 1969, p. 261.

69. J. Young, 'The Role of the Police as Amplifiers of Deviancy, Negotiators of Reality, and Translators of Fantasy', in S. Cohen (Ed.), *Images of Deviance*, Penguin Books, Middlesex, 1971, p. 41.

70. ibid., p. 43.

71. L. Taylor, *Deviance and Society*, Michael Joseph, London, 1971, pp. 90–1,

72. D. Maurer, *Whiz Mob*, College and University Press, New Haven, 1964. p. 11.

73. ibid., p. 43.

74. ibid., p. 52.

75. cf. P. Lerman, 'Gangs, Networks, and Subcultural Delinquency', *American Journal of Sociology*, July 1967, vol. 73, no. 1, esp. pp. 65–6.

76. cf. C. W. Mills, 'Situated Actions and Vocabularies of Motive', *American Sociological Review*, December 1940, vol. 5, no. 6.

77. B. Wilson, *Sects and Society*, Heinemann, London, 1961, p. 1.

78. E. Sutherland, *The Professional Thief*, University of Chicago Press, Chicago, 1956, pp. 165–6.

79. ibid., chs. IV and V.

80. K. Chesney, *The Victorian Underworld*, op. cit.

81. cf. A. Sutter, 'Worlds of Drug Use', in D. Cressey and D. Ward (Ed.), *Delinquency, Crime and Social Process*, Harper and Row, New York, 1969.

82. O. Klapp, *Collective Search for Identity*, Holt Rinehart Winston, New York, 1969, pp. vii–ix.

83. cf. M. Douglas, *Natural Symbols*, Cresset Press, London, 1970.

84. cf. N. Cohn, *The Pursuit of the Millennium*, Mercury, London, 1962; P. Worsley, *The Trumpet Shall Sound*, Paladin, London, 1968.

85. cf. L. Yablonsky, *The Hippy Trip*, Pegasus, New York, 1968.

86. J. Young, *The Drugtakers*, MacGibbon & Kee, London, 1970, p. 151.

87. M. Scott and S. Lyman, *The Revolt of the Students*, Merrill, Columbus, Ohio, 1970, p. 112.

88. cf. T. Shibutani, 'Reference Groups as Perspectives', *American Journal of Sociology*, 1955, vol. 60.

89. R. Cloward and L. Ohlin, *Delinquency and Opportunity*, Routledge & Kegan Paul, London, 1961, p. 183.

90. H. Finestone, 'Cats, Kicks, and Color', in H. S. Becker (Ed.), *The Other Side*, Free Press, New York, 1965, p. 286.

91. cf. T. Gautier, 'The Hashish Club' and C. Baudelaire, 'An Excerpt from the Seraphic Theatre', in D. Solomon (Ed.), *The Marijuana Papers*, Panther, London, 1969.

92. H. Finestone, op. cit., p. 285.

93. cf. K. Rexroth, 'Disengagement: The Art of the Beat Generation', in *New World Writing: No. 11*, New American Library, New York, 1957, pp. 28–41.

94. J. Ciardi, 'Epitaph for the Dead Beats', in T. Parkinson (Ed.), *A Casebook on the Beat*, T. Y. Crowell Co, New York, 1961, p. 258, Prentice-Hall, New Jersey, 1968, p. 164.

95. J. Carey, *The College Drug Scene*, Prentice-Hall, New Jersey, 1965, pp. 64–5.

96. ibid., p. 150.

97. Lancashire Constabulary, *Annual Report of the Chief Constable for the year 1969*, Hutton, Lancashire, 1970, p. 1.

98. T. Parkinson, 'Phenomenon or Generation', in T. Parkinson (Ed.), op. cit., pp. 278–9.

99. For an interesting discussion of politicised deviancy, see I. Horowitz and M. Liebowitz, 'Social Deviance and Political Marginality', *Social Problems*, 1968, vol. 15.

100. For an example of the rejection of the authority of imputational experts, see Millett's discussion of Freud on women: K. Millett, *Sexual Politics*, Rupert Hart-Davis, London, 1969.

101. M. Haug and M. Sussman, 'Professional Autonomy . . .', op. cit., p. 157.

102. B. Stone, *Sisterhood is Powerful*, Pathfinder Press, New York, 1970, p. 10.

103. cf. P. Rock and F. Heidensohn, 'New Reflections on Violence', in D. Martin (Ed.), *Anarchy and Culture*, Routledge & Kegan Paul, London, 1969.

104. N. Chomsky, *American Power and the New Mandarins*, Penguin Books, Middlesex, 1969, p. 295.

105. *Gay Liberation*, Red Butterfly, New York, 1970, p. 2. Similarly, the Manifesto of the London Gay Liberation Front states, 'the starting point of our liberation must be to rid ourselves of the oppression which lies in the head of everyone of us', Gay Liberation Front Manifesto, London, 1971, p. 15.

106. E. Essien-Udom, *Black Nationalism*, Dell, New York, 1964, p. 361.

107. E. Goffman, *Stigma*, op. cit., p. 7.

108. *Gay Liberation Front*, op. cit.

109. ibid., p. 4.

110. M. R. Karenga, 'The Quotable Karenga', in F. Barbour (Ed.), *The Black Power Revolt*, Collier, Toronto, 1968, p. 191.

111. cf. E. Essien-Udom, op. cit., ch. 5.

112. cf. T. Leary, *The Politics of Ecstasy*, Paladin, London, 1970.

113. E. Cleaver, 'The Primeval Mitosis', in *Soul on Ice*, Jonathan Cape, London, 1969.

114. E. Cleaver, 'The Courage to Kill: Meeting the Panthers', in *Eldridge Cleaver*, Random House, New York, 1969, p. 29.

115 B. Seale, *Seize The Time*, Hutchinson, London, 1970.

116. See the report in the *Guardian* newspaper, 6 April 1971, about the 343 Frenchwomen who signed their names to a manifesto about abortion which appeared in the *Nouvel Observateur*.

117. Quoted from the edited transcript of *United States of America Plaintiff, v. David T. Dellinger et al., Defendants, No. 69, Crim 180*, published as M. L. Levine et al. (Ed.), *The Tales of Hoffman*, Bantam, New York, 1970, pp. 144–5.

118. P. Maas, *The Canary that Sang: The Valachi Papers*, MacGibbon & Kee, London, 1969, p. 214.

119. cf. M. McIntosh, 'Changes in the Organization of Thieving', op. cit., pp. 98–133.

120. For a description of such an escalation, see W. H. Friedland and H.

Edwards, 'Confrontation at Cornell', in A. Meier (Ed.), *The Transformation of Activism*, Aldine, Chicago, 1970, pp. 69–90.

121. G. Simmel quoted in L. Coser, *The Functions of Social Conflict*, Routledge & Kegan Paul, London, 1968, p. 121.

122. P. Berger and T. Luckman, 'The Social Construction of Reality', Allen Lane, The Penguin Press, London, 1967, p. 117.

123. cf. L. Coser, 'Some Functions of Deviant Behavior and Normative Flexibility', in *Continuities in the Study of Social Conflict*, Free Press, New York, 1967.

124. cf. H. Garfinkel, *Studies in Ethnomethodology*, op. cit., ch. 1.

125. In M. Levine *et al.* (Ed.), op. cit., pp. 142–3.

126. cf. F. Henriques, *Stews and Strumpets: A Survey of Prostitution*, MacGibbon & Kee, London, 1961.

127. cf. H. Becker, 'Marihuana Use and Social Control', in *Outsiders*, Free Press, New York, 1963.

128. cf. T. Scheff, *Being Mentally Ill*, Weidenfeld & Nicolson, London, 1966.

129. cf. A. Strauss, *Mirrors and Masks*, Free Press, Chicago, 1959, ch. 4.

130. W. Einstadter, 'The Social Organization of Armed Robbery', *Social Problems*, Summer 1969, vol. 17, no. 1, p. 81.

131. W. Lippmann, 'The Underworld as Servant', in G. Tyler (Ed.), *Organized Crime in America*, University of Michigan Press, Michigan, 1967, p. 59.

132. For an interesting discussion of a thief's relationship with his receiver, see G. Smithson, *Raffles in Real Life*, Hutchinson, London, undated.

133. T. Rubin, *In the Life*, Ballantine, New York, 1961, p. 35.

134. Anon, *Streetwalker*, Bodley Head, London, 1959, p. 13.

135. cf. E. Goffman, *Behavior in Public Places*, Free Press, New York, 1963.

136. Anon, op. cit., p. 64.

137. C. Rolph (Ed.), *Women of the Streets*, New English Library, London, 1961, p. 63.

138. W. Young, *Eros Denied*, Corgi, London, 1969, p. 132.

139. cf. H. Asbury, *The French Quarter*, Capricorn, New York, 1968, esp. p. 352.

140. Sir W. Nott-Bower, *Fifty-Two Years a Policeman*, Edward Arnold, London, 1926, pp. 140–1.

141. C. Rolph (Ed.), op. cit., p. 26.

3

AUTHORITATIVE DEFINITIONS OF DEVIANCY

In this chapter I shall outline how definitions of deviancy are translated into recipes for effective social action. All major definitional systems shape social life but, in a society marked by conflict and dissensus about central meanings and understandings, many systems remain relatively inconsequential unless they are supported by coercion. Society can be regulated by a coherent and comprehensive system of definitions only when they are *imposed* on at least some dissident groups and individuals. Deviancy flows from the successful imposition of unwelcome status. The study of definitional processes must therefore be wedded to an analysis of the power structures which realise definitions in action. More particularly, it must focus on the groups which have the power to award lowly status and on the processes whereby such awards take place. As Erikson argues, 'The critical variable in the study of deviance . . . is the social audience rather than the individual actor, since it is the audience which eventually determines whether or not an episode of behavior or any class of episodes is labeled deviant.'[1] The social audience must, however, be structurally powerful enough to make its definitions fateful for the individual actor.

At least two major analytical areas emerge out of such a perspective: the generation of rules and the enforcement of rules. In complex societies there is a substantial fragmentation of rule-making and rule-enforcing effort. There are innumerable legislating, defining and policing agencies which collectively make up the formal structure of a society's system of social control. Legislators, judges, magistrates, policemen, bailiffs, psychiatrists, prison officers and traffic wardens form a loosely coordinated system with shifting internal boundaries; a differentiation of power and function; and intricate linkages forged out of internal conflict,* exchange and cooperation.† The overall structure is hierarchical; chains of command fashion the flow of power and decision-making. Each of the hierarchy's subsystems is shaped by its fellows. Each has the possibility of acquiring limited autonomy from the rest; each tends to have a drive towards maximising its control over resources and problem areas;‡ and each is concerned about defending its boundaries against outsiders. The higher strata have a greater capacity to exert influence over the whole but they are functionally dependent on and constrained by the lower strata.

Whilst there is some division of labour between those agencies which make and those which enforce rules, there is also considerable merging and overlap. Initiatives for action can emanate from almost any of the subsystems. Some minor agencies, such as the psychiatric and social work professions, have acquired the power to control substantial segments of social problems. Others have appropriated power in a covert fashion. They have evolved procedural rules, private understandings, alternative goals and monopolies of the right to provide authoritative definitions of their problematic populations. The delegation or channelling of power affords nominally subordinate systems opportunities for redefining the means and ends of social control. Very often they are responsible for transmitting information about the effects of control to those who made the rules and activated their enforcement. They can thereby shape their superiors' conception of the world of social problems which is to be managed and of the effects of that management. The police, for instance, have become experts in forming legislators' ideas about the nature and volume of crime. Command over information is one source of practical power, and control over the everyday business of enforcement is another. Rules undergo systematic changes as they are passed from their makers to their enforcers. It is the enforcers' particular interpretation of the meaning and applicability of rules that determines how a population experiences formal control.

Rather than discuss the workings of this structure at an abstract

* For an example of conflict between agencies, see the evident rivalry between the Customs and the police drugs squad revealed in the trial at Middlesex Area Sessions during June and July 1971. The London *Times* covered this trial during the period.

† For an interesting discussion of the way in which such relations were managed by one agency, an American juvenile court, see R. Emerson, *Judging Delinquents: Context and Process in Juvenile Court*, Aldine, Chicago, 1969.

‡ For an indication of such a process, in the case of attempts by various branches of the medical profession to gain control over the abortion problem, see K. Hindell and M. Simms, *Abortion Law Reformed*, Peter Owen, London, 1971.

level, I shall dwell on two concrete facets. In this chapter I shall examine the formal apex of the structure—the legislative process. In the next, I shall offer a model of police organisation as an instance of enforcement. These comparatively specific descriptions should demonstrate the interdependence of deviant organisation, systems of beliefs about deviancy, official attempts to make authoritative codes of those beliefs and their practical enforcement.

Law is a very special form of regulatory mechanism. Because of its artifice, it is qualitatively different in its initial stages from many other rule systems. It is imperialistic; supported by a powerful coercive apparatus; prone to reification; and relatively articulate and consistent.

LAW AS AN ARTIFICE

In Britain rules are not homogeneous in their salience, importance, structure or clarity. Rather than define social rules as an undifferentiated system of similar parts, it is more useful to regard them as stratified in layers of importance for members of a society. Some of the uppermost layers may be awarded legitimacy by only a few members; the deeper layers substantially unite members despite the existence of major fissures. The lower the strata, the less often are they recognised in everyday life. Few of us could precisely outline the rules which govern grammar, interaction or deportment. As Shibutani remarks:

The better established the norms are, the less likely it is that people will be aware of them. When there is a high degree of consensus, the assumptions are shared to such an extent that no one would even think of raising questions. What is important about any group . . . is what is taken for granted, what is silently and unconsciously presupposed.[2]

Such 'deep' rules do not require formal enunciation. Indeed, they are the very means by which such operations as enunciating 'surface' rules become possible. They form the materials out of which intelligible social action is built. Their breakdown is typically accompanied by the decomposition of identities and basic social order. Such *anomie* is not something which can be routinely managed by institutional control. Whilst wholesale infringement or collapse of these rules is tantamount to chaos, individual rule-breaking rarely needs direct and deliberate enforcement. Although the psychiatric profession has evolved to control residual deviancy, most cases are regulated by the constraints imposed by language and informal systems of relations.

The structural distribution of rules is also uneven. Some rules are accepted as fitting in certain areas but not in others. Whilst particular layers pertain to all members equally, others are extremely localised. Thus, strategies of analysis which accept as fundamental a conflict or consensus model of society do violence to the way in which activity is conducted in everyday life. Without a detailed map of rule systems, assumptions about the nature of normative order are simplistic. For example, many instances of what is taken to be significant conflict are disputes about outcrops of rules which are novel or unusually accessible to observation. We tend to define as particularly problematic those phenomena which are striking enough to challenge the natural attitude. The existence of sustained conflict is itself permitted only by the deeper strata of shared understandings concerning forms and sequences of meaningful interaction. It might even be argued that, since most expressions of conflict require a consciousness of the rules in dispute, conflict is unlikely to be waged directly about the most basic layers of rules.

Rules which become subject to debate and thought are peculiar in that they can be brought to consciousness. At least some of their properties no longer share with deep rules the characteristic of being silently presupposed. Instead, they acquire a quality of contrivance. In particular, the very existence of *law* suggests that situations are defined as problematic, that conformity cannot be taken for granted and that expectations must be clarified and authoritatively stated.

When activity is regulated by law, then, it is no longer solely the province of tacit and routinely binding understandings. Many laws are distillations of these understandings or mores, but the raising of the mores to awareness indicates that they have lost some of their potency. They become the thing to be judged rather than the criteria by which things are judged. There must always be some conflict between the intentions voiced in law and the beliefs of those subject to law:

Laws have accumulated because the mores have been weak and inconsistent; and because the laws have not had the support of the mores they have been relatively ineffective as a means of control. When the mores are adequate laws are unnecessary; when the mores are inadequate, the laws are ineffective.[3]

Law consequently signifies that there is some conflict over moral or technical assumptions; that certain actions are raised to a level of awareness at which they and their performance are not taken for granted but appraised; that there is a sizeable dissenting minority who challenge the propriety of the mores; or that, whilst relations *within* groups assume a taken for granted character, relations *between* them are rather more ambiguous. According to Sumner, the mores are so much a part of our thinking and acting that any detachment from them is impossible; law is qualitatively distinct from the mores because it does possess this detached aspect:

The thing to be noticed . . . is that the masses oppose a deaf ear to every argument against the mores. It is only in so far as things have been transferred from the mores into laws . . . that there is discussion about them or rationalizing upon them. The mores contain the norm by which, if we should discuss the mores, we should have to judge the mores. We learn the mores as unconsciously as we learn to walk and eat and breathe. The masses never learn how we walk, and eat, and breathe, and they never know any reason why the mores are what they are. The justification of them is that when we wake to consciousness of life we find them facts which already hold us in the bonds of tradition, custom, and habit.[4]

Law presupposes some dissent from a universal moral perspective and thereby tacitly recognises its own weakness. Law has another substantial element of contrivance. To the extent that we can become conscious of the existence of deeper rule structures, we frequently discover ambiguity in their use. As I have argued, the rules of everyday life are far from categorical; they are marked by uncertainty and problems of contextual application in certain cases. Laws in countries regulated by Anglo-American and Roman systems of jurisprudence are framed to dispel such issues. They impose a systematic rationality. Their drafting is supposed to minimise ambiguity. They clearly attempt an exhaustive classification of possible cases and proffer solutions in advance. Embellished by case law, they tend to cut a swath through the problems of applying mundane rules. Of course, no formal system can ever be completely exhaustive. Its use is possible only because there are subsidiary systems of evaluation which are not themselves codified. Nevertheless, law operates upon the basis of a logical system of clear alternatives which exclude the grey areas of everyday thinking. It is not a commonsense rationality and does not encompass the ambiguities and indecisiveness of most rules.

LAW AND REIFICATION

Reification, according to Berger and Luckman,

. . . is the apprehension of human phenomena as if they were things, that is, in non-human or possibly supra-human terms. Another way of saying this is that reification is the apprehension of the products of human activity *as if* they were something other than human products—such as facts of nature, results of cosmic laws, or manifestations of divine will. Reification implies that man is capable of forgetting his own authorship of the human world, and, further, that the dialectic between man, the producer, and his products is lost to consciousness. The reified world is, by definition, a dehumanized world. It is experienced by man as a strange facticity, an *opus alienum* over which he has no control rather than as *opus proprium* of his own productive activity.[5]

Law is particularly susceptible to reification. Initially contrived, an object of dispute, and distinguished by unusual clarity, it can become a phenomenon which is not associated with human authorship. Both to legislators and to men in their natural attitude, the artificiality of law becomes transformed into something incapable of being contrived. Law is a supremely powerful instrument of control because it has within it the tendency to become an end in itself. Although legalism is but one of the possible directions that perspectives on law can take,[6] there is always the possibility that law will become an ethical imperative because it *is* law. It is no longer the tool of a particular group but a formal embodiment of a society's ultimate values. As Simmel observes, the contents of law can become autonomous:

The requirements of social existence compel or legitimate certain types of individual behavior which thus are valid and followed, precisely because they meet these practical requirements. Yet with the emergence of 'law', this reason for their diffusion recedes into the background; now they are followed quite simply because they have become the 'law' and quite independently of the life which originally engendered and directed them. The furthest pole of this development is expressed by the idea of 'fiat justitia, pereat mundus'. In other words, although lawful behavior has its roots in the purposes of social life, law, properly speaking has no 'purpose' since it is not a means to an ulterior end. On the contrary, it determines, in its own right and not by legitimation through any higher, extrinsic agency, how the contents of life should be shaped.[7]

The production of this reified system is one of the few processes in Western societies which are embellished by potent symbolism, formalised behaviour and elaborate ritual. The transformation of a particular moral code into law thus tends to reify it, sanctify it and impersonalise it. Those who make laws are able to change once parochial interests into something qualitatively different. Law can thereby assume one of the properties of a moral system as described by Mandelbaum. He argued that moral experience is seen by the members of a society as external and given, not the arbitrary creation of particular men.[8] Subordination to the law is an expression of what Simmel calls 'subordination to a principle'.[9] It can conflict with an alternative kind of deference, subordination to a person. As a reified entity, law has an authority and concreteness which is independent of its creators. It typically constrains the legislator himself. Those who make law generate social facts which diminish their personal authority and freedom. It was presumably for this reason that Pharaohic Egypt did not possess a system of codified laws. Wilson argues of the pharaoh that 'He, as a god, *was* the state. . . . The customary law of the land was conceived to be the word of the pharaoh. . . . The authority of codified law would have competed with the personal authority of the pharaoh.'[10]

LAW AS AN IMPERIALISTIC CODE

Society can be described as a network of small social worlds. Each of the worlds is an organisation of roles, beliefs and loyalties. Each is somewhat differentiated from its neighbours, and the boundaries between them shape communication channels so that information and perspectives are unevenly distributed throughout the network. The organisation of each world provides a more or less definite structure for its members so that courses of action are outlined, co-ordinated and negotiated. The organisation is also a moral order in that its prescriptions and proscriptions are sources of identity and guidance.

Any order engenders the deviants whose activities might or do disrupt it. The moral organisation of families, groups of friends, communities and formal associations is simultaneously threatened and consolidated by their deviant members.[11] All such worlds tend to devise rudimentary or sophisticated means of identifying and managing deviancy in order to preserve the integrity of that moral organisation. An individual is thus continually beset by the possibility of becoming a local deviant.

There are a number of intersecting systems of rules which generate local deviancy. Within each social world there is a peculiar synthesis of individuated rules, general rules and foreign rules. Individuated rules stem from the more or less distinctive identity which a world confers upon each of its members. Roles are unique clusters of obligations and duties which are worked upon and transformed by their players. Role-playing is intelligible social behaviour, and intelligible social behaviour is constrained, orderly and predictable. Those who are unwilling or unable to maintain consistent roles are open to sanction. The rules that govern specific roles are so focused, adapted and negotiated that they are not immediately applicable to other roles. At another level, there are rules regulating the overall structure of intragroup relations. Although these are obviously translated into role-behaviour for their realisation, they refer to general properties of interaction as they are viewed through the world's particular perspective. They are not concerned with the proprieties of *specific* roles, but with those of general and standardised actions. There are differences between the ways in which a father, mother and children should behave. There are also routine expectations about how members of a family should behave. Similarly, within the organisation of a workplace, there is usually a well-defined system of rank and task. But work organisations themselves have recognisable styles of behaviour which distinguish them from one another.

The final rule system is foreign:

> . . . relationships may validate, redefine, or make irrelevant the rules from any other moral order—be that civil-legal, polite propriety, or another relationship of the same class. Herein lies their significance for the student of deviance, for they represent the ways in which members of any society make that society's rules of conduct meaningful in their daily interactions. Hence, each social relationship potentially contains a set of deviant values and ideologies which, if ever let out, would brand the member-participants as outsiders and deviants.[12]

Thus every moral world is also an organisation of rules current in settings outside itself. Out of the interplay between these modes of regulation there emerges a social control which is more or less binding and more or less categorical. A complex society is built on competing loyalties, priorities and postures which render many decisions morally problematic. Any person is the inhabitant of multiple social worlds and he frequently encounters conflicts of rules. An adherence to the structures of one moral system can always be represented as a betrayal of another.

Such conflict and potential deviancy must be continually neutralised if stable and uneventful relations between social worlds are to be possible. Without neutralisation, affairs could be peacefully conducted only when audiences are permanently segregated. Innumerable local deviancies are countenanced in everyday life. The moral bind of any minor world must be somewhat loosened if its members are to deal profitably with others foreign to it. It is this tacit recognition of the complexities wrought by moral diversity that makes social life viable. There must always be a class of local deviancies which a moral system recognises as excusable in particular circumstances. Few petty moral worlds can ever be categorical in their principles. The relaxation of moral constraints upon a world's members must be accompanied by an even greater tolerance towards nonmembers. Worlds differ in their demarcation of the size and content of the classes of permissible deviancies. Such demarcation will radically affect what a person must do in order to forfeit his membership of the world; it will also affect which groups of others members may safely and properly have relations with.

E

Of course, the chief determinant of the nature of demarcation is the degree to which moral worlds claim hegemony over their members' lives. Some groups attempt to serve as a comprehensive and total context for action. Contacts with other groups are reduced to a minimum for fear of contamination. Members' roles are progressively elaborated and expanded to isolate them from other kinds of experience. Such a response is typical of sectarian behaviour.[13] Thus, the Jehovah's Witnesses argue:

In an unrighteous society [outside] influence is not for your good and should be resisted. The closer you associate with such a community the more difficult will it be to combat its power to mould you to be like it. The safe course is to keep separate from it, and this can be done although you live in it.[14]

Similar control is exerted by those groups who are regarded as having an overarching position in the moral regulation of society. Their moral world is not parochial. Instead, they are entrusted with the overall coordination of petty worlds and cannot be permitted situational deviancy. Those groups which are presented as an integral part of the larger moral and symbolic fabric of society are regulated by unusually stringent systems of rules. They may stipulate that their members should not display any deviancy in any role whatsoever. Their hold on the member is not supposed to be released in any setting. Judges, civil servants and police officers are officially expected to act in such a way that no critical inference can be drawn about their moral *character*. Since any role-playing is taken to provide information about character and thus, by extension, the larger fabric, diffuse control can be exercised in defence of the wider order. A former Chief Constable of Sheffield remarked, for example:

. . . a great deal is asked of men who join the police. Every policeman lives, in a sense, a dedicated life. . . . He cannot merely perform certain routine duties during duty hours and consider that he has fulfilled his obligations. On the contrary, he is never free to behave irresponsibly at any time—to get drunk, for instance, or indulge in the sort of escapades which most young men are attracted to occasionally, or to hang around with pals who, while being excellent company, may not be above a little dishonesty now and then . . . the police officer in this country has to remember that he is a symbol of law and justice to other citizens, and, as such, he cannot permit himself ordinary peccadilloes which could be easily forgiven in other people.[15]

In many instances there is substantial compatibility between moral systems despite their differentiation. This is certainly the case with the deeper strata of rules. When the populations of different worlds agree upon common indices for identifying deviancy, or react suspiciously towards those who have been so identified by others, rule-breaking in one world can lead to penalties being inflicted in others. Here situationally permissible deviancies are also drastically reduced in number. The Teddy Boys, for instance, were systematically excluded from settings which they had not previously entered. The responses of those who had defined them as a social problem were taken as a warning by groups which had never encountered them. Understandings about the meanings of behaviour were diffused widely over local boundaries. One Teddy Boy recalled:

You started by being noisy and a bit of a show-off when you were with the others, you used a bit of bad language and had one or two fights amongst yourselves, and before you knew where you was the lot of you'd been told not to come around that place anymore—a cafe p'raps, or a cinema, something like that. Then you found people were even telling you not to come in to places before you'd ever been near them, they'd say if they saw you and your mates around they'd send for the Law straight off.[16]

When compatibility and consensus exist, deviancy generated in one world may well become deviancy in a whole system of worlds. When they do not exist, rule-breaking and its consequent status-forcing are localised. Deviants may then escape stigmatised positions by leaving one world and joining another. Despite the penal consequences of many such escapes (rule-breakers tend to acquire investments in their worlds), deviants of this sort are rarely involved in irreversible moral degradation. Nevertheless, whether consensus exists or not, few small worlds have the power to *impose* deviancy upon strangers. They have only a limited power over their *own* members. They depend instead on acquiescence with others and, more particularly, with the legal system. Although Simmons has observed, 'Almost every conceivable dimension of human behavior is considered deviant from the normative perspective of some existing persons and groups,'[17] few small groups have the power, authority or will to translate their beliefs into effective action against those whose acts they deplore. In a sense, many actions are simply the subject of a mute disapprobation felt by the powerless.

Law is a qualitatively different moral system. On occasion, it represents the moral order of a limited segment of society. On other occasions, it does represent something of a consensus of the majority. Different laws acquire different degrees of support from the society which they regulate. Some, like recent legislation on abortion, homosexuality and capital punishment, are expressions of an elitist culture. The main significance of law, however, is that it is imperialistic. It is buttressed by state agencies which enjoy a 'monopoly of the legitimate use of physical force'.[18] The edicts of a legal system are intended to cover the whole network of minor moral worlds irrespective of their acquiescence. Although other major moral codes attempt to achieve such a domination, law is the sole system which is vigorously enforced in a coercive fashion. The changing meanings of moral behaviour are not held to be of any moment to law. The only situational deviancies permitted legally are those covered by McNaghten, doctrines of *mens rea* and the like. There is no accommodation to situational morality. There is instead a categorical code which overrides every other. It is this facet of a legal system that generates the institutional agencies of control such as the police and prison services.

THE DIVERSITY OF LAWS

Just as social rules are varied in their structure and composition, so laws are anything but homogeneous. Few generalisations can be usefully made about the corporate body of laws. Laws differ in their intention and significance, their effects, their mode of development and in the extent to which people acquire commitments to their perpetuation and enforcement. Whilst the litter laws and laws on murder share some of the features which I have described, little else can be stated about them *qua* law. Instead, it is wise to distinguish between forms of law so that more internally consistent units are produced. One of the most satisfactory ways of breaking legal phenomena down into manageable parts is to construct a typology which focuses on the parts played by legislative inspiration, the intended consequences of legislation, and the actual consequences of legislation as they are realised in critical enforcement situations.*

Legislative inspiration is captured by Durkheim's distinction between retributive and restitutive justice. Retributive justice flows from the reactions expressed against particular deviancies committed in particular kinds of social structure. It is coloured by the *collective* nature of the response which deviancy evokes:

As for the social character of this reaction, it comes from the social nature of the offended sentiments. Because they are found in all consciences, the infraction committed arouses in those who have evidence of it or who learn of its existence the same indignation. Everybody is attacked; consequently everybody opposes the attack. Not only is the reaction general, but it is collective, which is not the same thing. It is not produced isolatedly in each one, but with a totality and a unity. . . .[19]

Retributive justice is a feature of relatively homogeneous societies, based on 'mechanical solidarity', in which moral worlds are not

* I am most grateful to Miss M. Durward, who suggested a substantial modification to my original scheme.

fragmented and reactions are relatively uniform. It is also to be discovered when deviancy breaks rules which stem from the deeper strata of a normative structure. Within even pluralist societies, there is a substantial unity centred around fundamental rules. Where sentiments are shared, affronts engender a response which is heightened by an awareness of common hostility to the rule-breaker. Hostility is not individual but reflected and reinforced in the known responses of others.

Restitutive justice, by contrast, marks a system of social control which is not buttressed by strongly held collective sentiments based on likemindedness. It is a means of adjusting relations rather than punishing the malefactor; it maintains a balance between disparate groups which are not united by a firm consensus:

> What distinguishes this sanction is that it is not expiatory, but consists of a simple *return in state*. Sufferance proportionate to the misdeed is not inflicted on the one who has violated the law or who disregards it; he is simply sentenced to comply with it. If certain things were done, the judge reinstates them as they would have been. He speaks of law; he says nothing of punishment. Damage-interests have no penal character; they are only a means of reviewing the past in order to reinstate it, as far as possible, to its normal form.[20]

Retributive justice characterises comparatively undifferentiated communities whilst restitutive justice emanates from complex societies structured by 'organic solidarity'. The latter also typifies attempts to regulate novel or noncontentious surface phenomena which are regulated by upper layers of rules. Retributive law is closer to a formal codification of the mores; restitutive law is a relatively deliberate and 'artificial' effort which organises relations that are not taken for granted. Both types exist in any one complex society: deviancies like murder, rape, assault and robbery exact a 'mechanical' response; and fraud, motoring and parking offences are likely to exact an 'organic' response.

It is interesting that retributive manifestations of law can have 'spurious' and 'genuine' forms. Powerful but atypical moral worlds can find support in law. They may react in a retributive manner towards deviancies about which there is no society-wide consensus. Durkheim's retributive justice was most fully realised in a society without a systematic division of labour. The inhabitants of internally fragmented communities are unlikely to be unanimous in their condemnation of all officially proscribed deviancies. Instead, some of the fragments display retributive reactions whilst others do not. When those who do display these reactions also make law, the initiative for the rules may be regarded as pseudo-mechanical in nature. There is probably virtually complete consensus in Britain about the shocking quality of murder, but dissensus exists about marihuana smoking. The penalties that are inflicted on the marihuana smoker are nevertheless punitive and consequential for him.

The conflict over the nature of law in a fragmented society was presumably the basis of the dispute between Hart and Devlin over the proper sphere of the criminal law. Devlin asserted, 'The criminal law as we know it is based upon moral principle. In a number of crimes its function is simply to enforce a moral principle and nothing else.' He furthered the doctrine of a retributive control over a wide range of behaviour by stating, 'The suppression of vice is as much the law's business as the suppression of subversive activities; it is no more possible to define a sphere of private morality than it is to define one of private subversive activity.'[21] As a jurist, he put forward a view of society which is organised around mechanical solidarity. The enforcement of laws against 'crimes without victims' is an expression of a consensus which exists in societies which are homogeneous enough to agree upon basic moral principles. Hart, however, conjures up an image of a community which is composed of diverse moral worlds. The enforcement of morals is nothing more than the act of an imperialistic moral world which seeks to dominate others. His is a society welded together by organic solidarity, and it thereby converts Devlin's mechanical control into a pseudo-mechanical form:

... a right to be protected from the distress which is inseparable from the knowledge that others are acting in ways you think wrong, cannot be acknowledged by anyone who recognises individual liberty as a value. For the extension of the utilitarian principle that coercion may be used to protect men from harm, so as to include their protection from this form of distress, cannot stop there. If distress incident to the belief that others are doing wrong is harm, so also is the distress incident to the belief that others are doing what you do not want them to do. To punish people for causing this form of distress would be tantamount to punishing them simply because others object to what they do; and the only liberty that could coexist with this extension of the utilitarian principle is liberty to do those things to which no one seriously objects.[22]

While mechanical and pseudo-mechanical laws have a retributive quality, it does not follow that a retributive control machinery is necessarily set up to implement them. Another feature of the typology must therefore emphasise legislative intent. It is useful to distinguish between symbolic and instrumental law. Not all law is enacted in the expectation that vigorous enforcement will ensue. Some legislation is designed primarily to affirm values, and it is therefore a largely expressive or symbolic display. Other laws are expressly intended to be activated. Rule-breakers are supposed to confront not only symbolic censure but also a range of penalties:

> . . . acts of officials, legislative enactments, and court decisions often affect behavior in an instrumental manner through a direct influence on the actions of peoples. . . . The instrumental function of such laws lies in their enforcement; unenforced they have little effect. . . . Symbolic aspects of law and government do not depend on enforcement for their effect. . . . The symbolic act 'invites consideration rather than overt reactions'. There is a dimension of meaning in symbolic behavior which is not given in its immediate and manifest significance but in what the action connotes for the audience that views it. . . . In analyzing laws as symbolic we are oriented less to behavioral consequences as a means to a fixed end; more to meaning as an act, a decision, a gesture important in itself.[23]

It is most unlikely that symbolic and instrumental laws are always and everywhere completely distinct categories. A strenuously enforced instrumental law is liable to become an end in itself both to its control agencies and to the larger society. It will acquire a symbolic significance which complements its 'purely' instrumental quality. As Blumberg remarks, 'Vested interests in deviance of all kinds tend to develop over a period of time . . . creating systems of deviance management and control which foster the growth of an industry and an attendant bureaucratic apparatus for its nurture, and dependent on it for political, psychic, religious or other forms of income.'[24] When an instrumental law is handed over to a specail agency for enforcement, that agency can well rework the meaning of the law so that it acquires a significance which is more pregnant than was intended by legislators.

Similarly, symbolic laws can be consequential in their positioning of scarecrows around the frontiers of deviancy. According to Matza, the mere act of ban does more than invite consideration:

> That ban imbues an activity with guilt is hardly surprising or unintended. The moral transformation of activity is the purpose of ban; the simplest way of summarizing the legislative and purportedly public attention is to predict that with time the activity will exist in guilt. . . . A self-evident consequence of so moral an act as ban is to restrict and discourage access to the designated phenomena at the invitational edge. An inculcated attitude of avoidance is intended by the sovereign and it would be the height of folly to imagine that a ban did not work towards that end.[25]

By publicly casting a particular role as deviant, an authoritative law-maker can translate the role player into a morally degraded outsider. Much social control in our society is structured by a rich demonology of deviant types. It often matters little whether the deviants are actively pursued. Rather, patterns of avoidance and fear can be generated by a legitimated act of classification:

. . . there are some categories that have an unusually strong ability to influence the judgement of a total person. These categories are so strong that men often cannot see any other part of the individual as independent of it. Such is the case with moral categories. . . . A moral category provides more than a partial identity of the person so characterized. It is more than simply a way of emphasizing and addressing a person in particular circumstances and situations. The moral category infuses every situation. . . .[26]

Whilst placement in a moral category can be consequential for the deviant and can influence how he is treated in other deviant roles structured by instrumental law, the enforcement that is activated by instrumental law has a qualitatively different impact on the rule-breaker. Threatened or real intervention in a deviant's affairs poses problems and restricts possibilities of action in a way that cannot be generated by an experience of guilt or shame alone. At the least, secondary deviation is more probable when law breaking is accompanied by a mechanical or pseudo-mechanical reaction which takes the form of instrumental law.

The final plank of the typology pays attention to the way in which law is actually translated into action by those who are entrusted with its enforcement. Obviously, any law can be managed by a number of agencies which impose different meanings upon it. The implementation of a law may entail the coordination of diverse institutions which display a variety of responses. Yet the intention of legislators may be realised or thwarted by the activities of one or more critical control agencies which play key roles in the enforcement process. Retributive or restitutive laws can be radically modified as they are taken up and applied in concrete situations. An understanding of the sources and intent of laws is incomplete until it is learned how those laws receive practical expression.

Organic laws with an ostensibly restitutive function can become instruments of retribution, for example. In an enforcement setting, definitions and assumptions can arise which are punitive towards the rule breaker. Secondary attributes of the rule breaker or the infraction itself prompt hostility which evokes more of the mechanical than the organic.[27] A rule-breaker's demeanour, stigma or stereotype can transform the execution of an administrative and neutral law into a matter of great moral significance to the law-enforcer. The enforcement agency may be so transformed by the routine difficulties which it encounters that a mechanical solidarity emerges to engender retributive justice. Debt-collectors,[28] factory inspectors[29] and traffic wardens may all, in time, redefine the meaning of particular laws and pursue deviants with a moral fervour more redolent of a desire to punish than of a concern with simple management. In the case of traffic wardens, for instance:

... cars begin to transform themselves from cars into biographical data concerning their and others' mutual experiences. On seeing such a vehicle a warden will recount a series of past events . . . which will permeate any future encounter he has with it. Cars begin to be sieved into a rudimentary classification of overlapping types. . . . [There are] the 'non-stayer' and 'sneaky' types. The commonest type, however, is the 'regular'—the driver who is always getting a ticket, but rarely uses complex, evasive tactics to avoid detection. Regulars can be subdivided into 'disgruntled regulars' and 'pleasant regulars'. To quote a traffic warden, the disgruntled regular is the 'motorist who knows the score [rules] but takes his tickets badly'. He is personally abusive if the warden is present. In the warden's absence he can communicate his feelings perfectly well by shredding his ticket and leaving the pieces in the gutter.[30]

Within the traffic warden's world, therefore, there is a crude differentiation of social and deviant types. Some of these types, such as the 'disgruntled regular', prompt a punitive response and an organic rule will have received effective redefinition. This kind of shift need not be an immediate result of the content or purpose of the rule itself; it can, instead, arise from everyday enforcement contingencies. Any ostensibly neutral law can be difficult to enforce and, when those difficulties are attributed to qualities of a deviant population, a desire for retribution emerges.

Just as any complex society contains rules which do not categorically belong to either the symbolic or the instrumental types of law, so there are many rules which cannot be neatly described as simply mechanical or organic in origin. Recent changes in the laws on homosexuality in England and Wales are an example of anomaly. It is more profitable to regard the pure mechanical and the pure organic as polar cases on a continuum.* Any one law can move its position on that continuum. There is a continuous series of shifts of law. In America, for instance, drugs were initially regulated by an organic law which became pseudo-mechanical and then mechanical. The practical translation of laws into rules-in-use is often responsible[31] for such movements. The actions of control institutions and organisations structurally linked to them can rework the meanings of much legislation. The press, for instance, can create 'crime waves' and

* Indeed, no society can probably be described as entirely mechanical or entirely organic in its mode of integration. As Coser remarks of complex societies, 'if it is affirmed *a priori* that the major social norms express the sentiments of the total collectivity, then one cannot recognize conflicting norms within a society; one cannot take cognizance of clashing values; one is unable to understand . . . that certain subordinated strata may accept a norm only because they passively submit to it, whereas it is the genuine expression of the moral sentiment of only a superordinate stratum'. (L. Coser, 'Durkheim's Conservatism and Its Implications', in *Continuities in the Study of Social Conflict*, Free Press, New York, 1967, p. 164.)

'moral panics' which alter the significance of laws. Control institutions themselves engage in covert or overt attempts to change key publics' stances towards the tasks which they perform. As Gusfield argues, definitions of deviancy are subject to constant negotiation:

... deviance designations have histories; the public definition of behavior is itself changeable. It is open to reversals of political power, twists of public opinion, and the development of social movements and moral crusades. What is attacked as criminal today may be seen as sick next year and fought over as possibly legitimate by the next generation. Movements to redefine behavior may eventuate in a moral passage, a transition of the behavior from one moral status to another.[32]

The resulting typology distinguishes between twelve forms of law:

Source	Legislative intent	Definitive enforcement style	
		Retributive	Restitutive
Mechanical solidarity	Symbolic	1	2
	Instrumental	3	4
Pseudo-mechanical solidarity	Symbolic	5	6
	Instrumental	7	8
Organic solidarity	Symbolic	9	10
	Instrumental	11	12

The 1920 Volstead Act which introduced Prohibition to America exemplifies a pseudo-mechanical symbolic law which was not enforced in a retributive manner (type 6). It was pseudo-mechanical in that it was prompted by a moral fervour which was confined to very few of America's moral worlds:

During prohibition many drinkers felt that forbidding drinking was an arbitrary assertion of State authority, based upon an unrealistic conception of alcohol and its effects. The accuracy of that assertion aside, it is important to understand that for sanctions to be meaningful they must be considered by potential violators as having a rational basis. Usually, when a sanction is invoked for a given activity, reasons are given for sanctioning that activity. If large groups in the population do not believe that the activity is wrong or harmful, especially if the 'reasons' do not stand up to experience, the rule loses its authoritative character.[33]

The law was symbolic in that it acted as a public affirmation of the moral superiority of the Prohibitionist moral world[34] but was never designed to be properly enforced. According to Sinclair, 'there was never any serious effort to enforce national prohibition until the early thirties, and by that time it was too late'.[35] Very little of the enforcement waged against bootleggers and speakeasies was vigorous. On the contrary, it was a period distinguished by exceptional corruption.*

Instances of the other types would include laws against incest (type 1)—the laws relating to incest cannot be readily organised by instrumental law because the discovery of the deviancy by outsiders is most difficult; the many capital offences of the early nineteenth century which were neutralised by juries reluctant to convict (2); laws relating to murder (3); a corrupt policing agency which refuses to pursue strenuous enforcement against consensually deplored criminals (4). Laws against homosexuality before the recent reforms could represent a marginal instance of legislation which did not reflect the pluralism of contemporary Britain; their implementation was always sporadic but it was occasionally marked by a retributive stance (type 5).† Many laws directed against the coloured and black populations of South Africa and Rhodesia can be characterised as examples of type 7. The enforcement of laws against marihuana is assuming an increasingly ritualistic quality in America and the retributive element appears to be ever slighter (type 8); the Race Relations Act should be construed as a piece of symbolic organic legislation which is applied in restitutive fashion (type 10); the early enforcement of the American Harrison Act of 1914 represents the enthusiastic activities of an agency which was set up to supervise fiscal and other details of the interstate traffic in drugs (type 11); the litter laws may be seen as organic laws which are primarily exhortatory in nature (type 10); and organic instrument laws which have a retributive character are represented by civil law relating to debts (type 12).

The usefulness of this classification is twofold. It is clear that the typology is clumsy and unwieldy, and its very ungainliness underlines the difficulties of confidently making assertions about law as a single entity. I believe that it is more prudent to describe the evolution and qualities of homogeneous *types* of law rather than embark on massive generalisation. Secondly, the classification directs attention at those laws which are likely to make the greatest contribution to the creation of deviant roles. While symbolic laws can become instrumental laws, and while they proffer authoritative definitions of correct behaviour,

* Thus Edgar Hoover observed of the FBI at that time, 'those of us who were honest kept quiet about where we worked. We didn't want people to think we were crooks.' Quoted in A. Hynd, *Con Man*, Paperback Library, New York, 1962, p. 104.

† For an interesting description of such retributive behaviour being experienced by a homosexual, see P. Wildeblood, *Against the Law*, Weidenfeld & Nicolson, London, 1955.

they are less likely to structure the social worlds of deviants and non-deviants. When laws are impelled by the reactions which stem from an affront to general or parochial mores, they will be enforced with a vigour which is most fateful for the deviant. They also bear with them the possibility of a moral reclassification of the deviant. Secondary deviation and the stabilisation of deviant behaviour are most likely to occur when types 3, 7 and 11 are brought into being through law-giving and law-enforcing, and it is with types 7 and 11 that the rest of this chapter will be predominantly concerned. These categories of law are not only the embodiment of a minority's world-views, they are also of the greatest moment to *changing* conceptions of deviancy. If the law were simply a reflection of a consensus or were inconsequential in the shaping of deviant roles, many of the problems of the sociology of deviancy would be much less taxing or interesting.

LAW AND POWER

The ideal-type of lawgiving which I shall offer in this chapter makes light of many of the difficulties entailed in an adequate description of power and social control. I shall proceed as if it were possible to discern one or two relatively distinct moral positions held by those who have access to legal machinery. I shall assume that legislators constitute a reasonably homogeneous group, an assumption which would not hold in more detailed analysis. In Schutz's terminology, my legislators are puppets or *homunculi* who are endowed with just enough substance to sustain an argument.[36] Nevertheless, a brief discussion must sacrifice sophistication and my homunculi may not violate understanding too much.

Power and privilege are unevenly distributed in a complex society. They are typically grounded in institutional structures which are themselves hierarchically organised. Amongst the network of moral worlds that makes up a society, therefore, particular groups enjoy unusual structural advantages in the exercise of power. They have acquired the capacity to impose their own conceptions of proper order on others. While the populations of most of a society's fragments are relatively impotent, those of a few are armed with a coercive apparatus which extends their dominion over a wide area.

At one level, it can be shown that laws are applied to further the peculiar interests of the powerful. Power is the ability of individuals to exert their will over others. It structures the flow and content of decisions which are made about the tolerable limits of behaviour in a group. Those with the least power can expect to have the greatest number of constraints imposed upon them by the criminal law. 'In the making of law, in their ability to secure protection under the law, and in advantages accruing from discretion in its enforcement, those with the greatest political and economic power benefit the most. Thus, the young and the economically and politically impotent have been the primary focus of attention . . . of laws.'[37]

Laws frequently mirror the forms of domination and subordination which prevail within a society. Laws which are supportive and neutral in their consequences for these forms are more likely to be enacted than those which are disruptive. Those which are not supportive are likely to be opposed. Unthreatening proposals may be actively championed or simply allowed to become effective without any intervention from the powerful. In a discussion of his own work on the English vagrancy laws and Jerome Hall's study of English theft laws, Chambliss observes:

In both these cases . . . the interest groups were sufficiently influential and sufficiently powerful (representing, as they did, the upper classes of the society) that their ability to influence legislation stemmed from the fact that the legislators and judges never questioned the desirability of passing laws which would benefit these groups. Consequently, no organized intervention by these social classes was really necessary to bring about legislation favorable to them.[38]

The powerful not only master law-making and law-enforcing institutions, they also control the channels which afford others access to these institutions.[39] Thus, although the initiative for making changes in the legal system does not always have to emanate from those in the higher positions of the social structure, power can manifest itself in the way in which the fate of that initiative is resolved. Whatever the source of potential legislative change may be, it is reasonable to suppose that the social organisation of power will influence the content, aims and scope of law. In the case of the American economic system, for instance, Weinstein claims:

Businessmen were not always, or even normally, the first to advocate reforms in the common interest. The original impetus for many reforms came from those at or near the bottom of the American social structure, from those who benefited least from the rapid increase in the productivity of the industrial plant of the United States. . . . But in the current century, particularly on the federal level, few reforms were enacted without the tacit approval, if not the guidance, of the large corporate interests. And much more important, businessmen were able to harness to their own ends the desires of intellectuals and middle-class reformers to bring together 'thoughtful men of all classes' in 'a vanguard for the building of the good community'. These ends were the stabilization, and continued expansion of the existing political economy, and subsumed under that, the circumscription of the Socialist movement. . . .[40]

Although I shall offer arguments expressing why I am dissatisfied with the idea that law is simply a direct embodiment of vested interests, it is clear that much legislation in America (and elsewhere) was governed by the concerns that Weinstein describes.[41] Indeed, it would be surprising if it were not. Something of this systematic bias in favour of the powerful appears in most areas of rule-making and rule-breaking. After all, if power is defined by a capacity to make and apply effective rules, such a bias is axiomatically built into social structure. The issues with which the law is concerned are quite frequently protection of the existing distribution of power and attacks on those who threaten its moral, economic and social basis.

Other contributors to such bias are the resources which the respectable and powerful can muster in minimising reactions to their own rule-breaking or, indeed, in preventing behaviour from falling under the aegis of the criminal law at all. The deviancy of the middle and upper classes is not infrequently associated with the pursuit of professional, institutional or entrepreneurial goals. When such deviancy is normalised as a stable feature of such occupational settings, the supporting service structures which are attached to the occupations may be deployed to aid the apprehended deviant. Legal, financial and other supports are available to the deviant in an unusually generous fashion. In many cases, too, the deviancy is simply not patrolled by conventional control agencies. As Douglas states:

Every significant urban [American] police force has a vice squad and a narcotics squad, but no police force has a 'professional squad', a 'medical squad', or a 'lawyer squad'.* Doctors, lawyers, and other professionals and businessmen are allowed to police themselves, so that their criminal activities do not often become officially categorized as crimes, whereas the lower classes have their policing done for them by the police.[42]

When deviancy is located in such occupational settings, moreover, conflicts of moral rules throw ambiguity on the meaning of the behaviour. The deviancy may be so routinised and so integrally a part of otherwise reputable activity that it is not easily separable as discreditable. Such deviants are also members of social strata and groups which tend to be awarded high moral status. The dissonance between the deviancy of a specific infraction and general respectability inhibits the ready imputation of immorality. In the case of violators of regulations governing the American black market during the Second World War, Mansfield states, 'The vast majority of them were respected members of their community. They were not professional criminals—on the contrary, they were regarded and regarded

---

* This is not perhaps strictly true (of Britain anyway); the police do maintain Fraud Squads and so on.

themselves as staunch supporters of the constituted order.'[43] Although the younger expressive deviants often emanate from the middle classes, other deviancies committed by relatively powerful groups are not marked by the visibility of expressive deviation. Again, compared with expressive and other visible deviants, these groups are capable of achieving a quiet accommodation with social control agencies. The 'impersonal' nature of their offences, coupled with the institutional setting in which they are committed, tends to neutralise the personal animus which characterises much reaction to deviancy. Reactions to behaviour are often stimulated by its garish and conspicuous nature and by the low status of those who display it:

In studying the problem-defining reactions of the community, it can be shown that public consciousness of 'problems' and aggregate moral reactions frequently center around forms of behavior which on closer analysis prove to be of minor importance in the social system. Conversely, community members not infrequently ignore behavior which is a major disruptive influence in their lives. We are all familiar with the way in which populations in various cities have been aroused to frenzied punitive action against sex offenders. Nevertheless, in these same areas the people as a whole often are indifferent toward crimes committed by businessmen or corporations—crimes which affect far more people and which may be far more serious over a period of time.[44]

There are other modes of defence available to the powerful. They can use physical and symbolic shields to disguise their activity or portray it as innocuous. In many cases, too, they are covered by special rules which are enforced with particular discretion and mildness. As Sutherland remarks:

Wealthy persons can employ skilled attorneys and in other ways influence the administration of justice in their own favor more effectively than can persons of the lower socio-economic class. . . . Much more important is the bias involved in the administration of criminal justice under laws which apply exclusively to business and the professions and which therefore involve only the upper socio-economic class. In America persons who violate laws regarding restraint of trade, advertising, pure food and drugs are not arrested by uniformed policemen, are not often tried in the criminal courts, and are not committed to prison; their illegal behavior generally receives the attention of administrative commissions and of courts operating under civil or equity jurisdiction.[45]

It is clear that my discussion has been something of an elaborated tautology. It does not substantially advance our understanding of the generation of legal rules. Adequate analysis would have to distinguish between and comprehend those groups who regularly engage in the interactions which culminate in law production. It would have to make possible the plotting out of typical sequences of law-making activity. It would focus on the taken-for-granted worlds of legislators and linked groups; account for their origins, maintenance and development; and assess how consensual was their basis. The absence of a sensitive differentiation between groups whose power is derived from access to economic, religious, military, political and other sources merely leads to simplistic speculation about movements of legislation. It cannot be maintained that there is a simple harmony which unites the diverse worlds of the powerful.

Yet I have necessarily bracketed all this intellectual terrain. Instead, I have pointed to one elementary feature of law, its emergence from asymmetrical power relations. Even so elementary a feature as this is not part of the conventional thinking of many legal theorists. I believe that much existing sociology of law can be dichotomised into naïve conspiracy theory and naïve consensus theory. The one poses an image of society which is dominated by an intellectualised version of International Freemasonry; a knowing, self-interested and capable elite. The other acknowledges virtually no structural or moral differentiation within society. Societal norms attain legal expression without mediation. There is, as it were, a magical transition from consensus to legal code. It is against this dichotomy that I have constructed my argument. In this section I have indicated the merest skeleton of the power dimensions of a legally ordered society. In succeeding sections I shall demonstrate how this skeleton is no guide *in itself* to the understanding of law. Neither the conspiracy nor the consensus theorists have attained mastery over the problem of what law, as a set of enforceable definitions of deviant phenomena, can be shown to consist of.

LAW AND AUTHORITY

In stable, complex societies, the coercive face of power is usually masked or partially replaced by a set of legitimations which exact a more or less willing compliance from the ruled:

Though force is the most effective instrument for seizing power in a society, and though it always remains the foundation of any system of inequality, it is not the most effective instrument for retaining and exploiting a position of power and deriving the maximum benefits from it. Therefore, regardless of the objectives of a . . . regime, once organized opposition has been destroyed it is to its advantage to make increasing use of other techniques . . . of control, and to allow force to recede into the background to be used only when other techniques fail.[46]

Similarly, McCleery remarks, 'In a stable social system . . . an "authoritative allocation of values" in that society becomes a matter of the creation and circulation of definitions rather than a matter of the application of force'.[47] In such societies, as I have argued, the 'authoritative allocation of values' receives its authority from at least two sources; the legitimacy of the forms of power and the legitimacy of the wielders of power. There is subordination to principles and to people.

These two sources are substantially interdependent; moral principles receive some of their structure and force from those who enunciate them, and enunciators receive authority and credibility from their utterances and acts. As principles become established, they grow progressively detached from their authors. They acquire anonymity and independent facticity but, in their initial stages, they can be discredited as invalid because of their identification with a particular human parentage. The legitimacy of legislators is based on a set of concepts which defend their right to rule. In a morally diverse world, an uncoerced peace can be achieved only when those in power are recognised as qualitatively superior to their subordinates. There are abundant means of claiming such superiority, but I shall focus on those three prevailing in industrialised societies which are grounded in a legal-rational order. The first means is the claim to moral superiority.

Moral superiority

If society is viewed as a stratified system of moral worlds, the system itself can be identified as a moral order which supports its parts. Compliance with this larger order must be elicited from the subordinate worlds and, in a stable society, such wider allegiance is generally obtained. 'Norms and values especially prevalent within a given class must direct behavior into channels that support the general class differential.'[48] When force is not the major defence of hierarchy, some voluntary recognition of the propriety of disprivilege must have been given. This being so, power in a legitimated stratification system will be accompanied by high moral standing. The powerful are usually located in communication networks at points which provide them with generous amounts of information; they can manipulate many of the symbols which evoke respect; and they are highly successful by achievement or ascriptive standards.[49] Wielding the law, they are doubly able to claim ethical worth. Becker states:

In any system of ranked groups, participants take it as given that members of the highest group have the right to define the way things really are ... from the point of view of a well socialized participant in the system, any tale told by those at the top intrinsically deserves to be regarded as the most credible account obtainable of the [system's] workings. And since ... matters of rank and status are contained in the mores, this belief has a

moral quality. We are, if we are proper members of the group, morally
bound to accept the definition imposed on reality by a superordinate group
in preference to the definitions espoused by subordinates. . . . Thus,
credibility and the right to be heard are differentially distributed through
the ranks of the system.[50]

It follows that only the powerful or the potentially powerful are
provided with the requisite stature to challenge the hierarchy's moral
structure. Outsiders and the impotent tend to be dismissed as illegitimate critics who have little right to reject the highest group's definitions or offer alternative moral perspectives. Indeed, even when an
issue is not defined in moral terms, it may become so defined if it
threatens the conceptual basis on which the hierarchy is built. 'The
men who govern must do so by "right". Any issue which is believed
to possibly alter the "right" to be on top is a likely candidate as a
moral issue in which men have strong commitments.'[51] Those who
resist either the specific content or legitimacy of deviant labels are
unlikely to be successful because they confront both a power structure and a moral system. In any case, very few deviants are ever total
strangers to that moral system and they may still accept its general
strictures although they challenge particular features:

Leviathan may have its say even when disobeyed. In making [deviant]
activity guilty, Leviathan bedevils the subject as he proceeds and thus is
partly compensated for its gross failure to deter. Under an authority more
weighty than his own, the subject will come to act as if innocent affiliation
with guilty activity is untenable—even if he does not see it in precisely that
way and despite the fact that he and his collaborators may claim to see
little guilt in the activity.[52]

Those who *are* successful in their challenge to Leviathan tend to be
equal in status to the definers. Those who can reject attempts to
impose the deviant label, foster guilt and exact submission must be
either very numerous or very powerful. Thus Bordua comments on
Erikson's study of witchcraft in Puritan New England:

. . . in the case of witchcraft prosecutions, not only were observers convinced that the accused were witches, but the accused seemed convinced
also. The witchcraft accusations came to have less and less defining criter-
iality, however, as the finger was pointed at persons eminent about whom
the accusations made much less 'sense'—persons whose eminence, we
might suppose, provided them not only with social protection from the
accusation but also self-protection. They seem to have had sufficient self-
esteem to refuse to entertain any self-doubt.[53]

Disinterestedness

The second support for the powerful is their alleged disinterestedness.
As I have argued, through reification the law can change the parochial

into the universal and the instrumental into the ultimate good. Those who make laws are already equipped to claim a disinterested stance. The criminal law supports this stance in another way. It tends to redefine the victims of deviancy.* In a crude sense, it may be argued that conceptions of the victim depend upon a society's organisation of power. A society which lacks a centralised, bureaucratised system of social control can do little to protect those who are harmed by deviants. The victim's defence lies not with state institutions but with smaller, more intimate groups such as the family, clan or local community. Redress must usually be obtained through personal confrontation:

> The basis of primitive and early Western law was personal reparation by the offender or the offender's family to the victim. When political institutions were largely based upon kinship ties or tribal organization, and when there was an absence of a central authority to determine guilt, and the form of punishment, some forms of revenge, blood-feud, vendetta, or pecuniary compensation were common practices.[54]

Thus, in a society without a clearly formulated and effective system of criminal law enforcement, the victims of deviancy were typically portrayed in personal terms. The specific groups who were harmed had to proclaim themselves. The state or 'society' were not victimised; instead an individual or kinship group was made the sufferer. With the consolidation of power structures, however, there appeared an interesting shift in the nature of the victim. Feudalism tended to reshape the nature of the relationship between the deviant and his victim. As power was assumed by ecclesiastical and secular authorities, the personal victim declined in importance. 'It was chiefly owing to the violent greed of feudal barons and medieval ecclesiastical powers that the rights of the injured party were gradually infringed upon, and finally to a large extent, appropriated by these authorities . . . the original victim was practically ignored.'[55]

The growing importance of central, regal authority accelerated this process. The king represented the apex of the power hierarchy and was closely identified with a reified state. The intense concentration of power in kingship generated an even more abstract victimology.[56] Deviancy was no longer the concern of individuals, but a matter that bound the offender and the state together. Jeudwine argued that a conception of the victimised state was entertained as early as the twelfth century when 'the Western world suddenly ceased to regard murder, arson, rape, and theft as regrettable torts which

---

* What follows is a compression of an important argument. For a much fuller treatment of the problem, see S. Schafer, *The Victim and His Criminal*, Random House, New York, 1968, especially his section entitled 'The Golden Age of the Victim'. My own argument is based on this work.

should be compensated by payment to the family—such and other offences came to be regarded not only as sins for which a penance was required by the Church, but as a crime against society at large to be prosecuted by the community through its chief. . . .'[57] Thus the very manifestation of deviancy in its clearest form, crime, was made possible by the creation of a metaphysical conception of social damage. The very term 'crime' connotes the appropriation of a judgmental function by the powerful.

The transformation of the victim, according to Ranulf, was further accelerated by the growing power of the bourgeoisie. An increasingly efficient and centralised control system was accompanied by a tendency to define an ever wider range of deviancies as crimes. The moral indignation of an ascendant middle class revealed itself in Reformation England as a crusade which criminalised activity in the name of the public good. This 'disinterested tendency to inflict punishment'[58] was a reflection of the ever closer identification of the powerful with the society they controlled. Thus deviancies became the subject of the criminal law and, as crimes, they were treated as wrongs inflicted on an abstraction—society. As Duster argues, 'Gradually, the middle-classes succeeded in establishing the principle that the general and anonymous community had its own interests in the prosecution of criminals.'[59] The specific moral world which had activated the system of labelling was lost behind its image as a dis-interested servant of the state or collectivity.* Only in civil law and the law of torts did a vestige of the personal victim remain. Definitions of crime tend to emphasise the universal threat it presents rather than its parochial aspects.† 'It is in the situation of a very powerful party opposing a very weak one that the powerful party sponsors the *idea* that the weak party is breaking the rules of society. The very concepts of "society" and its "rules" are appropriated by powerful parties and made synonomous with their interests.'[60]

It may well be true that most criminal laws are, in fact, instru-

---

* Thus Maruyama remarks, 'it is an outstanding characteristic of the European liberal *idea* of the state that it is neutral, that it adopts a *neutral* position in internal values, such as the problem of what truth and justice are; it leaves the choice and judgment of all values of this sort to special social groups . . . or to the conscience of the individual. The real basis of national sovereignty is a purely "formal" legal structure, divorced from all questions of internal value.' (M. Maruyama, *Thought and Behaviour in Japanese Politics*, Oxford University Press, London, 1963, p. 3.)

† Thus, in a classic definition, Blackstone stated, '. . . public wrongs, or crimes and misdemeanors, are a breach and violation of the public rights and duties due to the whole community, in its social aggregate capacity . . . treason, murder, and robbery are properly ranked among crimes; since besides the injury done the individual, they strike at the very being of society.' (W. Blackstone, *Commentaries on the Laws of England*, Clarendon Press, Oxford 1778, Book iv, p. 5.)

mental in preventing social harm. Yet it is mistaken to assume that law is enacted solely from a position of Olympian detachment. The transformation of behaviour into *crime* must be understood largely as a result of a moral world's active interpretation of that behaviour. It cannot be usefully discussed as if it were no more than a straightforward and rational response of a society to threatening acts. The emergence of law is founded on processes which mediate between behaviour, its construction as threatening by the powerful, and its translation into crime.

Representativeness

The third main legitimation of power-holders is their claim to representativeness, a claim which is clearly linked to ideas of superiority and disinterestedness. What is represented differs from society to society. It is rarely a simple numerical preponderance of the population (even if the perspectives of that preponderance could ever be assessed). Instead, it is usually the 'best' or the 'truest' traditions of a community. The ruled cannot resent the system which disprivileges them because their will, or some commendable facet of their will, moulds the decisions which are taken about them. The legislator is either subordinate to them or else he acts properly and 'in their own interests'. He does not behave capriciously or selfishly but with a regard to what deserves to be promoted and preserved.

Two examples, that of Russia and America, may serve to illustrate this kind of legitimacy. Both states have deliberately attempted to engineer new social systems populated by new kinds of men. They have used force to mould the old society into a new form. Both have been governed by élites which have claimed an infallible source of direction which legitimates their sovereignty and actions. Both have acted in the best interests of their populations.

After 1917 in Russia, power was administered by a 'dictatorship of the proletariat' which directly represented the true interests of the working class. Those who resisted such a regime were moral and social outcasts, in the same way as Talmon claimed Rousseau's conception of the 'people' excluded those who were hostile to the dominant interpretation of the 'general will'. 'The idea of a people becomes naturally restricted to those who identify themselves with the general will and the general interest. Those outside are not really of the nation. They are aliens.'[61] Power in Czarist Russia had been exercised by groups who were to become aliens in this sense. They were the restraints which imposed themselves on the emerging new society. '*Simultaneously*, with an immediate expansion of democracy, which *for the first time* becomes democracy for the poor, democracy for the people, and not democracy for the moneybags, the dictatorship of the proletariat imposes a series of restrictions on the freedom of the oppressors, the exploiters, the capitalists. We must suppress them in order to free humanity from wage slavery, their resistance must be crushed by force. . . .'[62]

Those who are to be emancipated and enfranchised are the proletariat, those whose legitimacy is totally withdrawn are representatives of a kind of ghost society which is fused with but not of the true society as it is represented by the Soviet legislator. Criminals and deviants in Russia are explained as anachronisms or as the contaminated. They emanate from the capitalist society which preceded Bolshevism or the capitalist societies which surround Bolshevism, they cannot be products of Bolshevism. Thus Feldbrugge argues, 'crime, according to Marxism, is a phenomenon which cannot take root in a socialist society and must inevitably die out there. The criminality which exists in such a society is explained as being due to remnants of capitalism in the consciousness of individual Soviet citizens and to outside influence.'[63] Minkovsky, too, remarks, 'the social causality of juvenile delinquency in the USSR does not signify that juvenile delinquency is predetermined by the nature of the socialist system. The phenomena and processes underlying juvenile delinquency are the result of the effect of survivals of the past in economics, ideology, culture and everyday life.'[64]

It is in this way that the principle of a hierarchy of credibility denies the deviant the moral right to criticise the bases of power. The deviant is an outsider, a pest or a parasite who is a stranger to the real society that is in the making.[65] It is the élite who has assumed a mandate to make authoritative definitions about the nature of society and those who are rightfully included within it. By affirming an ideal, it makes deviants of those who negate it. Thus legitimacy and deviancy are in a symbiotic relationship. The boundaries around the true proletariat are elastic and contractually negotiated. One can be proletarian only by adhering to élite conceptions of propriety. 'Officially the laws must be written for all citizens, but citizens enjoy the rights of these laws conditionally, only if they are not "enemies of socialism".'[66]

Soviet legislation is built on Marxist–Leninist science, a worldview which is held to offer unparalleled insights into the workings and development of society.* Those who are highest in the hierarchy are the wisest members of society and are consequently most representative of the essence of that society. They are a guiding force

* In the case of Chinese Communism, a standard official description of the party is 'great, glorious and consistently correct'. For an example, see Hu Chiao-Mu, *Thirty Years of the Communist Party of China*, Lawrence and Wishart, London, 1951, p. 95.

which is responsible for coaxing the less knowledgeable into greater awareness. Thus Berman maintains:

Soviet law cannot be understood unless it is recognised that the whole Soviet society is itself conceived to be a single great family, a gigantic school, a church, a labor union, a business enterprise. The state stands at its head, as the parent, the teacher, the priest, the chairman, the director. As the state, it acts officially through the legal system, but its purpose in so acting is to make its citizens into obedient children, good students, ardent believers, hard workers, successful managers.[67]

In such a society the notion of the victim that upholds the principle of disinterestedness acquires its most abstract formulation. When the state assumes the right to change rather than regulate men, its authority and legitimacy must penetrate almost every area of its subjects' lives. Inner states of mind, subjective intention and dissent are as important to the state as observable breaches of codified rules. Thus, in a decree of the Praesidium of the Supreme Soviet, it was announced that the penalties for hooliganism would be imprisonment for a period of between six months and a year, but 'malicious hooliganism—i.e. the same actions, but marked by their exceptional cynicism or special insolence, or connected with resisting a representative of authority . . . are punishable by deprivation of freedom for a period of one to five years'.[68]

In most complex societies, deviants offend against the moral as well as the political structure when they break rules. In totalitarian societies, the moral and political are indissolubly wedded together so that any deviancy will have political implications. 'Not the personal drama of the criminal and his victim, but the drama of the offender and ideology is of paramount and guiding importance, and crime is often confused with political sin. [This] concept of crime has substituted for the personal victim the idea of a victimized ideology. . . . Nonmaterial crimes like treason, libel, or others, are known in criminal law; but the suprauniversalistic orientation gave rise to the idea of the metaphysical victim.'[69]

Soviet legislation is thus a clear example of the interdependence of the forms of legitimacy, on the one hand, and the forms of deviancy on the other. It is clear that legislators claim a moral superiority, a disinterestedness and a representativeness which are transformed by the ideology of Russia. It is also clear that these claims generate peculiar kinds of deviancy.

American law-makers have claimed the same types of legitimacy but, again, their claims are phrased in a way that is shaped by a particular culture and ideology. I shall pursue only one aspect of this special phrasing although many others obviously exist. One of the principal features of American law-making has been its theocratic inspiration. The early American colonies constituted what Hartz has called the bearers of fragment cultures. The cultures from which the colonists emanated were marked by diversity and a certain balance between contrary moral perspectives. In seventeenth-century England, 'Puritanism represented an annoying exaggeration of conventional values, much like the fundamentalism of our own day.'[70] When the Puritans emigrated, however, they carried with them a culture which was no longer checked by competing views. What had grown in conflict and opposition was now unchallenged and sovereign:

It is not hard to see how the migration of a group from Europe heightens social consensus. The group does not have to deal with other groups possessing different values. Thus the French Canadian corporate community does not have to deal with the Enlightenment, and the American middle class does not have to deal with the institutions of the feudal order. . . . It is in the nature of the migration culture that it leads to a new sense of social peace based upon a new sense of community. And when these new emotions are fortified by the spirit of a new nationalism, as they almost always are, the moral world of the fragment is secured in an unusually powerful way.[71]

Earlier American legislation was justified by the claim that the law-makers acted as the vehicle of divine will: 'Nearly all the ordinary social usages, not to mention patterns of thought and faith, could be regulated according to the will of God as expressed in Holy Writ.'[72] Law stemmed from a theocratic élite composed of law and religious authorities united in the service of God: 'The magistrates could act as a secular arm in the service of the church, keeping order among the populace so that the gospel could be taught in peace and safety, while the ministers would provide the final authority for most questions related to longer-range policy.'[73] Thus legislators strove to realise the true, divinely ordained purpose of man's stay on earth. They were the representatives both of God and of God's society as it could be achieved, and their moral superiority and disinterestedness were derived from their access to sources of holy inspiration. As Merrill remarks:

The codes and crimes and pains and penalties of the early period in the Bay colony signally and more thoroughly than in most cultures measured not merely an attempt to punish what may be commonly accepted as wrong-doing. They represented beyond that an attempt to force intellectual and religious homogeneity on the whole community. . . . The civil and religious strait-jacket that the Massachusetts theocracy applied to dissenters was more rigorous than any that had been forced on the Puritans in England.[74]

The religious ideology which legitimated the power structure of the early American Puritans generated its own peculiar deviants. Whilst Soviet law makes deviants of capitalists and those who are corrupted by bourgeois thought, the colonists prescribed the death penalty for idolatry, witchcraft, blasphemy, adultery and perjury in capital cases. Erikson argues that the colony's three major crime waves, involving the Antinomian controversy, the Quakers and witches, reflected attempts to solve problems posed by uncertainties and weaknesses in the conceptual structure of religious legitimation. It is again no accident that deviancy manifested itself in a religious guise in this society. The ascetic stamp imposed on American society by this theocracy still remains a pronounced theme of law. Americans have probably been subjected to more laws curbing private morality than the population of any other country. Gambling, prostitution, abortion and certain forms of drug-taking and homosexuality are legal in Britain. They are not throughout the United States. The Puritan subculture of England had some impression on the criminal law; in America Puritanism was *the* culture for a long while. As Lipset argues, the fragment culture was not bounded or balanced: 'Although Puritanism is probably one of the main sources of American intolerance, there are certainly many other elements which have contributed to its continuance in American life. The lack of an aristocratic tradition in American politics helped to prevent the emergence of a moderate rhetoric in political life.'[75] The consequence for American patterns of deviancy has been profound: 'In America stands an enshrined puritanism, forbidding, illegalizing, censoring, reforming. Its purist ethic is the public face of our schizoid society.'[76]

The theocratic theme in American legislation was most pronounced during the colonial era, but it has been evident since then. In particular, it was revived by the trepidation felt by the native Americans about the massive immigration of Catholic Southern Europeans in the early decades of this century. Gusfield, for instance, has explained the Prohibition movement as an attempt to assert the moral and social supremacy of the heirs of the Puritan theocrats.[77] The Ku Klux Klan (which was probably the largest voluntary association formed in America) was also an organised attempt to establish the dominance of the white Protestant life-style over the Catholic, the Jew and the Negro. Its influence on local legislation was often quite marked.[78]

It is rather easier to trace legitimating themes in nation-building societies than in older, more stable countries where many traditions are fused. In England, for instance, there are elements of middle-class Puritanism co-mingled with aristocratic legitimations stressing something of a hereditary right to rule.[79] These concepts are framed in the context of a rational–legal structure of authority which stresses the propriety of decision-making processes rather than the infallibility or goodness of the decision-makers. Yet any group that assumes the role of imposing its moral position on others must hold that it has some ethical right to do so. The 'right' may be defended by the assertion that there can be no better legislature or legislative system, but laws cannot become authoritative if they are regarded as no more than the moral code of a minority group which exercises power in its own interests.

AUTHORITY AND CONSTRAINT

Authority makes law-giving possible in a society which is not dependent on coercion alone. It also acts as a major constraint on the ability of legislators freely to initiate criminal law. In many societies regulated by law, the authoritative nature of the legal process rests upon a clearly codified system of warnings and penalties. Assent is less likely to be given to power which is wielded in an unpredictable and arbitrary manner. While some communities have been controlled in this fashion,[80] their rulers have relied upon force or on a charismatic or traditional legitimation which is an unstable foundation for the maintenance of government in a changing, bureaucratic and complex setting. If 'the consent of the governed and, thus, a maximum degree of conformity, rests at least in part on a public belief that punishment will be imposed only for deliberate violations of regulations clearly stipulated in advance',[81] legislators seeking to make retrospective or unheralded laws are obviously threatened by a loss of authority.

Legislators are themselves restrained both by the forms of legitimate power and by the body of laws which has developed in the past. When lawmakers generate law, they create a code which remains authoritative only when they observe it themselves:

. . . the very commander subordinates himself to the law which he has made. The moment his will becomes law, it attains objective character, and thus separates itself from its subjective-person origin. As soon as the ruler gives the law as law, he documents himself, to this extent, as the organ of an ideal necessity. He merely reveals a norm which is plainly valid on the ground of its inner sense and that of the situation, whether or not the ruler actually enunciates it. What is more, even if instead of this more or less distinctly conceived legitimation, the will of the ruler itself becomes law, even then the ruler cannot avoid transcending the sphere of subjectivity; for in this case, he carries the super personal legitimation *a priori* in himself. . . . In this way, the inner form of law brings it about that the law-giver, in giving the law, subordinates himself to it as a person, in the same way as all others.[82]

Just as law must become a reified system to the legislator himself, so may its set of sustaining legitimations become external and compelling. The legislator must pay at least a token deference to the myths and ideas which validate his role. In time, that token deference can turn into a very real subordination. What was token for one generation of law-makers can assume a venerability and authenticity for succeeding generations. It may form the natural fabric of the taken-for-granted world which he enters when he starts to play the special roles attached to law-making. The ritual and symbolism of legislation are not intended for the ruled alone. They represent a non-verbal and potent language which can impress those who assume office. They are the materials out of which new identities are built. Legislators may thus be constrained by the very notions that make their actions authoritative. They may become self-disciplining and self-denying in the service of a public good.* The emergence of such legitimating perspectives as 'social facts' for the élite in Britain seems to have changed a sustaining myth into an organising reality. As Selznick points out:

In its early stages law emerges from and depends upon the assertion of power and the contest of wills; it confirms the outcome of the struggle and, at the same time, provides a moderating framework and a sublimating symbolism. In dialectical imagery, force is the thesis, law the disciplining antithesis. But as a system of discipline law has its own shortcomings. Standing alone, it cannot fulfill its own promise as an affirmative ideal. The latent historical outcome—the renewing synthesis—is the absorption of legal ideals into the political order and, at the same time the creation of supportive institutions, values, and modes of thought.[83]

It would be naïve to imagine that master legitimations are always and everywhere subscribed to by legislative élites. Yet it would be equally naïve to imagine that lawmakers are uniquely emancipated from a society's system of typifications and beliefs. They are not the inhabitants of a unique sphere which is marked by an instrumental rationality and an alienation from prevalent culture. Whilst they inevitably obtain a peculiar perspective on law and legitimacy, legislators are constrained by what passes for authoritative knowledge in their community. That they have the power to introduce some changes in that knowledge does not mean they do not employ segments of it to work those changes.

* Guttsman, for instance, claims that the Victorian 'public schools and the ancient universities tended to instil in those who passed through them a sentiment of superiority and a belief in predestined roles as the nation's leaders. In doing so they may equally well have sought to instil the idea of service and the duty of charity towards the less fortunate. . . .' (W. Guttsman, Ed., *The English Ruling Class*, Weidenfeld & Nicolson, London, 1969, pp. 14–15.)

An interesting example of the transformation of legitimacy working at the monarchical level is given in the case of the education of George V. When Bagehot wrote his *English Constitution*, he had little opportunity to study the manner in which Victoria actually played her regal and imperial roles. His book inaccurately portrayed her as a constitutional monarch who refrained from partisanship and intervention in state affairs. It did, however, become the source of George's knowledge about the workings of kingship. Before he ascended the throne, he was tutored on the basis of the *English Constitution*. It served as a manual for the structuring of his later behaviour. 'All that he aspired to do was to . . . represent all that was most straightforward in the national character; to give to the world an example of personal probity; to advise, to encourage and to warn.'[84]

Although a relatively tortuous argument could account for the powerful passing self-emasculating laws in terms of a deliberate quest for increasing legitimacy, it is simpler to conjecture that they do, on occasion, view themselves as a disinterested and representative body subordinate to the principles enunciated in law. Thus Chambliss states of America, 'it would be a mistake to [assume] that all laws represent the interests of persons in power at the expense of persons less influential . . . laws are passed which reflect the interests of the general population and which are antithetical to the interest of those in power'.[85]

LAWS AND RATIONALITY

Authority and its legitimating beliefs act as a set of checks on the exercise of a detached rationality. There are other, more fundamental, restraints which prevent a viable model of legislation being constructed in terms of pure consensus or pure conspiracy.

Any individual or group lives and acts within a society which is an accretion of the lives and activities of their predecessors. Modes of social control exerted in the past become part of the moral and definitional context of any present legislature's decision-making. Indeed, in a sense, these modes have created the very stuff of society. Following Durkheim, Erikson argues:

People who gather together in communities need to be able to describe and anticipate those areas of experience which lie outside the immediate compass of the group—the unseen dangers which in any culture and in any age seem to threaten its security. Traditional folklore depicting demons, devils, witches and evil spirits, may be one way to give form to otherwise formless dangers, but the visible deviant is another kind of reminder. As a trespasser against these group norms, he represents those forces which lie outside the group's boundaries; he informs us, as it were, what evil looks like, what shapes the devil can assume. . . . It may well be that without this ongoing drama at the outer edges of group space, the community would have no inner sense of identity and cohesion, no sense of the contrasts which set it off as a special place in the larger world.[86]

The deviant thus plays what is, in part, an educational role in structuring legislators' knowledge of society. Their conception of the community is organised around the recurrent interactions pursued between deviants and control agents. The understanding of a group's boundaries is acquired through the crystallisation of deviant roles.

At any point of time this crystallisation was achieved through the formation and enforcement of rules that took place in the past. Some of the deviancy-creating activity occurred very long ago. In effect, this means that a legislator's comprehension of society is inevitably dated and often markedly so. The boundaries are not fluid or flexible but are, instead, relatively frozen by the operations of the criminal law.

Law freezes social life in a number of ways. It codifies and reifies aspects of society but, more particularly, it acts as a continuing source of vitality to transactions between deviants and control agents. It supports deviancy in a threefold fashion. First, it adds a concreteness to the distinction between permitted and illicit behaviour and then entrusts enforcement agencies with the task of managing the illicit. Both in the initial act of classification and in the secondary act of management, clarity is built into the constructs upon which men act. Ambiguity is dispelled and distinctions heightened.

The creation of clear classes of acts is not limited to conceptualisation alone. These classes can, in fact, emerge as a product of agency and deviant behaviour.[87] The construction of deviant roles which can be managed by control agents and law-givers makes life more problematic for those who play the roles. It can force the deviant to reorganise his life so that his rule-breaking acquires a greater salience for him and for those who have dealings with him. In many instances, the criminalisation of activity can lead to what Matza terms 'bedevilment', the casting of the deviant into a daemonic role which 'virtually guarantees that further disaffiliation with convention will be a concomitant of affiliation with deviation; . . . that the subject will become even more deviant in order to deviate'.[88] The loading of extra meanings on to deviancy coupled with a sharp differentiation between the deviant and the nondeviant generates more significance in the behaviour than the rule-breaker perhaps originally intended or realised. An act or series of acts of rule-breaking which might have been of ephemeral importance to the deviant can become of such importance that he becomes trapped in a dramatised deviant role. Such secondary deviation is likely to be reinforced by the larger social context of deviation. Ostracism, guilt and the emergence of problems associated with the successful perpetuation of rule-breaking may propel the deviant towards others who are undergoing the same experiences. Drug-addiction provides an example. In the 1950s British policy towards the addict was medical and nonpunitive whilst American policy adopted a contrary course: 'As one might expect, there has been no pronounced development in Great Britain of an "addict subculture". In America, addicts have been driven by social stigma and by social, legal, and economic pressures to band together and to establish their own group way of life. For most American addicts it could rightly be said that addiction is their way of life. But the situation in Britain is quite different.'[89] The formation of groups which are centred on deviancy can add substance and permanence to the rule-breaking. The enforcement of the criminal law can thereby promote and prolong the behaviour which becomes illegal.

The third way in which the law 'freezes' social life is by its creation of sets of goals and understandings in which the enforcers acquire a considerable stake. The enforcers' careers may become founded on the crime which they combat and their lives may derive meaning from it. Becker argues that, although the interest which prompted legislation can evaporate, the very act of law-making and establishing a control apparatus can ensure that a passing concern will become the fount of enduring commitment for particular groups:

Once some organization takes charge of a problem, the group of aroused citizens whose collective concern prompted the development is likely to lose interest. They have, after all, turned the problem over to an organization so that they need no longer worry about it. One of the interesting features of this stage in the development of a social problem is that the personnel of the organization devoted to the problem tend to build their lives and careers around its continued existence. They become attached to 'their' problem, and anything that threatens to make it disappear or diminish in importance is a threat.[90]

The crystallisation of moral definitions is thus hastened by the institutionalisation of the reaction to a problem. By confirming the deviant in his deviant role and by setting up special enforcement roles, criminal law emphasises and stabilises the deviancy it purports to counteract. It thereby injects that deviancy into the larger moral system and allows it to become another one of the boundary defining and maintaining forces in society. When there is this possibility of a rule becoming the means whereby society itself is defined, not only will conceptions of society receive form and anchorage, the rule itself will enjoy a longer life:

Recurrent deviations and the growth of a deviant population bring alterations in the culture and social organization of the community within which they occur. Mythologies, stigma, stereotypes, patterns of exploitation, accommodation, segregation and methods of control spring up and crystallize in the interaction between the deviants and the rest of society. The informal societal reaction is extended and formalized in the routinized procedures of agents and agencies delegated with direct responsibility for penalizing and restraining or reforming the deviants.[91]

Technological and social changes may produce transformations in the forms of deviation that exist in a society. Deviancies are born, they flourish and they die. Yet the criminalisation of deviancy is a way of adding to the forces that sustain its existence. It is thus perfectly possible that law and the activities which it supports are liable to change at a slower rate than other, less formalised social phenomena. At the very least, the establishment of complex procedures, buttressed by dignity and isolation, can lead to lag. Rose, for instance, argued that whilst the law did not cause racial tensions in the Southern states of America, 'it "cemented" and "stabilized" the race problem so that the normal processes of change had a difficult time eroding it. . . .'[92]

One other source of freezing is the twin capacity of established law to act as a repository of legitimations for new forms of control and to be flexible in its range of application.[93] By forming a crucible for novel legislation, the existing body of law moulds and directs innovation. In his analysis of vagrancy laws, for example, Chambliss maintains:

. . . when changed social conditions create a perceived need for legal changes, these alterations will be effected through the revision and refocusing of existing statutes. . . . It also seems probable that when the social conditions change and previously useful laws are no longer useful there will be long periods when these laws will remain dormant. It is less likely that they will be officially negated.[94]

Deviancy can then be seen as the result of successive generations' attempts to clarify and control problematic behaviour. Some of this behaviour might not have been ratified as deviant had it emerged at a later stage than the one in which it was proscribed, but 'mythologies, stigma and stereotypes' have created outsiders whose wrongfulness is now simply taken for granted. This propensity to preserve earlier moral reactions means not only that much contemporary deviancy is a fossilised or frozen residue from the past, but that contemporary control is constrained and oriented by the past. Each new generation does not rewrite the social contract.

Deviants act as agents in structuring legislators' conceptions of the community and in warning them how it might be endangered. If past acts of social control were based on some informational poverty or limited perception, the present stock of social knowledge will be to that extent poverty-stricken and limited. The definition of a contemporary threat will be phrased in the context of this necessarily anachronistic and faulty knowledge of society. Two obstacles consequently prevent legislators from 'rationally' controlling deviancy; not only is the present threat likely to be misconceived, it is a misconceived threat to a misconceived model of society. Constructs of society and deviation can be coloured by imperfect knowledge and the combination of the two imperfect constructs can engender bizarre results.

No unsophisticated projection of economic or political vested interests on to law is likely to produce a satisfactory understanding of the nature of rules constraining deviancy. The knowledge that a society is 'capitalist', 'state capitalist' or 'socialist' will not furnish an unalloyed insight into legislative content: many moral definitions and deviancies will be, in a sense, foreign to the worlds of pure capitalism or socialism. As Hall argues in his analysis of the law of theft in England:

In the case-law there [are] many nice distinctions regarding, e.g., larceny by trick and obtaining property by false pretences, custody and possession, and interpretations of statutes which clearly opposed ordinary canons of construction; indeed, some of the decisions seemed to be utter nonsense. Yet, on the assumption that our predecessors in the Bar and on the Bench were thoughtful persons, there must have been some reason in their doings.[95]

The analysis of the links between law and moral positions is further complicated by the fact that legislation tends to generate unintended consequences. Laws resulting in social control can bring about a chain of unintended effects which then act as the framework of both the enforcement of those laws and the making of new ones. 'Laws are attempts to deal with social problems; they usually transform the social problems in some unanticipated way; in so doing they often create new problems. It is, of course, not correct that 'law creates problems', but that people—mainly law innovators—create problems through the formulation of laws intended to meet other problems.'[96] An excellent example of a law which created an abundance of secondary problems was the Volstead Act of 1920 which prohibited the manufacture and sale of alcohol in the United States. The Act, which was intended to coerce abstinence, resulted instead in a vast number of grave social problems. According to Sinclair:

The face of national prohibition presented insoluble problems to the machinery of law in the United States. Judges and prisons and policemen were few; stills and home-brewers and bootleggers were many. Yet this excess of law and lack of possible enforcement was . . . endemic to the national scene. The idea of moral perfection made the American people enshrine in their Constitution ideals which they could not fulfill, and made them outlaw habits in which they rather generally indulged. By their moral fervour as lawmakers, they made a large part of the people the allies and clients of lawbreakers. . . . The history of prohibition and crime shows how the tolerance exercised towards criminals by respectable citizens, labour, and capital allowed gangsters to take over local governments, as Capone did the government of Cicero, and even state governments. The loot of prohibition was sufficient to buy judges, state attorneys, and whole police forces. It enabled the gangsters to spread their influence into new areas of legitimate business. They were allowed to terrorize citizens so much that no Chicago jury would return a verdict of murder against a gunman, because of fear.[97]

Attempts to make law are never conducted in limbo. The tendency of strenuous enforcement to confirm and perpetuate deviancy results in the possibility of an ever more complicated set of interrelated social problems emerging. Contemporary control agencies in America have to contend with the social structures that arose out of the Volstead Act.[98] The corruption of these agencies has led to another chain of problems which demand further solutions. Past legislation thus has lingering effects whose control engenders new new difficulties. These primary, secondary and tertiary problems are the foci of legislative attention and the framers of legislators' conceptions of society. As Lyman and Scott argue, 'Some legislators may be astonished at the results of the laws they pass; others may be ignorant of them; and still others may claim that nothing like what happened was intended.'[99]

Another source of these secondary problems and unanticipated consequences is the increasing bureaucratisation of activities surrounding the application of law. In complex societies, legislators and the deviants they control rarely meet face-to-face. Instead, there is a vast array of mediating institutions which actively enforce, interpret and transform law and deviancy. Power is more and more diffused throughout the social control network with the result that substructures emerge which are defining agencies of some importance in their own right:

. . . only rarely, as in some very primitive, organizationally simple groupings of small populations, will those who formulate legal norms in symbols and those who actually enforce legal norms, especially at the immediate supervisory level, be the same persons. With increasingly complex organization of the control machinery of a political community come . . . problems of communication, interpretation, the scope of discretion, and

F

internal control . . .; the result is that there is always some 'play' between what is said at the top and what is done at the bottom of the structure.[100]

In the next chapter I shall present a case study of the police to show how this play works. All I shall emphasise here is that the courts, police, probation service, prison service and so on develop their own peculiar notions of what *really* constitutes deviancy, which forms of deviancy are the most significant, how they should be tackled and what should be done about the problems that ensue from such decisions. As Kitsuse and Cicourel state, 'In modern societies where bureaucratically organized agencies are increasingly invested with social control functions, the activities of such agencies are centrally important "sources and contexts" which generate as well as maintain definitions of deviance and produce populations of deviants.'[101] The interplay within and between these institutions can become a critical constraint on the abilities of lawmakers to realise their wills in action.

A literal realisation of legislative intentions may not occur because the actual contingencies of law enforcement complicate and distort law in a fashion that was never envisaged when the laws were made. The police, for instance, are constantly presented with dilemmas of discretion because they simply cannot take action about every single instance of rule-breaking they observe. An automatic arrest or intervention might conflict with such approved goals as successful peacekeeping; the pursuit of more severely condemned cases of lawbreaking; or the judicious and effective use of informal control methods. Police resources moreover cannot muster such automatic reactions.

Secondly, enforcement agencies are relatively isolated sectors of activity which fashion cultures and systems of interpretation peculiar to themselves. Such cultures can become progressively detached from the noninstitutional world and progressively incomprehensible to outsiders; 'Every social group, be it ever so small . . . , has its own private code, understandable only by those who have participated in the common past experiences in which it took rise or in the tradition connected with them.'[102] Whilst relations *between* institutions may be based on relatively intelligible conventions, those *within* them may be quite unintelligible to nonmembers. Checks may be available to powerful outsiders, but it is never entirely possible to grasp the ways in which the law undergoes subtle or crude changes in significance and usage. At the very least, the perspectives on law acquired by a patrolling policeman who is fearful of assault, by a prison officer who confronts routine problems of managing inmates or by the lawyer engaged in legal contest, will never be quite the same. The materials upon which the officials' understanding of law is built depend upon the immediate context of his work life and the problems which it throws up. Law then becomes translated into a stock of practical knowledge which is moulded and directed by routine contingencies.

At another level, institutions may direct law-enforcement towards goals which were never desired by the legislator. Goal displacement can occur in any institution, but it is more probable in many of the law-enforcing agencies. Those who work in such agencies master a body of practical and theoretical knowledge which places them somewhat beyond the reach of potential critics. When the agency can be characterised as a professional body, this inaccessibility is considerably reinforced; 'It is part of being a profession to be given the official power to define and therefore create the shape of problematic segments of social behaviour; the judge determines what is legal and who is guilty, the priest what is holy and who is profane, the physician what is normal and who is sick.'[103] Furthermore, control agents work in areas which are publicly regarded with a certain amount of ambivalence or fear and in which the public is extremely reluctant to participate. Many members of society accept authoritative definitions of the deviant as a person who is best avoided. By default, therefore, they allow the specialist to become more familiar with deviancy.

Such specialists are people to whom Becker applied the principle of the hierarchy of credibility. Not only are they approved by the state as authoritative bodies, they also have access to publicity-creating mechanisms. For instance, Dickson argues that the Federal Narcotics Division had the status of a public bureaucracy and 'the ability to develop propaganda and the means to communicate it were inherent in this status, as was the propensity of the public to accept this propaganda'.[104] (Later I shall show how this propaganda was employed.) This tendency of mediating institutions to acquire the right to make authoritative statements leads to their becoming extremely influential in defining law, crime and their own role in relation to law and crime:

Policing agencies tend to be unusually successful in campaigns to obtain favorable legislation in part because there is rarely any organized opposition to their efforts. Then, too, the fact that law-enforcement agencies are expected to publish 'authoritative' reports on crime and criminals has the effect of having interest groups defined culturally as authorities on matters which are of direct concern to their own welfare.[105]

Another source of information control is available to the members of such bureaucracies. Quite frequently they alone are able to gauge the extent and nature of the rule-breaking activity that is pursued in their own province. For instance, although the police rely on the public for reports of crime, they also generate a considerable amount of data themselves.[106] Patrolling policemen can choose to ignore or act upon the deviancy which they witness and, in many cases, the decision to ignore it will lead to that deviancy remaining known to the deviant and policeman alone. Agencies can thus influence how much deviancy and what kinds of deviancy are knowable to outsiders. By extension, they not only tend to administer their own tests of effectiveness, they can also affect the findings. Few people other than psychiatrists are equipped to know how much mental illness abounds in a community or what effects different treatment programmes produce.

It is probable that many agencies exploit their power only to ease the performance of particularly troublesome tasks. Others do, however, transform the law into an instrument of aggrandisement. Dickson's discussion of the growing imperialism of the Federal Narcotics Division illustrate how an exceptional campaign transformed a minor fiscal law into a major means of social control:

While most if not all bureaucracies attempt to maintain their moral commitment or ideology . . . , some go further and initiate moral crusades, whereby they attempt to instil this commitment in groups and individuals outside their bureaus. . . . [After the passing of the 1914 Harrison Act] the public's attitude toward narcotics could be characterised as only slightly opposed. Faced with a situation where adaptation to the existing legislation was bureaucratically unfeasible, where expansion was desirable, and where environmental support—from both congress and the public—was necessary for continued existence, the Division launched a two-pronged campaign: 1) a barrage of reports and newspaper articles which generated a public outcry against narcotics use, and 2) a series of Division-sponsored test cases in the courts which resulted in a re-interpretation of the Harrison Act and substantially broadened powers for the Narcotics Division. Thus the Division attained its goals by altering a weakly-held public value regarding narcotics use from neutrality or slight opposition and by persuading the courts that it should have increased power.[107]

Thus, agencies which are nominally subordinate to the legislature can achieve substantial autonomy. In the creation of their own goals and interpretations they can bring about a considerable thwarting or transformation of legislative wishes. Information upon which a legislator acts is frequently relayed to him by agencies which again bring about changes in the reality of law.

Law-giving can consequently be viewed as a process which is carried on in one part of a larger system of communication and control. The kinds of knowledge which law represents, and the effects of that knowledge, depend upon the practical workings of that system. The workings have an overt face and a covert: the overt face displays a unity and consensus which support the master legitimations, principles and structures of social control; the covert face reveals an abundance of conflicts and discontinuities which belie them.

Although no research has explicitly focused on the cultural organisation of the system, it is plausible that the social control network is characterised by a number of overlapping paradigms which structure its members' understanding of their tasks.[108] Functional areas of the network—for example, those dealing with juvenile delinquency or fraud—are dominated by sets of implicit and explicit ideas about the nature of the problem they manage, their role in that management and their relations to other agencies.

While I have concentrated on the manner in which the forms and contents of law are shaped by the system's responses, it is clear that the same model can be applied to the analysis of how new laws emerge. The system not only transforms law, it also affects what deviancies are going to be brought to the attention of legislators in the first instance. Built into the paradigms will be identifying procedures which enable agencies' members to recognise and react to change or novelty in their problematic areas. The paradigms are systems of relevance which highlight certain phenomena and obscure others. They are also systems of interpretation which impose meaning on the world. Identifying procedures are therefore likely to systematically select out particular kinds of novelty and change whilst they fail to apprehend others. Very often, too, they are likely to impute old meanings to new events so that those events are comfortably accommodated by the paradigm.[109]

Because of such differential sensitivity, agencies and legislators are not always immediately responsive to new events which are potentially deviant. Furthermore, they need not share *unofficial* concern about these events even when they *can* respond. In consequence, initiatives for introducing social control measures frequently emanate from groups outside the network who do not share the constraining perspectives. These groups are either marginal or completely foreign to the world of formal control.[110]

Legislators are usually socially and structurally distant from those people whose activities they come to proscribe. It is the work of intermediary organisations—the media, control agencies and outside groups—which brings about their attention being drawn to the possibly deviant. As Fuller and Myers argue:

Social problems do not arise full-blown, commanding community attention and evoking adequate policies and machinery for their solution. On the contrary, we believe that social problems exhibit a temporal course of development in which different phases or stages may be distinguished. Each stage anticipates its successor in time and each succeeding stage contains new elements which mark it off from its predecessor. A social problem thus conceived as always being in a dynamic state of 'becoming' passes through the natural history stages of awareness, policy determination, and reform.[111]

The generation of awareness is often the task of unofficial reforming agencies who do not share the official paradigm. The press, 'moral entrepreneurs'[112] or 'moral crusaders' exert pressure on the official system to take cognisance of what concerns them. The fate of their pressures will be determined by master interpretations held by authorities and legislators, but it may well be that the pressures will affect the interpretations themselves. An early survey of social control discovered the immense responsiveness of the Cleveland courts and police to newspaper-created 'crime waves'. 'Crime waves' were the result of lavish press coverage of criminal acts. Cleveland papers gave the impression that a surge of criminality had occurred but 'the response was out of all proportion to the actual increase in crime'.[113] The survey reported that a consequence of the presentation of crime waves was 'a tendency to demand summary action and quickly reportable results on the part of police, prosecutors and judges . . . where the community is whipped up to demand "results" of its system of criminal justice, officials responsive to popular whims, as this survey discloses them to be, will, at least unconsciously, care more to satisfy popular demands than to be observant of the tried processes of law'.[114] The effects of crime waves can move even further up the social control network, reaching the legislative apex.[115]

It should be clear that authoritative definitions of deviancy are an outcome of an immensely complicated series of transactions between the definers' interpretations of their own and the general interest, the conceptual structures upon which law and legitimacy rest and the institutions which are collectively engaged in casting the forms of deviant behaviour. Official definitions of deviation emerge from unequal power relationships, but the preconditions for an effective use of this power themselves hinder possibilities of a clear expression of authority's intentions. They also shape the ways in which these intentions are formed by the powerful.

I have focused on one facet of law as an official system of proscribing behaviour. The content and forms of law can be understood, in part, as the products of a system of beliefs and the structures that shape those beliefs. The system and the structures are dispersed over the whole social control network that is formally established to manage deviant behaviour. Law can be understood neither as a pure expression of vested interests, nor as a purely 'rational' response to phenomena threatening harm. Instead, it is vastly more complex. Because of its critical role in fashioning legislative and popular understanding of the composition and contours of society, law is simultaneously the creature and the creator of conceptions of propriety and impropriety. As such, it has the tendency to impose an anachronistic colouring upon official versions of deviation. A legislature is constrained by its predecessors' ideas and is thereby rarely free to initiate laws reflecting its own unalloyed interests. It is also constrained by ideas which percolate up through the social control network, by the press and by its exposure to current typifications. Out of this amalgam, definitions of deviancy are codified and set into action as instructions for enforcement. Enforcement then feeds back data which structure ensuing legislative decisions. Law cannot be conceived as a one-way flow of influence, it is the outcome of constant, complicated exchanges.

1. K. Erikson, 'Notes on the Sociology of Deviance', in H. S. Becker (Ed.), *The Other Side*, Free Press, New York, 1964, p. 11.

2. T. Shibutani, *Society and Personality*, Prentice-Hall, New Jersey, 1964, p. 44.

3. E. Sutherland and D. Cressey, *Principles of Criminology* (6th ed.), Lippincott, Chicago, 1960, p. 11.

4. W. Sumner, *Folkways*, Dover, New York, 1959, p. 77.

5. P. Berger and T. Luckman, *The Social Construction of Reality*, Allen Lane, The Penguin Press, London, 1967, p. 106.

6. cf. P. Selznick, 'The Sociology of Law', *International Encyclopaedia of the Social Sciences*, Crowell, Collier and Macmillan, New York, 1968, vol. 9, esp. p. 57.

7. G. Simmel, 'The Autonomization of Contents', in K. Wolff (Ed.), *The Sociology of Georg Simmel*, Free Press, New York, 1950, p. 42.

8. M. Mandelbaum, *The Phenomenology of Moral Experience*, Free Press, New York, 1955.

9. G. Simmel, 'Subordination under a Principle vs. a Person', in K. Wolff (Ed.), op. cit.

10. J. Wilson, *The Burden of Egypt*, University of Chicago Press, Chicago, 1951, pp. 49–50.

11. cf. R. Dentler and K. Erikson, 'The Functions of Deviance in Groups', *Social Problems*, Fall 1959, vol. 7, no. 2.

12. N. Denzin, 'Rules of Conduct and the Study of Deviant Behavior', in J. Douglas (Ed.), *Deviance and Respectability*, Basic Books, New York, 1970, pp. 131–2.

13. cf. B. Wilson, *Sects and Society*, Heinemann, London, 1961.

14. *Watchtower*, 1 July 1961, p. 394.

15. Sir P. Sillitoe, *Cloak Without Dagger*, Cassell, London, 1955, pp. 77, 78.

16. Quoted in T. Parker, *The Ploughboy*, Hutchinson, London, 1965, p. 27.

17. J. Simmons, 'Public Stereotypes of Deviants', *Social Problems*, Fall 1965, vol. 13, no. 2, p. 225.

18. M. Weber, 'Politics as a Vocation', in H. Gerth and C. Wright Mills, *From Max Weber*, Routledge & Kegan Paul, London, 1961, p. 78.

19. E. Durkheim, *The Division of Labor in Society*, Free Press, New York, 1964, p. 102.

20. ibid., p. 111.

21. P. Devlin, *The Enforcement of Morals*, Oxford University Press, London, 1965, pp. 7, 13–14.

22. H. Hart, *Law, Liberty and Morality*, Stanford University Press, Stanford. 1963, pp. 46–7.

23. J. Gusfield, 'Moral Passage: The Symbolic Process in Public Designations of Deviance', in C. A. Bersani (Ed.), *Crime and Delinquency*, Macmillan, New York, 1970, p. 65.

24. A. Blumberg, review of N. Walker's 'Crime and Insanity in England', *Journal of Criminal Law, Criminology and Police Science*, March 1970, vol. 61, no. 1, p. 90.

25. D. Matza, *Becoming Deviant*, Prentice-Hall, New Jersey, 1969, pp. 146–7.

26. T. Duster, 'The Legislation of Morality', Free Press, New York, 1970, p. 67.

27. cf. I. Piliavin and S. Briar, 'Police Encounters with Juveniles', *American Journal of Sociology*, September 1964, vol. 69.

28. See my unpublished D. Phil. dissertation, 1969, Bodleian Library, Oxford.

29. cf. W. Carson, 'White-Collar Crime and the Enforcement of Factory Legislation', *British Journal of Criminology*, October 1970, vol. 10; and 'Sociological Aspects of Strict Liability and the Enforcement of Factory Legislation', *Modern Law Review*, July 1970.

30. J. Richman, 'Coming Between a Man and His Car', *New Society*, 30 April, 1970, p. 726.

31. cf. A. Lindesmith, *Opiate Addiction*, Principia Press, Indiana, 1947.

32. J. Gusfield, op. cit., p. 76.

33. J. Skolnick, 'Coercion to Virtue: The Enforcement of Morals', *Southern California Law Review*, 1968, no. 588, p. 626.

34. cf. J. Gusfield, op. cit., p. 66, and *Symbolic Crusade: Status Politics and the American Temperance Movement*, University of Illinois Press, Urbana, 1963.

35. A. Sinclair, *Prohibition: The Era of Excess*, Faber & Faber, London, 1962, p. 204.

36. A. Schutz, *Alfred Schutz: Collected Papers*, vol. 1, Martinus Nijhoff, The Hague, 1967, pp. 41–3.

37. J. Short Jr, *Modern Criminals*, Aldine, Chicago, 1970, p. 2.

38. W. Chambliss (Ed.), *Crime and the Legal Process*, McGraw-Hill, New York, 1969, p. 8.

39. cf. P. Bachrach and M. Baratz, 'Two Faces of Power', *American Political Science Review*, December 1962, vol. 56, no. 4, pp. 947–52.

40. J. Weinstein, *The Corporate Ideal in the Liberal State: 1900–1918*, Beacon Press, Boston, 1969, p. x.

41. For a series of instances of such concerns, see P. Taft and P. Ross, 'American Labor Violence', in H. Graham and T. Gurr (Ed.), *The History of Violence in America*, Bantam Books, New York, 1968.

42. J. Douglas, 'American Social Order', Free Press, New York, 1971, p. 92.

43. H. Mansfield *et al.*, *A Short History of OPA*, General Publication of the Historical Reports on War Administration, Government Printing Office, Washington, 1947, p. 257.

44. E. Lemert, *Social Pathology*, McGraw-Hill, New York, 1963, p. 4.

45. E. Sutherland, *White Collar Crime*, Holt, Rinehart and Winston, New York, 1967, p. 8.

46. G. Lenski, *Power and Privilege*, McGraw-Hill, New York, 1966, p. 51.

47. R. McCleery, 'Communication Patterns as Bases of Systems of Authority and Power', in *Theoretical Studies in Social Organization of the Prison*, Social Science Research Council, New York, 1960, p. 49.

48. R. Turner, 'Sponsored and Contest Mobility and the School System', *American Sociological Review*, December 1960, vol. 25, no. 6, p. 859.

49. cf. R. Michels, *Political Parties*, Free Press, Glencoe, 1949.

50. H. S. Becker, 'Whose Side Are We On?', *Social Problems*, Winter 1967, vol. 14, no. 3, p. 241.

51. T. Duster, op. cit., p. 88.

52. D. Matza, *Becoming Deviant*, Prentice-Hall, New Jersey, 1969, pp. 147–8.

53. D. J. Bordua, 'Recent Trends: Deviant Behavior and Social Control', in C. A. Bersani (Ed.), *Crime and Delinquency*, Macmillan, New York, 1970, p. 455; cf. also J. Bednarski, 'The Salem Witch-Scare Viewed Sociologically', in M. Marwick, *Witchcraft and Sorcery*, Penguin Books, 1970, pp. 151–63, esp. p. 155.

54. S. Schafer, *The Victim and his Criminal*, Random House, New York, 1968, p. 8.

55. W. Tallack, *Reparation to the Injured, and the Rights of the Victim of Crime to Compensation*, London, 1900, pp. 11–12.

56. For an excellent analysis of how the growth of regal authority aided changes in conceptions of deviancy and victimology, see J. Hall, 'The Carrier's Case', in *Theft, Law and Society*, Bobbs-Merrill, Indianapolis, 1952, p. 15.

57. J. Jeudwine, *Tort, Crime and the Police in Medieval England*, Williams and Norgate, London, 1917, p. 84.

58. S. Ranulf, *Moral Indignation and Middle Class Psychology*, Schocken, New York, 1964, p. 1.

59. T. Duster, op. cit., p. ix.

60. J. Lofland, *Deviance and Identity*, Prentice-Hall, New Jersey, 1969, p. 19.

61. J. Talmon, *The Origins of Totalitarian Democracy*, Sphere Books, London, 1970, p. 48.

62. V. Lenin, *The State and Revolution*, Foreign Language Publishing House, Moscow, undated, p. 151.

63. F. Feldbrugge, 'Soviet Criminal Law—The Last Six Years', *Journal of Criminal Law, Criminology, and Police Science*, September 1963, vol. 54, no. 3, p. 263.

64. G. Minkovsky, 'Some Causes of Juvenile Delinquency in the USSR and Measures to Prevent It', reproduced in *Current Digest of the Soviet Press*, vol. 18, no. 30, p. 9.

65. cf. L. Lipson, 'Hosts and Pests: The Fight Against Parasites', *Problems of Communism*, March–April 1965, vol. 14, no. 2.

65. M. Djilas, *The New Class*, Thames and Hudson, London, 1958, p. 89.

67. H. Berman, *Justice in the USSR*, Random House, New York, 1963, p. 366.

68. Decree of the Praesidium of the USSR Supreme Soviet: 'On the Formation of a USSR Union-Republic Ministry for Safeguarding Public Order', 26 July 1966.

69. S. Schafer, op. cit., p. 36.

70. K. T. Erikson, *Wayward Puritans*, Wiley, New York, 1966, p. 45.

71. L. Hartz, 'A Comparative Study of Fragment Cultures', in H. D. Graham and T. D. Gurr (Ed.), *The History of Violence in America*, Bantam Books, New York, 1969, pp. 107–8.

72. L. Merrill, 'The Puritan Policeman', *American Sociological Review*, December 1945, vol. 10, no. 6, p. 766.

73. K. Erikson, 'Wayward Puritans', op. cit., p. 58.

74. L. Merrill, op. cit., p. 766.

75. S. M. Lipset, 'The Sources of the "Radical Right"', in D. Bell (Ed.), *The Radical Right*, Doubleday Anchor, New York, 1964, p. 318.

76. G. Tyler, *Organized Crime in America*, Ann Arbor, Michigan, 1967, p. 47.

77. cf. J. Gusfield, *Symbolic Crusade: States Politics and the American Temperance Movement*, University of Illinois Press, Urbana, 1963.

78. cf. K. T. Jackson, *The Ku Klux Klan in the City: 1915–1930*, Oxford University Press, New York, 1967.

79. For a classic rendering of this position as it was maintained in the last century, see B. Disraeli, 'A Vindication of the English Constitution', in W. L. Guttsman (Ed.), *The English Ruling Class*, Weidenfeld and Nicolson, London, 1969, esp. p. 26.

80. cf. L. Preuss, 'Punishment by Analogy in National Socialist Penal Law', *Journal of Criminal Law and Criminology*, March–April 1936, vol. 26; and M. Rheinstein (Ed.), *Max Weber on Law in Economy and Society*, Harvard University Press, Mass., 1954, especially the section on kadi justice.

81. D. Cressey, *Theft of the Nation*, Harper Colophon, New York, 1969, p. 204.

82. G. Simmel, op. cit., p. 262.

83. P. Selznick, *Law, Society, and Industrial Justice*, Russell Sage Foundation, New York, 1969, p. 28.

84. H. Nicolson, *King George V: His Life and Reign*, Constable, London, 1953, p. 63.

85. W. Chambliss (Ed.), op. cit., p. 10. It would be a mistake, however, to assume that the enforcement of laws which restrain élites is always as vigilant as that of those which control other groups. cf. E. Sutherland; *White Collar Crime*, op. cit.

86. K. Erikson, 'Notes on the Sociology of Deviance', op. cit., p. 15.

87. cf. J. Young, 'The Role of the Police as Amplifiers of Deviancy, Negotiators of Reality and Translators of Fantasy', in S. Cohn (Ed.), *Images of Deviance*, Penguin Books, Middlesex, 1971.

88. D. Matza, 'Becoming Deviant', Prentice-Hall, New Jersey, 1969, p. 148.

89. E. M. Schur, *Narcotic Addiction in Britain and America*, Tavistock, London, 1963, p. 144.

90. H. S. Becker, *Social Problems*, John Wiley, New York, 1966, p. 13.

91. E. Lemert, 'Social Pathology', op. cit., p. 55.

92. A. Rose, 'Law and the Causation of Social Problems', *Social Problems*, Summer 1968, vol. 16, no. 1, p. 41.

93. cf. K. Renner, *The Institutions of Private Law and their Social Functions*, Routledge & Kegan Paul, London, 1949.

94. W. Chambliss, 'The Law of Vagrancy', in W. Chambliss (Ed.), op. cit., p. 62.

95. J. Hall, *Theft, Law and Society*, Bobbs-Merrill, Indianapolis, 1952, p. vi.

96. A. M. Rose, op. cit., p. 35.

97. A. Sinclair, *Prohibition; The Era of Excess*, Faber & Faber, London, 1962, pp. 239, 249.

98. cf. D. R. Cressey, op. cit.

99. M. Scott and S. Lyman, 'Accounts, Deviance, and Social Order', in J. Douglas (Ed.), *Deviance and Respectability*, Basic Books, New York, 1970, p. 106.

100. A. Turk, *Criminality and Legal Order*, Rand McNally, Chicago, 1969, p. 39.

101. J. Kitsuse and A. Cicourel, 'A Note on the Uses of Official Statistics', *Social Problems*, Fall, 1963, vol. 11, no. 2, p. 139.

102. A. Schutz, 'The Stranger: An Essay in Social Psychology', *American Journal of Sociology*, May 1944, vol. 49, no. 6, p. 505.

103. E. Freidson, *Profession of Medicine*, Dodd, Mead and Co, New York, 1970, p. 206.

104. D. Dickson, 'Bureaucracy and Morality', *Social Problems*, fall 1968, vol. 16, no. 2, pp. 149–50.

105. W. Chambliss (Ed.), op. cit., p. 9.

106. cf. D. Black and A. Reiss, 'Studies of Crime and Law Enforcement in Major Metropolitan Areas', vol. 2, sec. 1, *Field Survey 3, A Report of a Research Study submitted to the President's Commission on Law Enforcement and Administration of Justice*, United States Government Printing Office, Washington, 1967.

107. D. Dickson, op. cit., pp. 144, 149.

108. cf. E. Lemert, *Social Action and Legal Change*, Aldine, Chicago, 1970.

109. cf. P. Rock and F. Heidensohn, 'New Reflections on Violence', in D. A. Martin (Ed.), *Anarchy and Culture*, Routledge & Kegan Paul, London, 1969, and P. Rock and S. Cohen, 'The Teddy Boy', in V. Bogdanor and R. Skidelsky, *The Age of Affluence*, Macmillan, London, 1970.

110. cf. E. Lemert; 'Social Action and Legal Change', op. cit.

111. R. Fuller and R. Myers, 'The Natural History of a Social Problem', *American Sociological Review*, June 1941, vol. 6, p. 321.

112. cf. H. Becker, *Outsiders*, Free Press, New York, 1963.

113. M. Wiseheart, 'Newspapers and Criminal Justice', in R. Pound and F. Frankfurter (Ed.), *Criminal Justice in Cleveland*, Cleveland Foundation, Cleveland, Ohio, 1922, p. 545.

114. ibid., p. 546.

115. cf. E. Sutherland, 'The Diffusion of Sexual Psychopath Laws', in W. J. Chambliss (Ed.), op. cit.

4

THE ENFORCEMENT OF LAWS

Law structures a society's system of typifications. It affects a population's stock of knowledge about the nature, extent and distribution of deviancy. It establishes patterns of guilt, shame and motivation. Yet it cannot be universal without coercion because it is an imperialistic code whose very existence presupposes dissent. It depends upon supporting coercive agencies for its effectiveness. Chief amongst these enforcement agencies is the police.

I shall dwell exclusively upon police organisation in this chapter. I shall do so in order to furnish a detailed case study of the way in which authoritative definitions of deviancy undergo changes as they become translated into action. My model should hold for most industrial societies and especially Britain, but the material upon which it is based is principally American because the sociology of the police has been a largely American pursuit.

Four issues have directed the construction of my model:

The police as inhibitors. Deviancy rarely flourishes unchecked in a society. Its growth, maintenance and forms are shaped by critical features in its environment and by the police in particular.

The police as transformers. The police are not merely one of the agencies which inhibit or permit the forms assumed by deviancy, they also transform it. Because transactions between the police and deviants have significant effects on both groups, police actions, policies and decisions are themselves causal agents in the structuring of deviancy.

The police as translators. The police are one of the vehicles through which powerful social groups enforce their definitions of proper social order. Without such a vehicle, these definitions would be substantially less consequential. But the translation and enforcement are never literal because the police are recruited from special segments of the community, form themselves into institutions with peculiar cultures and traditions and encounter special problems. Legal definitions are forced to undergo subtle or crude changes before they are realised in action. Without a knowledge of concrete police practices, conjectures about the manner in which law affects a population remain no more than conjectures. As Skolnick argues, 'the police define the operative legality of the system of administering criminal law . . . if the criminal law is especially salient to a population which has more or less recurrent interactions with the police, it is the police who define the system of order to this population'.[1]

The police as creators of reality. The police create one reality for the population which they manage. They create another by generating the matter out of which knowledge is constructed about the nature and volume of deviancy. Official statistics and records of crime underpin authoritative conceptions of deviancy and socially problematic areas. Such rates are not a *direct* reflection of any 'real' amount of rule-breaking. Primarily, they are indices of official activity.[2] They are a collapsed version of the innumerable decisions which are taken about the social management of deviation. If, for instance, the police act against drug-taking, drug-taking will become a rate. If they decide to refrain from combating witchcraft, witchcraft will not be a rate. Police policies thus shape the manner in which the members of a society can map out their social world.

POLICE GOALS

The police constitute a bureaucracy which is designed to serve specific goals; primary goals are explicitly laid down by external institutions as the justification of ongoing police work; secondary goals arise internally as a response to recurring problems confronted by the bureaucracy; and tertiary goals are the incidental, unintended consequences of the nature of enforcement work.

Primary goals: symbolic support

The head of the Thames Valley Police drugs squad was reported to have said, 'We like to give people the impression they are always being watched, and always being involved with the police if they experiment with dangerous drugs.'[3] The police play a continuous and complicated dramatic role which serves to underline the pervasiveness and importance of official definitions of rectitude. The ubiquity of the police in the community leads to the weaving of a kind of symbolic web which is intended to be an everpresent check on potential and actual rule-breakers. Wenninger and Clark argue:

... the police operate as part of the background or social milieu affecting all members of a society. This milieu is 'given' from the moment of entrance of a member into the society and is consciously or unconsciously taken into account in most social behavior. ... [4]

The police are hags who ride deviants and nondeviants alike. Their role is as much representational and symbolic as it is one centring on instrumental action. As such some observers can no longer see them in their individuality and diversity. They can become abstract manifestations of legal order. As a writer of the *London Quarterly Review* of 1856 remarked:

Amid the bustle of Piccadilly or the roar of Oxford Street, P.C.X.59 stalks along, an institution rather than a man. We seem to have no more hold of his personality than we could possibly get of his coat buttoned up to the throttling-point. Go, however, to the section-house ... and you no longer see policemen, but men. ... They are positively laughing with one another! [5]

Symbolic support may receive a more precise form in the provision of a calculus of pains and pleasures to be derived from law-breaking. Whilst nondeviants appear to be more convinced of the inevitability of the detection and punishment which follow upon rule-breaking, [6] the deterrent role of the police generates a state of apprehensiveness in a great many instances of deviancy. Such apprehensiveness is a major structuring influence on the expression of rule-breaking behaviour.

Active intervention

The police play instrumental as well as expressive roles. They actively intervene in those situations where rule-breaking has occurred or is threatened. They are responsible for the boundary-patrolling tasks of a system of social control. They control those deviancies which are proscribed both by external law-giving institutions and by their own law-interpreting behaviour.

There is a systematic division of labour between enforcement agencies. Police are rarely called upon to deal with matters arising out of civil law litigation and, in this respect, they are primarily instruments of retributive justice. Many forms of deviancy are tackled by institutions of private control: store detectives, security firms, insurance companies, private detectives, debt-collectors and so on. The police confront only a limited range of deviant behaviour.

The most obvious targets for police attention are actions which have broken the criminal law. The ostensible function of the police in these cases is to provide a bridging service between law-breakers and law-administering bodies such as the courts. In practice, however, the police often act as terminal agents of control;[7] the processing of deviancy does not go beyond them but ends instead in alternative sanctions or cautioning. On other occasions, too, rule-breaking may only be imminent. In these situations the police may attempt to freeze affairs so that what might be an otherwise inevitable deterioration in lawlessness does not ensue. Indeed, the capacity of individual officers to 'handle a situation' may become the key criterion by which their performance is assessed.[8]

The police are not only required to enforce laws because they are skilled and organised people with a licence to use violence in the interests of the state. Their role is not to be entirely attributed to the replacement of informal mechanical modes of control by a formal and specialised system.[9] It is also a product of their peculiar relation to the victim and offender. The civil law still permits the offended to pursue the offender some way before the state intervenes. The criminal law does not do so for at least three reasons: the state has usurped some of the victim's rights and obligations; it affords the offender some measure of protection from his victim or those who sympathise with the victim (in the extreme cases, such sympathies can take the form of vigilante action or lynching); and, lastly, it allows for the possibility of peaceful relations being resumed between offender and victim. Feuds or private enforcement tend to exacerbate and perpetuate conflicts which might have been terminated by a seemingly dispassionate administration of external control.[10] As a government commission of 1839 observed of riots:

. . we have been informed that the animosities created or increased, and rendered permanent by arming master against servant, neighbour against neighbour, by triumph on one side and failure on the other, were even more deplorable than the outrages originally committed. . . . The necessity for such painful and demoralising conflicts between connected persons could be avoided by providing a trained and independent force for action in such emergencies.[11]

The police are a state's main defence against activity which is officially defined as threatening. Threats may be levelled against the complex political and moral structure which is held to constitute the state itself. They may also take the form of minor behaviours which are not regarded as subversive to the structure but are manageable within it. Theft, rape, assault and crimes without victims would be members of the second class; whilst treason, political subversion and radical politicised deviation would be members of the first. The proper classification of deviancy is frequently a matter of terminological dispute. As I have argued in Chapter 2, there is inevitably some ambiguity about the significance of deviations. Many deviants point to the political consequentiality of acts which conventionally fall under the second class and, as Turk has indicated, controlling élites are predisposed to apply the label 'criminal' to as many subversive acts as possible. *Crime* denotes evil intention, individual pathology and the possibility of suppression to a much greater extent than such words as *revolution* or *political action*.

While the police are primarily occupied with the second class, they are also regarded by their administrators as the chief bulwark against threats stemming from the first. The routine tasks of monitoring political deviants are usually undertaken by such bodies as the Special Branch.[12] However, conventional police forces may also be deployed against political deviants when, for instance, demonstrations become violent. In such cases the police become the major shield of the state. The shielding role of a police force becomes particularly important when the administrative centre of a nation also houses a large population.[13] As Lloyd George observed in 1919, 'The police force is so essential to the stability of social order that at all hazards we must take steps to ensure that we have a body of men at the disposal of the state who can be relied upon.'[14]

Secondary goals

The police also have a subsidiary set of goals which are largely instrumental in allowing them to achieve the first set. Any institution must organise itself so that it is capable of realising its ostensible objectives. The process of organisation establishes a new, lower order of objectives which can, in time, displace higher ones.* At the very least, the police must be able to maintain their efficiency by co-ordinating their activities into a system; controlling deviant members of that system; providing the system with information, resources and commitments; and protecting itself from outside interference. Any police bureaucracy must also organise knowledge about itself and its place in the larger world. It must attempt to understand how deviant processes occur and what effects its own actions will have upon them. That is, the police must evolve a lay sociology of crime and enforcement which will direct them. Werthman and Piliavin state:

* Thus Skolnick lists a number of American examples of the way in which the police employ their power to attain organisational goals (such as wage increases) rather than first order goals. cf. J. Skolnick, *The Politics of Protest*, Ballantine, New York, 1969, esp. p. 273.

... patrolmen are forced to operate like social scientists. In order to locate 'suspicious persons' they must use indicators, each with a specific but by no means perfect probability of leading them either to the discovery or prevention of a crime. Policemen develop indicators of suspicion by a method of pragmatic induction . . . the police divide the population and physical territory under surveillance into a variety of categories, make some initial assumptions about the moral character of the people and places in these categories, and then focus attention on those categories of persons and places felt to have the shadiest moral characteristics.[15]

This lay sociology may be called the 'police theory'. It will stress certain themes. It will, for example, map out an area in terms of the social relations that can typically be expected there. A policeman will identify certain areas as properly containing certain kinds of people. Those who are 'out of place' will attract suspicion. The way in which particular offenders can be located in an area's social networks will also affect action. Their location will structure the effects of possible enforcement. Deviants who can expect a reasonable mobilisation of local resources will be treated rather differently from those who are more vulnerable. Different kinds of area will also make the officer himself more or less vulnerable. He believes that he can expect certain kinds of support or hindrance in the districts of a city, and his strategies will be resolved appropriately. In individual encounters, too, the police are alert to possibilities of violence and obstruction. They develop a superior sensitivity to those cues which might signify an assault or other danger. Skolnick observes:

The policeman, because his work requires him to be occupied continually with potential violence, develops a perceptual short-hand to identify certain kinds of people as symbolic assailants, that is, as persons who use gesture, language and attire that the policeman has come to recognise as a prelude to violence. This does not mean that violence by the symbolic assailant is necessarily predictable. On the contrary, the policeman responds to the vague indication of danger suggested by appearance. Like the animals of the experimental psychologist, the policeman finds the threat of random damage more compelling than a predetermined and inevitable punishment.[16]

The definitions which the police use to organise their environment highlight most of the features which are pertinent to the police role. They search for incongruities between things, situations and people. For example, Adams cites a list of some twenty suspicious circumstances which should trigger off an officer's interest. They include 'Persons who do not "belong" where they are observed. Businesses opened at odd hours, or not according to routine or custom. Emaciated-appearing alcoholics and narcotics users who invariably turn to crime to pay for the cost of habit. Any person observed in the immediate vicinity of a crime very recently committed or reported to be "in progress". Persons who attempt to avoid or evade the officer. Exaggerated unconcern over contact with the officer. Visibly "rattled" when near the policeman. "Lovers" in an industrial area (make good lookouts). Persons wearing coats on hot days,'[17] and so on. Such cues generate suspicion. Other cues suggest who might have committed an offence. Certain groups are assumed to be in a much higher risk category than others. Wearing particular clothes, associating with certain people and, in particular, possessing a police record are likely to lead to interrogation. The police theory's conception of typical criminal processes prompts officers to look for an offender amongst the ranks of those who have committed the same offence in the past. There are low-risk categories as well, and categories of people whom it is dangerous to interrogate unless there is a high degree of certainty about their guilt.[18]

Not only are the offender and potential offender assessed, the police theory provides criteria for judging victims, informers, informants and witnesses. Any policeman must rapidly comprehend a situation and arrange its crucial components together so that likely outcomes can be predicted.

In his encounters with the victim, for instance:

. . . the tendency of the [American] patrolman to be and act suspicious arises not simply from the danger inherent in his function but from his doubts as to the 'legitimacy' of the victim. Middle-class victims who have suffered a street attack . . . are generally considered most legitimate; middle-class victims of burglary are seen as somewhat less legitimate (it *could* be an effort to make a fraudulent insurance claim); lower-class victims of theft are still less legitimate (they probably brought it on themselves).[19]

For any police action to be possible, officers must juggle with these organisationally derived perspectives and reach decisions. The generation of these perspectives arises out of the suspension of the *epoché* of the natural attitude, and it places the policeman in a position which is somewhat estranged from the commonsense thinking that prevails in everyday life. The ground for his thinking and the decisions he reaches are quite frequently esoteric and unfamiliar to most lay members of society.

Perspectives must be organised because the policeman is constantly confronted by problems of choice which he must resolve independently and quickly. Choice arises because he is simply unable to respond to deviancy in an indiscriminate manner. There is too much deviancy and there are too few policemen for all deviants to be always apprehended when their rule-breaking comes to official attention. Not only are the police unable to process all the deviation they encounter, there are numerous reasons why they do not wish to do so:

(1) They are constrained by the processing capacities of the courts, prisons and so on. Over-enthusiastic enforcement would engender stresses in the social control network; stresses that would generally be resolved by pressure being placed on the police to slacken their effort.

(2) Indiscriminate action would antagonise many people who have been safely insulated from the police in the past. Mass antagonism would engender instabilities in the patterns of accommodation that the police and lay members of society jointly attain. Excessive resort to coercion would also transform a great deal of primary deviation into an unmanageable secondary deviation. Furthermore, it would undermine the presentation of the police as *authoritative* agents and render them agents dependent upon *force*:

. . . a conflict arises for the policeman between carrying out the social role which the prevention of crime requires and performing the 'thief-catching' role, where he is exercising delegated authority. The police want to be respected and not questioned in the execution of their duty, but at the same time to have understanding and help from the public.[20]

(3) Additional stress would be induced by sending crime rates up to vast heights. Total enforcement would so boost reported rates that public concern could well become a state of near panic. With some slight exaggeration, Blumberg states, 'Any society that committed the energy, resources and personnel to root out and punish all wrongdoers would set off enough mass paranoia, violent conflict and savage repression to become a charnel house, and pass into oblivion.'[21]

(4) Total enforcement would depend upon either a complete absence of flexibility in police work or upon complete police agreement with legal norms. Such flexibility is an inherent component of police organisation and such agreement is unlikely to occur.

(5) Finally, a policy of total enforcement would rest upon an inability or refusal of the police to differentiate between offences, victims and offenders. Even if the police applauded the wisdom of all laws that were passed, it would be impossible for them to apply those laws with equal severity in all cases.

Because the police are required to exercise continuous discretion, the police theory must also specify how choices should be made. The theory will outline which offences can be ignored, which can be treated in an informal and lenient manner, which necessitate the show of force, and which compel the actual use of formal sanctions. In some cases, for instance, a policeman may believe that official punitive or therapeutic measures are simply inappropriate. Piliavin and Briar argue that officers are occasionally reluctant 'to expose certain youths to the stigmatisation presumed to be associated with official police action. Few juvenile officers believed that correctional agencies serving the community could effectively help delinquents.'[22] Similarly, a policeman who arrests too many people might be thought unable to 'handle his beat'. He cannot exercise the appropriate amount of personal authority which is required to stabilise relations in an area.[23] The arrests of certain kinds of offender might be equally damaging to his reputation.[24] As a result, the police theory must evolve some means whereby priorities can be established, the amount of discretion can be fixed and resources can be most effectively deployed. A policeman will have informal guidelines upon which to work if he can assume that there is a taken-for-granted policy on most matters. He will know whether he can ignore a mild delinquency or an instance of drug-taking. Without this reassurance, his work will be slowed up and he will lay himself open to formal and informal sanctions. To the extent that he adheres to the precepts of the local version of the police theory, he is unlikely to find himself without support, respect or effective remedies. Policies become institutional-ised in different police organisations and they are subject to immense variation.[25] It seems probable that policemen who enter a new department must undergo a period of 'learning the ropes' before they become fully coordinated members.

While consensus exists amongst officers, and while the cases that they handle are manageable in terms of the police theory, the control bureaucracy will function in a smooth manner. It will categorise the population which it encounters and apply standard patterns of processing to each of the categories. Such a system reduces the time which is devoted to each case, permits rapid decision-making, promotes organisational stability and the coordination of the organisation's roles. In time, the theory will acquire an objective quality so that it will no longer be regarded as a product of the organisation. It will be treated as an accurate, commonsensical perspective on the world. It will impose a structure on that world so that it transforms it. McNamara states:

. . . police officers frequently failed to assess the motives and behavior of citizens with whom they were interacting because of the categories which they used in classifying these citizens. Classifications based on legal cate-gories particularly reduced the likelihood of accurate interpersonal test-ing. . . . Perhaps more relevant is the tendency to formulate initially a plan of action based upon whether a citizen is labeled a criminal. In this respect the legal categories often had an effect similar to that of stereotypes. That is, criminals were selectively perceived by officers in terms of (1) the legal prescriptions and proscriptions regarding appropriate police authority and procedures relative to the type and degree of the crime, and (2) the actions past and future that were considered to be associated with the type and degree of crime. This labeling, in turn, provided a base for a 'self-fulfilling prophecy' in situations where the labels and their imputed or associated characteristics were communicated to citizens who responded with indignation and often physically assaulted the officers. . . . The legal categories also interfered with the process of predicting a citizens's response to a police officer simply because of the salience for police officers of the legal categories when applied to citizens. That is, officers acted as though their understanding of the citizens with whom they were interacting were complete once they found the appropriate legal and/or departmental designation for the citizens.[26]

Such an application of normal cases will stabilise the police world so that typical events and personalities will recur time and again in an orderly and intelligible fashion. The untoward is likely to be redefined as the familiar and placed in an appropriate category. Yet there is another important way in which organisationally generated notions prevail over those which emanate from the world outside the organisation. According to Reiss and Bordua, the police, unlike most other service organisations, are their own clients:

the police in a sense are a service without clients. The police serve the public as a collectivity rather than distributively. Enforcement must be initiated where there is no victim and/or complainant. Given the lack of guidelines either from the public as client or from a specific victim or complainant as client, the police can become in effect their own clients. We take this to be one of the fundamental features in the oft mentioned tendency of the police to develop a supermoralistic perspective and to see themselves as engaged in a 'private' war on crime.[27]

As I shall show later, there are other organisational features of the police, their isolation in particular, which promote the formation of an esoteric culture that sets its own goals for its adherents. It is this kind of transition that permits this goal displacement which I mentioned before.

There is another secondary goal which tends to become an end in its own right as well as acting as an influence on the police theory. In order to achieve first-order goals, the police must acquire an authority which is not instantly granted them. The effectiveness of the police, especially in Britain, rests very largely on the way in which they can gain compliance. Although any policeman is supported by reserves which can be called upon, the existence of support may

provide scant reassurance in an ongoing enforcement situation.
Not only is there an inevitable time-lag between an appeal for help
and succour, there are also powerful pressures which restrain an
officer from making such an appeal in the first place. A policeman
who is unable to cope will be exposed to the risk of being thought
inefficient and unprofessional by his colleagues. He also places a
burden on those colleagues who must be deployed to aid him. The
maintenance of authority over a territory in general, and over certain
deviants in particular, may become one of an officer's overriding
concerns. It may even transcend the need to enforce the law wisely
and in a legally judicious manner. Instead, the criminal law can
become transformed into an instrument which is used to engineer the
personal control of a policeman. A preoccupation with respect,
especially in America, can become the dominant influence on an
officer's handling of his work. Westley suggests that in the United
States:

The policeman finds his most pressing problems in his relationships to the
public. His is a service occupation but of an incongruous kind, since he
must discipline those whom he serves. He is regarded as corrupt and
inefficient by, and meets with hostility and criticism from, the public. He
regards the public as his enemy, feels his occupation to be in conflict with
the community, and regards himself to be a pariah. The experience and the
feeling give rise to a collective emphasis on secrecy, an attempt to coerce
respect from the public, and a belief that almost any means are legitimate
in completing an important arrest. These are for the policeman basic
occupational values. They arise from his experience, take precedence over
his legal responsibilities, are central to an understanding of his conduct
and form the occupational contexts within which violence gains its
meaning.[28]

The need to exact respect from an occasionally disrespectful
population shapes the policeman's handling of his role. It makes the
classification of a type of deviant as subversive to authority extremely important for the handling of that person. It means that the
police may spend more time and effort in the enforcement of the law
against those kinds of deviancy which undermine respect. It also
means that the role-style of deviants becomes as important as the
deviant role itself. It is not only the fact that a person is deviant which
determines enforcement outcomes, it is also the demeanour of the
deviant. Such demeanour can become critical in deciding whether an
incident will lead to an arrest, the manner in which the arrest is
carried out, the charge which is made and the nature of the evidence
which may be offered in court. When, for example, a policeman
intervenes in a fracas:

There is one major exception to the generalisation that the patrolman will be reluctant to make an arrest as a result of a dispute or fight he has not witnessed. This situation arises when one or the other of the quarrelling parties turns on the officer and abuses, resists, or attacks him.[29]

Respect is not only important because it is a prerequisite of authority; it is also conducive to other ends. A policeman's colleagues will deplore messy enforcement which attracts publicity and which may generate an escalation of lawlessness. Their disapproval will aggravate the policeman's own feelings of discomposure. Any interaction is a precarious activity, and embarrassment is often caused by benign role partners. The psychic costs of ordinary discomposure are much greater when the policeman not only fears assault but also invests himself in his occupational identity. Lack of respect may also be taken to signify the possibility that a policeman's contacts with respectful others will be contaminated by the subversive. Above all, disrespect upsets a definition of the situation which must be congenial to most policemen. A deviant who readily complies with an officer, admits his guilt and seeks guidance, reassures the policeman that the job which he is doing is a beneficial and legitimate role. Those who challenge this conception of police work also offer some threat to the morality and rationality of enforcement. In consequence, an officer's stock of respect is jealously defended:

Uncoerced responsiveness to police authority in the immediate situation, that is respect—uncoerced in the immediate situation at least—is the most valuable resource available to the police. Much excessive police coercion can be attributed to the perception that respect must be re-established in a situation where it has broken down or to building up future respect credits in populations where police expect disrespect as a routine matter.[30]

Hence the respectfulness of different groups in a society and the ways in which deference may be secured from them can be built into the police theory and inform the way in which much routine police work is carried on. The criterion of respect will affect who will be arrested for what offences in what circumstances.

There are other second-tier goals which influence behaviour, but these are an aspect of the way in which the police organise their internal and external relations. I shall therefore discuss the structuring of links with the courts, public, press and so on when I describe police organisation itself. At this point, it can be simply pointed out that the successful articulation of a police service with its environment is a self-evident secondary goal.

Tertiary goals

The third set of goals I described as being the incidental, unintended consequences of police work. The policeman enters a surprising diversity of situations and the demands which are placed upon him in those situations are not necessarily those which he or his superiors would choose. It may nevertheless be essential for him to satisfy these demands in order for him to continue to function as an effective agent of control. In an article entitled the 'Policeman as philosopher, friend and guide', it is suggested:

While it is probably impossible to perform acts of support and control simultaneously, support without control is overprotection and invites passivity and dependency, while control without support is tyranny and invites rebellion. While the agent may specialise in one aspect of social control of deviance, the other must, nevertheless, be part of his repertoire.[31]

The apex of the social control system, the legislature, depends upon authority for its continued effectiveness. The rest of the units of the system also attempt to acquire a willing compliance from the population which they manage. Unadulterated coercion is an unreliable method of attaining long-term compliance. In Britain, where each police officer is responsible for the control of some six hundred people,[32] coercion alone cannot secure police objectives. Of course, potentially abrasive contacts between the police and public are concentrated in certain areas only, so that control dilemmas are to that extent diminished. Nevertheless, a willing acquiescence to police work is an indispensable component of effective action. When the policeman's coercive role-style is tempered by a benign complexion, he may become enrolled as an agent of support and called upon to perform a large number of extraneous services. The Cummings and Edell analysed some 650 incoming calls that were received at an American police station in an urban area over an eighty-two-hour period. They discovered that about half of these were taken up with matters which did not relate strictly to law enforcement issues.[33] Instead, information was sought about health services, children's problems, help for incapacitated people and so on. A proliferation of such subsidiary role-requirements tends to transform the nature of the policeman for many people. He may become a working-class analogue of the specialist upon whom the middle class relies for advice upon problems of living. Whitaker remarked:

One village constable said that eighteen families regularly bring him their income-tax forms to fill in, besides looking on him as their doctor, marriage counsellor, and general adviser.[34]

It is clear that such a development of role-style serves at least the secondary goals of a police organisation. It permits the police to maintain a network of informants and contacts who will make law enforcement proper more manageable. The maintenance of such a network is of vital importance to any policeman. It allows him to gain access to authoritative information about the characteristics and movements of those whom he is seeking. The policeman may build up a set of reciprocal relations which will become a valuable resource that can be exploited for both its psychic and its instrumental value.

The evolution of such a style will be significant in another way. Like all people who are engaged in a continuous, delicate and possibly troublesome interaction with others, a policeman becomes immensely preoccupied with the dramaturgical properties of his performance. He must sustain a persuasive and authoritative front before people whose freedom he threatens. This concern with successful role-playing dominates much of the working life of the police. As I have argued, the ability to 'handle situations' is one of the criteria by which the police judge themselves. The policeman may normally adopt an impersonal front which conveys the impression that he is the impartial representative of an abstract system of laws. In particular circumstances, he may employ a paternalistic role-style which suggests that the deviant is a sympathetic person whose infraction provokes anxiety. This is most likely to happen when the deviant is of lower status and power than himself, and when he is not likely to be subversive to his authority. With those of higher status, he may hide as much of his nonofficial self as possible behind an impassive, deferential demeanour. The role-strain induced in such situations can often be allayed when the officer discovers a flaw in the superior person which will so degrade him that unequal relations are equalised or reversed. With others, especially committed, professional criminals, the policeman may transform himself into the unwilling player of a game whose rules are understood by both partners in the interaction. Such role-distance can relieve tension. An illustration is recalled by a thief who had been arrested in Scotland:

I found two men awaiting me. The Chief introduced them as Detective-Inspector Goodwillie and Detective-Inspector Mitchell, both of the 'Yard'. We shook hands, just to show there was no animosity.

'I don't suppose you know either of us, do you?' inquired Goodwillie.

'No. I have not had the pleasure of meeting you before, I think,' I answered as amiably as I could.

'Well, we've come all the way from London to see you', said Goodwillie. 'We want to see if you can help us clear up your English crimes. A lot of them have been placed in our hands and we understand that you are anxious to come down to England to be tried for them.'

That was perfectly true. The ten days I had been in Edinburgh had been sufficient for me to realise that the game was up. When that is the case, it is no use giving more trouble than is absolutely necessary. I told Good-willie so. 'That's a good chap', he replied. 'We're going to give you a trip down to London so that you can help us.'[35]

The goals and skills of the police in specific interactions will suggest appropriate strategies. Those who wish to produce a smooth, trouble-free enforcement situation will choose that role-style which is most likely to dispel or redirect hostility. Paternalism, impassivity or game-playing, however, may not be seen as obvious solutions to all enforcement problems. Degradation may be regarded as a necessary process in order to render the deviant malleable. It may be an intervening phase or it may colour the whole of the policeman's treatment of the deviant.

It may be, however, that a compliant deviant is not the sole good which the officer seeks. The deviancy may be defined as so outrageous that the officer cannot or is unwilling to restrain himself. The role-style of the deviant may also cause affront. In these cases, the officer may wish to use the arrest or encounter as an opportunity to punish rather than as a preliminary to the punitive work of the courts. In other cases, too, the policeman may anticipate that the court or his colleagues will not concur in his definition of the deviant or the deviancy. He may then subject the deviant to a punishment which would not be meted out by others. His degradation work here is a compensation for the work which should be, but is not likely to be, performed by others. A perennial concern with the interactional properties of his work is an inevitable product of the police occupation.

It is apparent that these three tiers of goals are not easily separable from one another. The typology may, indeed, be misleading because no one objective can be situationally divorced from any others. Instead, the goals form an interrelated system which pervades the policeman's orientation towards his work.

POLICING AS A BUREAUCRATIC PHENOMENON

To understand how these foregoing goals and characteristics of the police are institutionalised and patterned, one must grasp the organisational character of policing. The police are a fairly mono-lithic, centralised bureaucracy with a strict allocation of roles, rights, duties and obligations. The division of labour is symbolically rein-forced by uniform, by differentials in rank and all the etiquette that signifies a strictly hierarchical quasi-military organisation. The police, in fact, straddle occupational styles: they cannot be properly described as a 'civilian' occupation because they are subject to extraordinary restraints and expectations; at the same time, they do not conform to a strict military model of organisation. It is not quite clear what the dominating bureaucratic model should be. One definition, which is still prevalent, suggests that the policeman is a civilian with an unusual role. Thus, the Report of the Desborough Committee of 1919 stated:

We consider it important to bear in mind that the constable, even in the execution of his duty for the preservation of the peace, acts not as an agent of the Government, exercising powers derived from that fact, but as a citizen, representing the rest of the community, and exercising powers which, at any rate, in their elements, are possessed by all citizens alike.[36]

Nevertheless, the year before, the Home Secretary, Sir George Cave, released a press statement about the attempts of the police to organise themselves into a trade union:

The Prime Minister said to the deputation of policemen who saw him that he could not in wartime sanction recognition of a Police Union. He pointed out that the trouble in Russia had to a great extent arisen from the existence of a Union or a committee among the soldiers. He thought the Police were a semi-military force, and that to a great extent the same condition applied to them. . . .[37]

While control *within* the British police is carefully supervised, and the police are not allowed to resort to the collective defences available to other occupations, the police themselves are relatively free from *direct external control*. The head of a British police force wields an authority (either rational, legal or charismatic)[38] which is not subject to much formal restraint. Hart observes that '. . . a constable is not the servant of the police authority and cannot be given orders by them',[39] and the important case of *Fisher* v. *Oldham Corporation* established that 'if a police officer arrested a man for a serious felony and the Watch Committee passed a resolution directing that the felon should be released, the resolution would be of no value. . . .'[40] The Home Office can exercise some influence by wielding financial sanctions and issuing memoranda which are accepted as instructions, but a police chief enjoys unusual autonomy. Autonomy is reinforced by the tendency of the police to be their own clients, to formulate their own interpretations of first-order goals and to devise appropriate strategies. Changes of chief constable can result in substantial shifts of policy. For instance, the 1963 *Police Review* stated:

Manchester is evidently one of the Forces which believe that the law should be strictly enforced, and some figures included in the Chief Constable's annual report in fact reveal a radical change of policy during the past few years. In 1955 there was one prosecution for importuning. In 1956 and

1957 there were none, and in 1958 there were two. Mr. J. A. McKay was appointed Chief Constable at the end of that year, and the number of prosecutions rose to thirty in 1959 and 105 in 1960, to 135 in 1961 to 216 last year. The inescapable conclusion to be drawn from these figures is that until 1958 a blind eye was turned on importuning and that prosecutions were not encouraged by the Chief Constable.[41]

Another feature of the organisation which supports its ability to function as an independent unit generating its own goals is the unusual solidarity which prevails within the police. Solidarity is sustained in a number of ways. Its prime buttress is the relative homogeneity of the police, a homogeneity which is not encountered in other, similar hierarchies. Apart from the abortive Trenchard scheme of the 1930s and the more recent recruitment of graduates, the police are exempt from control by an officer stratum drawn from the middle and upper classes. As Bordua and Reiss argue:

The fact that all police-command personnel come up through the ranks means not only that there is relatively little class distinction among police but that the sharp difference between managers and workers in industry is less apparent for the police.[42]

Internal solidarity is also bolstered up by the social isolation of the police. Most officers carry out their work in uniform and they are subject to monitoring by innumerable others. The police are additionally segregated by time, function, geography and by patterns of sociability. The police work when many people are at home, asleep or engaged in leisure. In many cases they are temporally out of phase with the normal population and their encounters with it are correspondingly restricted. The inquisitorial and deterrent functions of the police also serve to promote social distance between the two groups. Distance increases when the police are confined to living in certain areas, whether they be the suburbs or, more particularly, in special police dwellings. Lambert states:

The growth of the police profession, the tendency for colonies of police houses to be built in certain neighbourhoods, the growing social and geographical mobility of the aspiring middle class with whom the policeman identifies, have all broken the old style links with the community. . . . Inevitably the policeman's own suburban view of life conflicts with that held in a heterogeneous central residential area. A policeman has only limited contact with his clients. He sees them as a social category . . . not as a whole person. He is himself seen as a social category, as an outsider.[43]

Attitudes engendered by such isolation are reported by a survey of the 1962 Royal Commission on the Police:[44] 67% of the officers interviewed believed that their job had an adverse effect on friendships with people outside the force. Their beliefs were mirrored by statements made by the public: 42% of the public thought that some police took bribes, 35% believed that the police used illicit methods of obtaining information and 32% believed that the police might distort evidence given in court. Such alienation encourages the development of solidarity and the formation of a distinctive police subculture which centres around the police theory which I described above. Such isolation appears more pronounced in the United States than in Britain. In America, the police seem to be rather more socially distant from the population around them, they also more frequently tend to imagine that they have been assigned a lower status than that which is appropriate. Bordua argues that:

Among the most significant consequences . . . is the fact that isolation from the community without careful bureaucratic organisation can result in police occupational cultures which can become private subcommunities heavily involved in illegally determining the distribution of law enforcement and the use of violence.[45]

Such subcultures can be undermined and fragmented: disrupting influences include civilian penetration of the police organisation, and the pressures induced by bureaucratisation and by internal divisions within the subculture itself. Civilian review boards and disciplinary bodies can threaten the authority of the police theory. Similarly, Wilson suggests that public penetration can make 'the "crime rate" go up by having offense reports recorded by persons who . . . are not constrained by the norms of the uniformed force'.[46] If the process of bureaucratisation is viewed as a progressive substitution of impartial, externally imposed rules for private initiatives and attitudes,[47] bureaucratisation will work something of a transformation on police discretion and private morality. The subculture can be further undermined by a lack of cohesion within the police force itself. While the organisation may seem monolithic and integrated from the outside, it is actually split in a number of ways. Apart from the functional differentiation into departments which may generate disputes about how the law should be administered and by whom, there are faults in the hierarchy. Although the police are ordered into a neat hierarchy with power attached to rank, in practice police officers cannot be rigorously controlled by their superiors.

A superficially centralised organisation is, in fact, extremely decentralised. The police are spread over the whole of the country and many police operations cannot be scrutinised. Gibbons comments on the ecological peculiarities of the police:

Many formal organisations are located in a single place, such as a college, a prison, or a factory. Control of individuals is made easier by virtue of the visual surveillance which can be maintained over them. But the police organisation is scattered about the community in headquarters and precinct stations. It is further scattered due to the fact that the largest single group of police employees are the patrolmen, most of whom are in patrol cars and not at the station house at all. These conditions make it difficult for police officials to conduct systematic evaluations of job performance of the workers, save through such devices as recording the number of arrests made by officers. The ecological structure of police work also creates difficulties in the way of control over deviant workers. Many of the deviant acts in which policemen sometimes engage, such as drinking on the job, are extremely difficult for administrators to observe.[48]

A police chief's difficulties in monitoring his officers are exacerbated in other ways. The officers' deviant behaviour may never reach his attention, not only because they are often careful to practise it in a covert manner or because the victim, if any, may not be aware of what constitutes correct procedure; it may also be concealed by the willing participation of outsiders who benefit from such deviance. A corrupt or partial officer may be welcomed by those whose interests he advances. Furthermore, much deviancy is *not* carried out by solitary erring officers who receive no group support. Instead, there may be powerful combinations amongst the junior officers which promote and defend unusual actions. As the US President's Crime Commission Task Force Report on the Police observed:

While neither articulated nor officially recognised, common responses obviously tend to develop in frequently recurring situations. A new police officer quickly learns these responses through his associations with more seasoned officers. The fact that a response is routine does not mean that it is satisfactory. To the contrary, many routine responses are applied on the basis of indefensible and improper criteria. But once developed, the routine response is generally immune to critical re-evaluation unless a crisis situation should arise. Because of their informal character, such responses tend not to be influenced by developments in police training. And, because they consist of the accumulated experiences of frontline officers, they tend to take on a vitality which sometimes continues even without the active support of the higher echelon of police administration.[49]

The evolution of such routine response has another effect on the police administrator's ability to control his organisation. While a great many reports of crime are forwarded to the police by individuals outside the force, many others depend on police activity. In their role as agents of 'aggressive patrol', the police actively seek deviancy out. Moreover, many forms of deviancy are unlikely to be voluntarily reported by outsiders. They may involve no victims, the victims may be compromised by reporting, or the deviancy may be carried out in such a discreet manner that it has no witnesses. Other kinds of deviancy may never be recognised—embezzlement or fraud may not be discovered. No administrator can ever know the extent of deviancy in the area which his force is supposed to control. He depends precisely on those deviant officers for information when he investigates their efficiency. Wilson states:

... the police chief has only the most rudimentary knowledge of how well his patrolmen are preventing crime, apprehending criminals, and maintaining order. No police department, however competently led or organized, can know how much crime and disorder a community produces or how much would be produced if the police functioned differently.[50]

Of course, the deviancy of officers may be supported or viewed with equanimity by their superiors. There is a continual conflict between 'due process' and 'crime control' patterns which involves superior officials as well as junior policemen. The chairman of the Durham police authority stated, for instance, that the police may have to employ illegal methods but 'the point is they have not got to be found out breaking the law'.[51] Whether organisational rule-breaking is condoned or not, the lower ranks of the police hierarchy are nevertheless capable of achieving autonomy from the constraints nominally imposed by their seniors.

This peculiar organisation must become integrated with its environment, an environment peopled by such publics as criminals, the 'community', the courts and rival enforcement agencies. The force's links with other formal institutions impose constraints on the manner in which it can define its goals and devise strategies to attain them. If, for example, the courts are critical of the kinds of deviants who are brought before them, or sanction the police for employing particular techniques, the police organisation itself must make some adaptive response. It is convenient, therefore, to look upon these institutions as forming a system whose parts affect one another. As Reiss and Bordua argue:

Transactions among police officers, public prosecutors, and the judiciary not infrequently have the effect of subverting the goals of law enforcement, since each is in a position to sanction the other's behavior.[52]

If each of these institutional parts of the larger system has a somewhat different interpretation of the aims and practices of law enforcement, it will follow that there is always the possibility of competition between the parts for greater control. Each institution will evolve its own subcultural definition of the proper place of itself and others in the overall system. These definitions are likely to conflict and there may be considerable jockeying for power between police officers, probation officers, lawyers and the judiciary. The police may employ extra-legal or illegal means of control; the probation service may make recommendations and apply theories which run counter to the soft determinism of the police or courts; the courts may emphasise the due process model rather than the crime control pattern;[53] and so on. In the case of the management of delinquency, Wheeler *et al.* state:

If we assume that each of these occupational groups is interested in expanding its domain of control over delinquents, it is clear that the police do so by keeping delinquents out of the courts and in the hands of police departments and juvenile bureaus, while the probation officers and judges do so by expanding into the police territory and absorbing a large proportion of the youth population into the court. A simple hypothesis that each group attempts to expand its own range of control over children in trouble would also explain the greater readiness to see youths in court among . . . judges and probation officers.[54]

Police defences of such bureaucratic imperialism may invoke the peculiar expertise of the police in handling certain problems, the inability of other organisations to provide effective remedies for these problems, the difficulties caused by a strict observance of the due process model. The officers of Piliavin and Briar's study of police encounters with juveniles relied on an unofficial 'administrative legitimation of discretion' which maintained that 'strict enforcement practices would overcrowd court calendars and detention facilities, as well as dramatically increase juvenile crime rates—consequences to be avoided because they would expose the police department to community criticism'.[55]

The most nebulous external group with whom the police interact is the 'public' or 'community'. At the very least, the police are somewhat vulnerable to the vagaries of 'public opinion'. The publics can be more or less obstructive; they can, for example, refuse to provide the police with information so that enforcement becomes transformed into a proactive rather than a predominantly reactive activity, or they can mobilise themselves into pressure groups which might cause discomfort.[56] Most police forces have some interest, therefore, in placating the public. By so doing, they can change the basis of their control from pure coercion to a partially legitimated authority. Their orientation can vary immensely in the degree of responsiveness which they are prepared to make, yet some responses must be made.

Other things being equal, the consistent and zealous enforcement of unpopular laws will promote the isolation of the police from the population which it is supposed to serve and discipline. Similarly, as constraining agents, the police may be perceived as threatening even when they enforce laws which receive fairly widespread popular support. Clark suggests that isolation may be reinforced because the police are 'visible reminders of the seamy and recalcitrant portion of human behavior'.[57] Such an association would presumably stigmatise those who associated with the police. The dangers presented by the poor integration of a force with the community can be offset by deliberate strategies. The police may dull their collective response to consensually approved illegality or treat with circumspection those actions which the public regards with ambivalence. In any case, the police are themselves likely to be somewhat less than eager to enforce such laws. They must also be aware of the hostility which certain techniques can engender. The use of peremptory methods of interrogation, the employment of dogs and horses, and the resort to what others define as gratuitous violence can all alienate a community from its police. As the Royal Commission observed, 'departments may utilise procedures, such as the use of dogs, to control crowds, without balancing the potential harm to police–community relations'.[58]

Another more amorphous restraint imposed by the public is the demand that the police cope with crime without causing alarm. The police cannot make public too little crime because they will be thought inefficient and the account of their activities may conflict with popular notions about the frequency and distribution of deviancy. On the other hand, it might be dangerous to process too much deviancy in case the public became alarmed at the apparent ubiquity of threatening behaviour. The police may informally tailor their rates so that they reconcile these two demands. If, for example, too little rule-breaking has been handled over a period of time, they may inflate their records by comparatively artificial means. All officers know where traffic offences are often committed, and it is possible that they will satisfy a tacit quota of reports by visiting these places.[59] Other methods may be employed as well, as Reiss and Bordua observe:

The dilemma created by the necessity to maintain a public image of success in the face of aggregative measures of lack of success can readily lead to the manipulation of the statistics to create a favourable public image. Police departments, in fact, build up their *volume* of production largely out of misdemeanours rather than felonies, out of crimes against property rather than against persons, and in these days from juveniles and traffic. Tradition oriented departments often artificially inflate their success rate by getting arrested persons to 'cop out' to additional offenses or by charging offenses to an arrested person on the basis of a *modus operandi*.[60]

Not only may there be a careful preparation of the overall volume of crime processed during a period of time; the police are alert to the need to present the kinds of *specific* rates which are demanded by an

G

influential public. In America a residual populist tradition and a greater involvement of the police in community political structures have rendered crime statistics extremely responsive to perceived and legitimated demands. While the American responsiveness described by Niederhoffer may not be quite so frequently encountered in Britain, his observations still indicate how critical relations between police and public produce predictable outcomes:

With monotonous regularity the statistics reported are collated and often manipulated, so that they prove how successfully the department is performing its duties. If newspapers complain that delinquency is rising, the next police report will inevitably reveal a great increase in arrests of juvenile delinquents. When a safety council alleges that motorists are speeding dangerously, 'by coincidence' the police publish statistics of a tremendous number of summonses issued for speeding violations. . . .[61]

Another construct built into the police theory will thus be a combination of an internalised 'generalised other' and a conscious responsiveness to what are perceived as legitimate or significant community pressures. The ways in which these pressures are articulated will, of course, have a strong effect on their consequences for the police. It is plausible that the police compound out of their own sentiments and the sentiments which they attribute to authoritative and respectable others a model of generalised expectations of behaviour. As Banton argues, 'to explain what a policeman actually does it is necessary to see his activities as being governed more by popular morality than by the letter of the law'.[62]

EQUILIBRIUM AND THE POLICE

The nature of the police organisation is thus shaped by its goals, its structure and its relations with others. The outcome of the interactions of these factors will be a bureaucracy which tackles deviancy in an ordered and reasonably stable manner. The *amount* of the deviancy which it tackles will be a direct consequence of the ways in which it is directed by these pressures, the freedom with which it has to act, its technology and its size. It is transparently clear that the number of personnel that can be deployed to combat deviancy will determine the amount of deviancy that will be discovered and, perhaps, how much deviancy is thought to be *discoverable*. Erikson suggests:

the amount of deviation a community encounters is apt to remain fairly constant over time . . . it is a simple logistic fact that the number of deviancies which come to a community's attention are limited by the kinds of equipment it uses to detect and handle them, and to that extent the rate of deviation found in a community is at least in part a function of the size and complexity of its social control apparatus . . . when the community calibrates its control machinery to handle a certain volume of deviant behavior, it tends to adjust its legal and psychiatric definitions of the problem in such a way that this volume is in fact realised. After all, every control agent and every control facility is 'needed' by society. If the police should somehow learn to contain most of the crimes it now contends with . . . it is still improbable that the existing control machinery would go unused. More likely, the agencies of control would turn their attention to other forms of behavior, even to the point of defining as deviant certain styles of conduct which were not regarded so earlier.[63]

Such an orientation suggests an interesting model of police–deviant interaction. The matrix of the police theory, police adaption and organisation, and processing capacities will generate a particular product. This product will be a drive towards the stabilisation, routinisation and conventionalisation of police–deviant relations. No bureaucracy can function smoothly when the population it serves and controls changes in an erratic manner. The police theory will direct officers to deal with certain people in certain areas who commit certain kinds of deviancy. Through self-fulfilling prophecies, the effectiveness of such a policy will generally be proved.[64] When a police organisation settles down to working in a community in this way, the result will be an uneasy equilibrium. The equilibrium is constantly changing and can be upset in a number of ways. The relations between competing pressures, the consistent deployment of resources and the viability of the police theory will strive towards a stability that can be threatened by (amongst other factors): (1) changing legislation, (2) changes in political or internally generated pressures on the police (the demands expressed in the 1950s to 'clean up' the teddy boys led to the mounting of such campaigns as 'Operation Teddy Boy'), (3) actual changes in the deviant behaviour itself, (4) changes in technology (the introduction of the telephone, pocket radios for the police, 'panda' cars, etc.), and so on.

When a stable state enters disequilibrium, the once relatively balanced forces within it can become more and more out of joint with one another. For instance, the familiar deviancy amplification cycle, which will demand an ever greater share of police resources, can be triggered off. Viewed from one perspective, the cycle entails the appearance of a crime wave which prompts an increase in public concern. Public concern, expressed by the press, pressure groups and political demands, tends to push police attention on to the deviant phenomenon. An increase in attention will generally boost arrest rates which, in turn, will further mobilise public sentiment. An increasing range of neutral or ambiguous phenomena may become defined as manifestations of the threatening rise in the deviancy and this, in itself, will accelerate the rise of the crime wave. This process may have an autonomy which is quite independent of any change in the deviant behaviour itself. Sutherland's work on the sexual psychopath laws in America, and such articles as 'The phantom anesthetist of Matoon: a field study of mass hysteria'[65] and 'The phantom slasher of Taipei',[66] demonstrate how spurious the causes of such disequilibrating cycles can be.

When a reasonably stable system of police–deviant relations is upset, there are consequences for areas other than the one which is immediately affected. If a deviancy amplification process starts, or unusual attention is devoted to a particular action or series of actions (the Moors Murders or the kidnapping and murder of Mrs McKay are examples), there must, if police resources are fully deployed, be a corresponding decrease in enforcement activity elsewhere. Other things being equal, fuller enforcement against one form of deviancy will entail lesser activity against other deviancies. It is reasonable to suppose that the withdrawal of police attention will not be conducted in a random fashion. Instead, the police theory will contain a set of priorities which will dictate how important and how marginal certain deviancies are. Such a set was certainly suggested by a statement of the Chief Constable of Southend-on-Sea: 'There are many cases where offences of shoplifting entail trifling values and I am not prepared to prosecute at the public expense if no good purpose can be served.'[67]

In part, the set of priorities will be shaped by the moral indignation which various deviancies evoke. For example, Clark has shown how his sample of police attach differing degrees of moral seriousness to situations. Whilst 13% believed that breaking 'Sunday Blue Laws' was wrong, 62% condemned instances of racial prejudice, 85% deplored 'drunken bums' and 94% disapproved of obscene literature.[68] The priorities are structured by other factors. Ease of enforcement, perception of public concern, visibility of the deviancy, departmental specialisation (and thus occupational commitment) may be involved. The issue might be phrased more usefully if police–deviant relations were thought to be susceptible to classification in a model of different styles of accommodation. Each type within this classification will constitute a separate mode of enforcement behaviour and its consequences and each, to some extent, will be governed by its own peculiar laws. Withdrawal from one type will have vastly different effects from those precipitated by withdrawal elsewhere. While the police theory might prescribe inaction in the case of one type, or token action in another, it might regard the neglect of another type as a decision involving heavy opportunity-costs.

Collusion

The most obvious example of collusion, a state of criminal–police liaison established to defend joint interests against other groups, is that of the relations that can unite the police with organised crime structures. Here, the police may be effectively controlled by the deviant. Gardiner illustrates this well in his description of the 'politics of corruption'. He explains the mastery exercised by a criminal, 'Stern', over the lesser criminals in a community:

... since he controlled the police department, he could arrest any gamblers or bookies who were not paying tribute. Some of the local gambling and prostitution arrests which took place during the Stern era served another purpose—to placate newspaper demands for a crackdown. As one police chief from this era phrased it, 'Hollywood should have given us an Oscar for some of our performances when we had to pull a phony raid to keep the papers happy'.[69]

Control by criminals in such an ideal-typical case of police corruption depends upon at least two things.[70] The criminal must be able to establish an exchange relationship so that there is a reciprocity of benefit. The exchange may, for instance, be based on votes or money. The principle that bolstered up Stern's power was 'pay top personnel as much as necessary to keep them happy . . . and pay something to as many others as possible to implicate them in the system and to keep them from talking'.[71] A second basis is the necessary structuring of social control institutions and criminal organisation so that they are able to articulate with one another. When political and social control agencies are decentralised and locally based, when they are able to defend themselves against outside intervention, and when they are closely implicated in power structures which dominate a community the basis is laid for corruption. When, additionally, crime is transformed into a stable organisation which generates a steady income, engages in a multitude of petty transactions and supports a network of dependants in a community, integration is enhanced. Police action in this relationship will tend to focus on protecting it from disruption by other criminals or other agencies, on ensuring that the activity of the organised criminal is confined within mutually defined limits of licence, and on maintaining a token display of control. When other segments of deviancy require extra attention, this particular form of rule-breaking can become virtually unpoliced.

Cooperation

Criminals and police may coexist in some state of mutual reciprocity which is characterised by neither one controlling the other. Relations may be similar to those experienced in a game; the partners define one another as legitimately placed and rule-abiding. The contrast between the cooperative deviant and the expressive deviant is given prominence in a report on the Thames Valley Police drug squad:

The squad regards itself as unique in that drug users are unlike the typical criminal. 'Villains do not argue about getting pinched', Inspector Warren says, 'but the kids do.' The squad's members are only too well aware that they are vulnerable to public criticism, and that one of the commonest defences against possession of a dangerous drug is: 'It must have been planted by the police'. 'The drug user is much more prepared to argue whether what he is doing should even be against the law', the detective-inspector explains. He also points out the drug user is much more aware of his rights.[72]

In contrast to the drug user, the cooperative 'villain' respects some of the game-like conventions which contribute to uneventful and, in some cases, beneficial exchanges between rule-breakers and rule-conformers. Cooperation may lead to tacit understandings about what crimes are likely to generate public anxiety and thus restrain the criminal from committing them (the Mafia's reluctance to embark on drug-trafficking is an example);[73] the surrender by criminals of colleagues who upset a stabilised order; the system of limited protection afforded informers. On this last, Skolnick remarks:

. . . what commodities are exchanged by informer and informed, and under what conditions are such commodities created? The most important and valuable of these commodities, from the informer's point of view, is some sort of 'break' in the criminal process. This can be achieved by with-holding arrest of an informer when he has committed a crime, bringing about a reduction of charge, making a recommendation for lesser sentence. . . . But this 'leverage' does not necessarily constitute a 'license' to engage in illicit activities.[74]

Police inattention to the deviancies committed in this kind of relationship might well lead to a damaging increase in criminal activity. Temporary withdrawal, however, might result in a minor system of self-policing until enforcement is waged again. Such a relationship is organised around the capacity of deviant groups to impose some order upon themselves. There are shared understandings about what deviancies are likely to lead to the alerting of important groups outside the relationship, and there are attempts to suppress those disruptions. Billy Hill, a London thief of some importance, remarked:

After all, when you've worked it out, trouble only attracted the attention of the police. If any two mobs started trouble the guv'nor of the C.I.D. usually got busy and wanted to know what it was all about. Then when their reports went into the Yard the high-ups down there got on to the uniformed branch whose job it is to supervise all clubs and spielers. So gang warfare didn't do anyone any good.[75]

Coexistence

Coexistence can characterise relationships when the crimes lack victims. Some implicit understanding is reached so that, as long as the deviancy is carried out in a discreet manner, enforcement will not be pursued. Thus Lambert remarks of Varna Road in Birmingham, 'the activities of prostitutes are restricted to certain areas. On the fringe of [F] Division . . . is a notorious, nationally-famed area for prostitution, where for many decades the oldest trade has flourished neither unnoticed by the police nor unchecked '[76] The social accommodation between deviant and policeman can be maintained provided the public, senior police officers, the press and others remain ignorant of or indifferent to the deviancy. Because it is dependent upon an implicit acquiescence, the conditions allowing coexistence are marked by variation and instability. In the case of the enforcement of laws relating to homosexuality, the Wolfenden Committee observed:

we have found that there are variations in the ways in which different police forces administer these laws. In some parts of the country, they appear to be administered with 'discretion'; that is to say, in some police districts no proceedings are initiated unless there has been a complaint or the offence has otherwise obtruded itself upon the notice of the police, for instance by a breach of public order and decency. In other parts of the country, on the other hand, it appears that a firm effort is made to apply the full rigour of the law as it stands.[77]

While there may be no overt system of exchange, the homosexual or prostitute rewards social control agencies by his self-policing, and the control agents provide an unwritten licence to deviate. There is the maintenance of a token control, what I have described as a 'beating of the bounds of deviancy', which confirms the limits of the areas in which rule-breaking is tacitly condoned. A disequilibrium in the total system of police–deviant relations can result in the effective removal of police supervision.

This kind of continuum is built up on the possibilities of exchange between deviants and police, threats to various levels of police goals and possibilities of self-policing. It would also include instances of: *mild antagonism* where the deviancy causes some offence, is not self-policing, offers no reward to the police, is witnessed with some ambivalence and is socially visible (drunk and disorderly conduct is an example); *antagonism* where there is some congruence between police, public and legal perspectives on the deviancy but where the offences are sporadic, not expressive, explicitly political or the basis of group organisation (amateurish robbery, for instance); and *conflict* where there is a threat to more than one level of police goal, public agitation about the deviancy, no possibility of stabilisation and an aggressive posture (recurrent and violent political action, serious sexual assaults, and kidnappings).

Within the larger equilibrium which I have described above is a set of lesser, interacting equilibria which impose their own demands on the police. Upset in one of the lesser police–deviant worlds will have characteristic and predictable effects on the others and on the larger system. A crisis will not have a random impact upon police strategy. There will be an orderly redeployment of resources and attention. Thus, a decision to impose control on organised crime will be unlikely to deflect attention away from political demonstrations but it *will* ease pressure on criminals without victims. Interestingly, the defence of the structure and stability of this larger equilibrium and the smaller equilibria within it is an extremely important second-order goal in itself. It acts as a means of ensuring predictability in police work, perpetuating the system of police rewards, confirming departmental specialisation, and so on. As Chambliss remarks:

Where a symbiotic relationship exists between the legal system and criminal organisation, the potential for severe disruption of the ongoing process is omnipresent. Much of the criminal-law effort must therefore be devoted to protecting the system against outsiders' becoming aware of such a relationship. Since the only really reliable information about the system must ultimately come from persons who are themselves involved, considerable protection is automatically afforded.[78]

As inhibitors, transformers, translators and creators of reality, therefore, the police are considerably more than a simple instrument of legislative intentions. Confronting routine problems and operating with a special setting, they evolve a systematic and intricate series of relationships with the population they manage. In this evolutionary process, 'The abstract "laws" and policies of the [police] departments themselves become important only in so far as they are *used* by the police in constructing their situational meanings; the abstract meanings are important only as *resources for practical use*. This is precisely the way the police make use of the legal categories of crime: they use them to get the "job done adequately", as they define this, and they *see* the situational contingencies as defining the nature of the "job" and its "adequate" performance, hence, as necessarily defining how one should *use* the legal categories.'[79]

The translation of laws into 'resources for practical use' structures the flow and content of legislative definitions as they are encountered by deviant and nondeviant members of a society. Thus translated, the law provides meanings, experiences and problems for deviants. Activity and understanding develop within this context and affect enforcement, legislative interpretations of social order, and popular conceptions of rule-breaking. Policing is consequently an integral part of a community's scheme of social control, social definitions and behaviour.

1. J. Skolnick, *Justice Without Trial*, John Wiley, New York, 1966, p. 14.

2. cf. J. Douglas, *The Social Meanings of Suicide*, Princeton University Press, Princeton, 1967, and *American Social Order*, Free Press, New York, 1971.

3. *The Times*, 5 February 1971.

4. E. Wenninger and J. Clark, 'A Theoretical Orientation for Police Studies', in M. Klein (Ed.), *Juvenile Gangs in Context*, Prentice-Hall, New Jersey, 1967, p. 163.

5. Quoted in A. Silver, 'The Demand for Order in Civil Society', in D. Bordua (Ed.), *The Police*, John Wiley, New York, 1967, pp. 13–14.

6. cf. G. Jensen, ' "Crime Doesn't Pay": Correlates of a Shared Misunderstanding', *Social Problems*, fall 1969, vol. 17, no. 2.

7. cf. E. Bittner, 'The Police on Skid-Row', *American Sociological Review*, October, 1967, vol. 32, no. 5, p. 702.

8. cf. J. Wilson, *Varieties of Police Behavior*, Harvard University Press, Massachusetts, 1968, p. 31.

9. cf. E. Durkheim, 'The Divison of Labor in Society', Free Press, New York, 1964, chs. 2, 3, 4 and 5.

10. cf. G. Simmel, *Conflict and the Web of Group Affiliations*, Free Press, New York, 1955, esp. pp. 35–8.

11. First Report of the Commissioners Appointed as to the Best Means of Establishing an Efficient Constabulary Force in the Counties of England and Wales, London, 1839, p. 205.

12. cf. J. Hart, *The British Police*, Allen & Unwin, London, 1951, esp. p. 117.

13. cf. D. Bordua, 'Police', *International Encyclopaedia of the Social Sciences*, Macmillan, New York, 1968, vol. 12.

14. Letter to Sir Edward Shortt, quoted in G. Reynolds and A. Judge, *The Night the Police Went on Strike*, Weidenfeld & Nicolson, London, 1968, p. 119.

15. C. Werthman and I. Piliavin, 'Gang Members and the Police', in D. Bordua (Ed.), *The Police*, op. cit., p. 75.

16. J. Skolnick, op. cit., pp. 45–6.

17. T. F. Adams, 'Field interrogation', *Police*, March–April 1963, p. 28.

18. cf. W. J. Chambliss and J. T. Liel, 'Mistakes in Police Work', in E. Rubington and M. S. Weinberg (Ed.), *Deviance*, Macmillan, New York, 1968.

19. J. Wilson, op. cit., p. 27.

20. E. Rose, *et al.*, *Colour and Citizenship*, Oxford University Press, London, 1969, p. 350.

21. A. Blumberg, *The Scales of Justice*, Aldine, Chicago, 1970, p. 8.

22. I. Piliavin and S. Briar; 'Police Encounters with Juveniles', in E. Rubington and M. S. Weinberg (Ed.), *Deviance*, p. 139.

23. J. Wilson, op. cit., p. 31.

24. cf. J. Wilson, 'The Police and the Delinquent in Two Cities', in S. Wheeler (Ed.), *Controlling Delinquents*, Wiley, New York, 1966, p. 23.

25. For a description of some of this diversity, cf. J. Wilson, *Varieties of Police Behaviour*.

26. J. H. McNamara, 'Uncertainties in police work', in D. J. Bordua (Ed.), *The Police*, pp. 170, 171.

27. A. J. Reiss and D. J. Bordua, 'Environment and Organisation: a Perspective on the Police', in D. J. Bordua (Ed.), *The Police*, p. 30.

28. W. A. Westley, 'Violence and the Police', *American Journal of Sociology*, July 1953, vol. 49, p. 35.

29. J. Wilson, *Varieties of Police Behavior*, p. 130.

30. A. Reiss and D. J. Bordua, in D. J. Bordua (Ed.), *The Police*, pp. 47–8.

31. E. Cumming, I. Cumming and L. Edell, 'Policeman as Philosopher, Friend and Guide', *Social Problems*, Winter 1965, vol. 12, no. 3, p. 277.

32. ibid.

33. An estimate based on Institute of Municipal Treasurers and Accountants, *Police Force Statistics 1966–67*, London, 1968.

34. B. Whitaker, *The Police*, Penguin Books, Middlesex, 1964, p. 25.

35. G. Smithson, *Raffles in Real Life: The Confessions of George Smithson* alias *Gentleman George*, Hutchinson, London, undated, p. 229.

36. *Report on the Police Service of England, Wales and Scotland (1919)*, Cmd. 253.

37. Quoted in G. Reynolds and A. Judge, *The Night the Police Went on Strike*, Weidenfeld & Nicolson, London, 1968, p. 69.

38. cf. D. J. Bordua and A. J. Reiss, 'Command, Control and Charisma', *American Journal of Sociology*, 1966, vol. 72, no. 1, pp. 68–76.

39. J. M. Hart, op. cit., p. 12.

40. ibid., p. 11.

41. *Police Review*, 3 August 1963, p. 721.

42. D. J. Bordua and A. J. Reiss, 'Command, Control and Charisma', *American Journal of Sociology*, 1966, vol. 72, p. 72.

43. J. Lambert, 'The Police Can Choose', *New Society*, 18 September 1969, no. 364.

44. cf. also M. E. Cain, 'Conflict and its Solution', unpublished Ph.D. thesis, University of London, 1969, p. 118.

45. D. J. Bordua, *The Police*, p. 177.

46. J. Wilson, *Varieties of Police Behavior*, p. 154.

47. cf. D. J. Bordua, *The Police*, p. 176.

48. D. C. Gibbons, *Society, Crime and Criminal Careers*, Prentice-Hall, New Jersey, 1968, p. 67.

49. U.S. President's Commission on Law Enforcement and Administration of Justice: *Task Force Report*, 'The Police', US Government Printing Office, Washington, 1967, p. 16.

50. J. Wilson, *Varieties of Police Behavior*, p. 58.

51. *The Times*, 15 June 1971.

52. A. J. Reiss and D. J. Bordua, in D. J. Bordua (Ed.), *The Police*, p. 33.

53. cf. H. L. Packer, 'The Courts, the Police, and the Rest of Us', *Journal of Criminal Law, Criminology, and Police Science*, September 1966, vol. 57, esp. p. 239.

54. S. Wheeler, E. Bonacich, M. R. Cramer and I. K. Zola, 'Agents of Delinquency Control', in S. Wheeler (Ed.), *Controlling Delinquents*, pp. 48–9.

55. I. Piliavin and S. Briar, in Rubington and Weinberg (Ed.), *Deviance*, pp. 139–140.

56. cf. J. Wilson, *Varieties of Police Behavior*, p. 70.

57. J. P. Clark, 'Isolation of the Police', *Journal of Criminal Law, Criminology, and Police Science*, vol. 56, no. 3, 1965, p. 308.

58. *Final Report of the Royal Commission on the Police*, HMSO, London, 1962, p. 278.

59. cf. J. Wilson, *Varieties of Police Behavior*, p. 97.

60. A. J. Reiss and D. J. Bordua, in D. J. Bordua (Ed.), *The Police*, p. 35.

61. A. Niederhoffer, *Behind the Badge*, Doubleday, New York, 1967, p. 14.

62. M. Banton, *The Policeman in the Community*, Tavistock, London, 1964, p.146.

63. K. T. Erikson, *Wayward Puritans*, Wiley, New York, 1966, pp. 24, 25–6.

64. cf. C. Werthman and I. Piliavin, in D. J. Bordua (Ed.), *The Police*, p. 75.

65. D. M. Johnson, *Journal of Abnormal and Social Psychology*, April 1945, vol. 40, pp. 175–86.

66. N. Jacobs, *Social Problems*, Winter 1965, vol. 12, no. 5, pp. 318–28.

67. *The Times*, February 1963.

68. J. P. Clark, *Journal of Criminal Law, Criminology, and Police Science*, 1965, vol. 56, p. 314.

69. J. Gardiner, 'Wincanton: The Politics of Corruption', Appendix B of the US President's Commission on Law Enforcement and Administration of Justice; Task Force Report on Organized Crime, US Government Printing Office, Washington, 1967, p. 65.

70. For a fuller treatment of corruption, see M. McMullan, 'A Theory of Corruption', *Sociological Review* (New Series), July 1961, vol. 9, no. 2.

71. J. Gardiner, op. cit., p. 66.

72. *The Times*, 5 February 1971.

73. cf. P. Maas, *The Canary that Sang: The Valachi Papers*, McGibbon & Kee, London, 1969, pp. 214–15.

74. J. Skolnick, op. cit., p. 137.

75. B. Hill, *Boss of Britain's Underworld*, Naldrett Press, London, 1955, p. 149.

76. J. Lambert, *Crime, Police and Race Relations*, Oxford University Press, London, 1970, p. 75.

77. *Report of the Committee on Homosexual Offences and Prostitution*, Cmd. 247, 1957, p. 46.

78. W. Chambliss (Ed.), *Crime and the Legal Process*, McGraw-Hill, New York, 1969, p. 97.

79. J. Douglas, 'American Social Order', op. cit., p. 104.

CONCLUSION

Each of the four chapters has contributed to a single theme. My argument has been that deviancy is a central societal concern; that its character is complex and negotiated; and that the processes which aid its production cannot be reduced to neat causal episodes which have a beginning, a middle and an end.

Societal centrality

Deviancy is not simply a set of pathological events which occasionally break out at the furthest margins of a society; it is the very stuff of social order. Only when the structure of a social world is marked out in terms of its contrasts, can social life be organised and co-ordinated. Deviancy sustains and produces order by engendering commitments and tensions, by dispelling ambiguities and by setting defined limits on possible action. By being portrayed as discontinuous with everyday life, deviancy sets up boundaries around most forms of behaviour. It encloses what might otherwise be an anomic confusion. Moral meanings are many-layered and conflicting. Without deviancy and its depiction, fateful decision-making would be rendered enormously difficult. Deviation thus infuses almost every major social process.

Complexity and negotiation

Pluralist societies are made up of innumerable groups who never meet. Its structures are supported by beliefs and myths about itself and its members. Perspectives on deviancy are rarely formed on the basis of face-to-face encounters between deviants and others. Instead, what passes for deviancy is shaped by social distance, intermediary interpretative institutions and the attribution of putative characteristics. The presentation of deviancy rests upon the manner in which rule-breaking is organised, its identification by the knowing and the naïve and its relevance to numerous interests held by different social worlds. No one can ever know deviancy or its component episodes in their totality. The vision acquired by any one individual or group is segmented and negotiated. Transactions between deviants and others give rise to a multiplicity of different versions of reality. The organisation of those versions is always fluid and incomplete. Contradictions abound.* The realities that inform and motivate a society's subworlds conflict. When the subworlds are articulated as institutions, particularly social control agencies which must work cooperatively, secondary systems of negotiation emerge. Working compromises translate these realities into practically useful knowledge. Fed back into everyday life, these perspectives are again worked upon. The cycle of resolution, conflict, organisation and disorganisation is virtually endless.

Interdependence of processes

Deviancy cannot be carved up into cause and effect sequences which are discrete and finite. Rather, deviancy is sustained by a mutual dependence of processes. Deviancy cannot be imagined without social control, and social control would be formless without deviancy. Beliefs about deviancy, deviant organisation, actions against and by deviants, are all parts of a seamless system which is marked by the relative simultaneity of its operation. They are both the causes and the effects of each other, and the ramifications of change in them spread far within the system. There is a circularity about processes involving deviation: a change in deviant behaviour modifies control effort, legislative understanding and popular knowledge which, in turn, inevitably generate further changes in deviancy itself. Portions of the cycle can be prised out for purposes of analysis, but the residue must not be forgotten nor must the portions be taken for anything but incomplete items. In a sense, then, the arrangement of my chapters has been arbitrary. Any one chapter could have been first, any second, without destroying the model which I have tried to construct.

* cf. B. Wilson; 'Mass Media and Public Attitudes to Crime', *Criminal Law Review*, June 1961.

INDEX